S0-BBM-117

AN INTRODUCTION TO ANCIENT EGYPT

Published for the Trustees of the British Museum by British Museum Publications Limited

© 1979, The Trustees of the British Museum
ISBN 0 7141 0924 X (*cased*)
ISBN 0 7141 0923 1 (*paper*)
Published by British Museum Publications Ltd
6 Bedford Square, London, WC1B 3RA

First published in 1964 as *A General Introductory
Guide to the Egyptian Collections in the British Museum*
(ISBN 0 7141 0908, *paper*; 0 7141 0909 6, *cased*)
Reprinted 1971 and 1975
Revised and reset with additional illustrations, 1979

British Library Cataloguing in Publication Data

British Museum
   An introduction to Ancient
   Egypt.—Revised ed.
   1. British Museum 2. Egypt—
   Antiquities—Exhibitions
   I. Title II. General introductory
   guide to the Egyptian collections
   in the British Museum
   932' .0074'02142   DT59.L

Designed by Patrick Yapp

Set in Photina 10 on 12 point
Printed in Great Britain
at the University Press, Oxford
by Eric Buckley
Printer to the University

CONTENTS

LIST OF COLOUR PLATES

NOTE: *The page numbers given are those opposite the colour plates, or, in the case of a double-page spread, those either side of the plate.*

LIST OF BLACK AND WHITE ILLUSTRATIONS

PREFACE

The text of this volume is based closely on that of *A General Introductory Guide to the Egyptian Collections in the British Museum*, first published in 1964. In its title the 1964 *Guide* followed the example of earlier publications of 1909 and 1930, but its content written by I. E. S. Edwards, A. F. Shore and T. G. H. James, was planned along somewhat different lines. Its aim was to provide an outline of the physical, historical, and cultural background of the collection; it was not intended to be a comprehensive catalogue of the sixty-five thousand objects in the Department of Egyptian Antiquities. In the present revision it has been decided to modify the title, emphasizing thereby that the book is an *Introduction* to the culture of ancient Egypt, not a *Guide* in the strictest sense.

In preparing this new edition, the framework of the old *Guide* has been preserved, but the opportunity has been taken to bring the text up to date in the light of recent discoveries, and to introduce many new illustrations. As in the old *Guide* royal names have, in accordance with current practice, been given mostly in the forms in which they were preserved in the Classical histories. Likewise, spellings of place-names, with very few exceptions, follow the style found on the maps of the Survey of Egypt. The dates used in this revision show many small variations from those adopted in 1964. For all periods down to the end of the New Kingdom, the chronology set out in the third edition of the *Cambridge Ancient History*, vols. I and II (Cambridge, 1970–75), has been adopted. For the subsequent, very controversial, period down to the Twenty-sixth Dynasty (when relatively precise dating can be achieved), the system proposed by K. A. Kitchen in his *Third Intermediate Period in Egypt* (Aris and Phillips, Warminster, 1973) is followed.

The revisions of the text have been carried out by members of the staff of the Department, Miss Carol Andrews, Dr M. L. Bierbrier, Mr W. V. Davies, Miss Alexandrina Logan-Smith and Dr A. J. Spencer. Miss Logan-Smith has acted also as general editor of the whole.

T. G. H. JAMES
Keeper,
Department of Egyptian Antiquities,
The British Museum

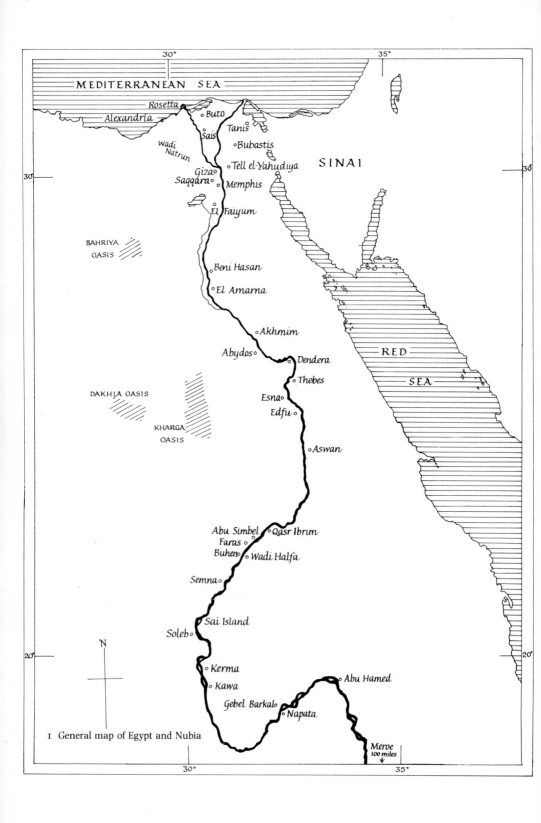

MEDITERRANEAN SEA

30°　　　　　　　　　　　　　　　35°

Rosetta
Alexandria　　　　○ Buto
　　　　　　　　Sais
　　　　　　　　　○ Tanis
　　　　　　　　　　○ Bubastis
Wadi
Natrun　　　　　　○ Tell el-Yahudiya　　　SINAI

Giza ○　　　　　　　○ Memphis
Saqqara ○

El Faiyum

BAHRIYA
OASIS

Beni Hasan

El Amarna

Akhmim

Abydos ○　　　○ Dendera

Thebes

Esna ○
Edfu ○

○ Aswan

DAKHLA OASIS

KHARGA
OASIS

RED

SEA

Abu Simbel ○　○ Qasr Ibrim
Faras ○
Buhen ○　○ Wadi Halfa

Semna ○

Sai Island

Soleb ○

N

○ Kerma　　　　　　○ Abu Hamed

○ Kawa

Gebel Barkal ○
　　　　　○ Napata

1　General map of Egypt and Nubia

Meroe
100 miles

30°　　　　　　　　　　　　　　　35°

CHAPTER ONE

THE LAND OF EGYPT
AND ITS NATURAL RESOURCES

The land

Egypt has been called the gift of the Nile, and it is true that without the Nile Egypt as a fertile, well-populated country would not exist. In ancient times the country stretched from the Mediterranean Sea in the north to the First Cataract at Aswan in the south, a distance of about 750 miles by river. Today the southern boundary lies only a few miles north of Wadi Halfa in the Sudan, but the effective land of Egypt is still that area to the north of Aswan. After passing through the formidable granite barrier of the First Cataract the Nile follows a course northwards through a sandstone belt that stretches almost as far as Edfu. Thereafter the valley is composed of limestone deposits which continue as far north as Cairo. A short distance to the north of Cairo the river divides and forms the Delta, which is a region about 14,500 square miles in area, composed of alluvial deposits. Today the Nile flows through the Delta in two principal channels, of which the eastern enters the Mediterranean at Damietta and the western at Rosetta. In antiquity there were three principal channels known in the Pharaonic Period as 'the water of Pre', 'the water of Ptah', and 'the water of Amun', and in classical times as the Pelusiac, the Sebennytic, and the Canopic branches. The other branches mentioned by classical writers such as Herodotus were not principal channels, but subsidiary branches from the Sebennytic (the Mendesian and Saitic or Tanite) or artificially cut (the Bolbitine and Bucolic).

The land of Egypt is principally the valley of the Nile and, more precisely, that part of the valley that is cultivated. In antiquity the cultivated area was determined by the height to which the Nile rose in its annual inundation. The flood-waters (p. 21) not only watered the fields; they also brought with them a deposit of rich alluvium which renewed the fertility of the land with almost unfailing regularity. This black deposit provided a contrast between the inhabited land of Egypt and the uninhabited tawny-coloured desert which was so striking that it caused the ancient Egyptians to name their land Kemet 'The Black' (⌂𓈖𓊖). The desert lands were known as Deshret 'The Red' (𓈖𓃭𓊖). The modern name Egypt is derived from the Greek *Aigyptos* which probably represents 𓉗𓉐𓂓𓏤𓊪𓏏𓎛 *ḥwt-kꜣ-Ptḥ* 'Hikuptah', one of the ancient names of Memphis, the capital of the country during the Old Kingdom.

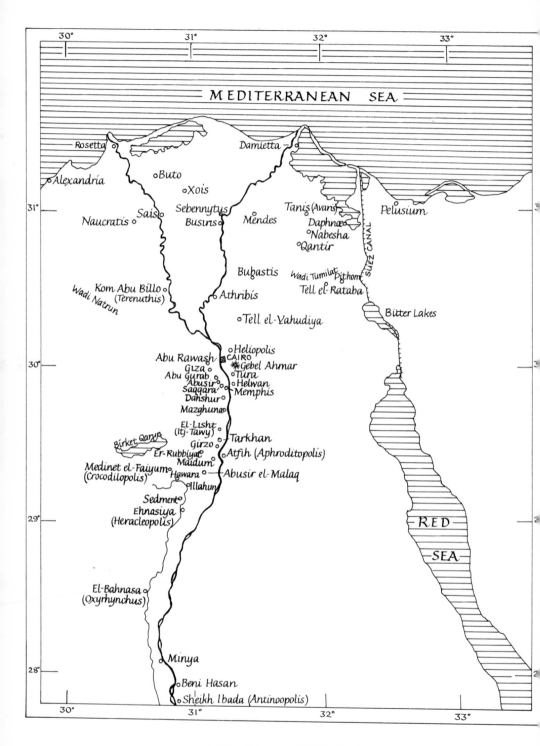

2 Map of Lower and Middle Egypt

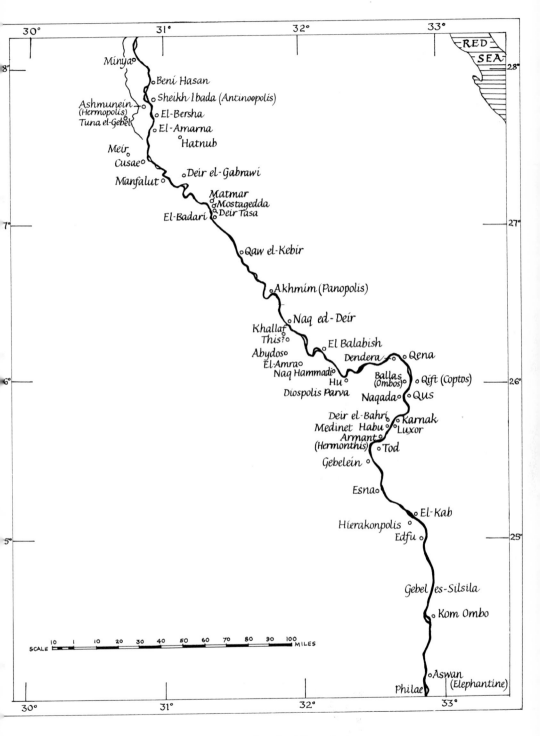

3 Map of Upper Egypt from Beni Hasan to Aswan

The administrative organization of the country was confined to the same habitable, cultivated land, the valley proper with such oases as were easily reached from the valley. From early times the land was divided into two principal regions, today called Upper and Lower Egypt. Upper Egypt, known in pharaonic times as Shemau, was divided into twenty-two administrative areas which are called nomes, the Greek term for these districts. The ancient name for a nome was 𓈖, more simply, 𓈖 (*sp3t*). The first nome was that of Elephantine (modern Aswan), just north of the First Cataract and the twenty-second was that of Aphroditopolis (modern Atfih) to the south of Cairo. The frontier between Upper and Lower Egypt has never been precisely determined. The twenty-first nome comprised the region known as the Faiyum, a natural depression lying a few miles from the Nile Valley to the west of Aphroditopolis and watered by an offshoot of the Nile called the Bahr Yusuf. The Faiyum, which today has an area of about 850 square miles, was first exploited by the kings of the Middle Kingdom who established their capital not far from its entrance at Itj-towy near the modern El-Lisht. In the north of the Faiyum is a lake, the Birket Qarun, which has always been a haunt of wild fowl and a centre for hunting.

In the Western Desert there are several oases which may be considered as having been part of Egypt in ancient times although they were always regarded more as frontier regions, to be exploited, than as integral parts of the country itself. Such administration as they had was based on the seventh Upper Egyptian nome, the capital city of which was Diospolis Parva (modern Hu). Chief among these oases was El-Kharga, known in antiquity as the Southern Oasis. It lies eighty miles to the west of the Nile Valley, and a further forty miles to the west is El-Dakhla, a smaller oasis. North of Kharga on the latitude of El-Hiba and seventy miles west of the Nile is El-Bahriya, the Northern Oasis.

Lower Egypt, known in ancient times as To-mehu ('The Northern Land'), was, like Upper Egypt, divided into nomes. This part of the land of Egypt consisted chiefly of the Delta, which in early antiquity was very largely still an undeveloped region of marshland and scrub. Its organization into nomes was, therefore, a process that suffered modification from time to time as the country was opened up and developed. Ultimately the number of nomes was twenty, of which the first was the nome of Memphis.

In antiquity the desert-lands that bordered the cultivated Nile Valley, while coming under the control of the government of Egypt, were not considered, it would seem, as integral parts of the country itself. The Libyan desert on the west of the Nile Valley is a desolate area of sand dunes and rocky wastes (Plate 1).

Apart from the large oases of El-Kharga, El-Dakhla, and El-Bahriya and a few smaller oases which were sporadically occupied and cultivated and used as places of banishment for political and other prisoners, this desert had little to attract the ancient Egyptian. It was, however, crossed by a network of ancient tracks that linked the Nile Valley with the Sudan and the cultivated coastal strips and oases of Libya. The Eastern or Arabian Desert, on the contrary, was much exploited in antiquity. Different in character from the Libyan desert, it is largely a mountainous, rocky region, the source of many minerals and hard stones which were used in great quantities by ancient craftsmen. It is, however, without oases, and wells are few and widely separated.

Inasmuch as these desert-lands were not parts of Egypt proper, they were treated in the same way as the peninsula of Sinai and the land of Nubia: they were areas to be exploited, but not incorporated into the administrative organization of the land of Egypt. The nome-structure was reserved, therefore, for the cultivated lands of the valley together with the Delta.

The Nile and the inundation

The Nile, which both made possible and maintained life in Egypt, was also the principal highway of the land. Until the early New Kingdom (c. 1600 BC) the Egyptians lacked wheeled conveyances and the horse. Travel on land was carried out either on foot or by donkey. The river offered the obvious means for travel and traffic by boat was considerable from an early date. As no point in the valley was more than a few miles from the river, it became a highway that could take the traveller, the trader, or the royal official anywhere in the realm. During the period of the annual inundation when most of the cultivated area was covered by water this usefulness of the Nile could further be exploited. Flat-bottomed barges could convey heavy cargoes such as building-stones and monumental sculptures directly from the quarries, situated in the cliffs bordering the flooded valley, to their destinations in temples and cemeteries, which were situated just beyond the limits of the flood-waters.

Travel on the Nile was facilitated by the direction of the prevailing wind which, with almost unceasing regularity, blows from the north. A boat travelling south, therefore, against the flow of the stream, could use sails; one travelling north could proceed with the current. In times of calm or when the wind and the current were adverse, oars were used. The river was used for travel to such an extent that the regular words for 'go north' and 'go south' were determined in the hieroglyphic script by boats: 'go north' or perhaps more strictly 'go downstream' has a boat with no sail (⟶): 'go south' or 'go upstream' has a boat with

a sail ($\Downarrow$) e.g. 35292 (fig. 4). Egyptians thought of travel in terms of movement on the Nile and they had difficulty in describing properly direction outside Egypt. There is a famous sentence in the Tombos stele of Tuthmosis I in which the Euphrates, a river that flows from north to south, is called 'that reversed water that goes downstream [i.e. the Egyptian word which equally means 'go north' in terms of the Nile] in going upstream [i.e. 'going south']'.

4 Wooden model boat

The Nile, which for its last 900 miles runs through the land of Egypt, has its origins in the heart of Africa. Of the two principal streams which unite at Khartum, the longer, the White Nile, derives its main flow from the waters of Lake Victoria. Other contributory sources are Lake Edward and Lake Albert.

About 600 miles south of Khartum lies Lake No, where the main stream is joined by another tributary, the Bahr el-Ghazal (Gazelle River), flowing in from the west. A further tributary, the Bahr el-Zaraf (Giraffe River), joins the main stream, from the east, about 60 miles north of Lake No, and between this point and Khartum the river is enlarged by the water of the Sobat, which also flows from the east. The total length of the tributaries, which make up the White Nile as far as Khartum, is about 1,560 miles. At Khartum, the modern capital of the Republic of the Sudan, the White Nile is joined by the second principal stream, the Blue Nile, which rises in Lake Tana in Ethiopia and is about 1,000 miles long. From Khartum to the sea the united streams, which form the river known as the Nile, follow a course about 1,913 miles long and are joined by one tributary only, the Atbara, which also rises in the Ethiopian highlands. Between Khartum and Aswan the Nile in six places runs through regions where the flow of the stream is broken up by the exceptionally rocky nature of its bed. These six stretches of the river are known as the cataracts and they are all to a greater or lesser extent difficult for navigation.

The special characteristic of the Nile, which has made it so important for Egypt, is its annual inundation, caused ultimately by rains which fall in Central Africa, and melting snow and rains in the Ethiopian highlands. By the end of May in Egypt, the river was at its lowest level. During the month of June the Nile, between Cairo and Aswan, began to rise, and a quantity of 'green water' appeared at this time. The cause of the colour is said to be myriads of minute organisms which subsequently putrefy and disappear. During August the river rose rapidly and its waters assumed a red muddy colour, which was due to the presence of the rich red earth brought into the Nile by the Blue Nile and the Atbara. The rising of the waters continued until the middle of September, after which they remained stationary for two or three weeks. In October a further slight rise occurred, and then they began to fall; the fall continued gradually until, in the May following, they were at their lowest level once more. The order of the rising of the various tributaries in the south, swollen by spring rains, is as follows: the Sobat rises about 15 April, the Gazelle and Giraffe rivers about 15 May, the Blue Nile at the end of May, and the Atbara a little later. The united waters of these streams reached Egypt about the end of August and caused the inundation to reach its highest point. Vast quantities of rich earth were brought down by the floods of the Blue Nile and Atbara and much of this matter was deposited in a thin layer over the land which was flooded.

Until recent years when the flow of the river has been controlled, even during the inundation season, by the Sudd el-'Ali dam at Aswan and by barrages at Esna, Nag Hammadi, Asyut, and to the north of Cairo, the average rise during the inundation period seems to have been approximately the same as it was in antiquity. Ancient records, both those preserved in classical authors and the visible evidence of ancient Nilometers, show that a flood of 6 metres was perilously low and that one of 9 metres was so high as to cause much damage: a flood of 7–8 metres was ideal for every purpose. In effect this meant that the whole valley of the Nile was flooded up to the edge of the rising ground of the desert. Towns and villages and the dykes that carried paths as well as serving as water barriers, remained above the water-level except in years of very heavy floods. When the waters fell back within the banks of the river in the autumn the land was covered with a deposit of the soil brought down in the flood-waters; it was this regular addition to the land that made the country so exceptionally fertile.

The ancient Egyptians understood fully to what extent their life and prosperity depended on the unfailing regularity of the inundation. The occasional phenomenon of an insufficient rise and the consequent shortage of food were enough to remind them that they could not expect a good flood as inevitable. They never, therefore, regarded the river and its gifts with com-placency. The Nile was known in antiquity by the name *iteru*, usually translated as 'river'; the inundation was called Hapy and was worshipped as a god. The religious and secular litera-ture from very early times is full of references to the desirability of high inundations and the misery attendant on the failure of the flood. Nomarchs regularly boasted that they were able, through their providence, to feed the people of their nomes even in years when the Nile ran low. Hapy was, therefore, constantly the subject of the prayers of the Egyptians. He was represented as a bearded god with a cluster of water-plants on his head: he was shown with pendent female breasts indicative of his fertility and sometimes pouring water in libation. In mythology it was held that the inundation originated in underground caverns situated in the region of the First Cataract to the south of Aswan. The gods of this region, Khnum, Anukis, and Satis, possessed especial importance inasmuch as they could interfere with the inundation. An inscription carved during the Ptolemaic Period on the island of Siheil records a famine which supposedly took place throughout Egypt during the reign of a king identified by some historians as Djoser of the Third Dynasty (*c.* 2660 BC). In a dream Khnum announced to the king that the failure of the inundation was due to the neglect of the gods of the cataract region. The king by a decree re-established the territories and offerings of the gods, ensuring thereby that the flood should rise unfailingly thereafter to the required height.

Agriculture

In ancient times the economy of Egypt was based primarily on agriculture. It has been said that the lot of the Egyptian farmer

Plate 1
View of Saqqara and the Western Desert from the ancient town of Memphis

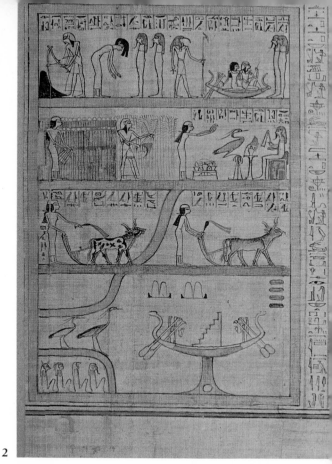

Plate 2
Agricultural scenes from the *Book of the Dead* of the priestess Anhai

Plate 3
Theban tomb painting showing the checking of a boundary stone

Plate 4
Fowling scene from a Theban tomb

2

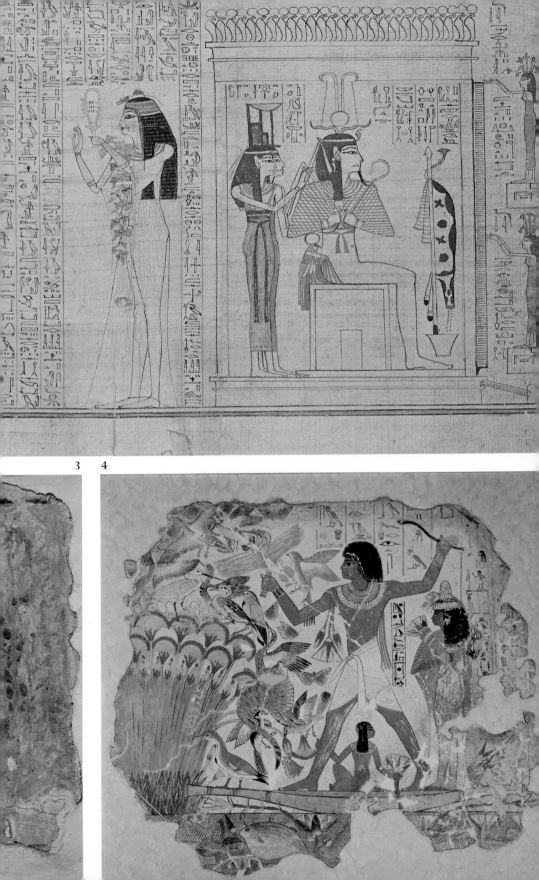

Plate 5
Tribute from Nubia
(rings of gold,
ebony, panther-skins,
apes)

was far happier than that of his contemporaries in other countries. Yet ancient texts from Egypt contain many jibes aimed at the life of the peasant in the field; but these jibes are probably not to be accepted literally because they were written by scribes who had a professional bias against manual labour. There is plenty of evidence that the Egyptian farmer worked hard, but it is also certain that, except in years when the inundation was inadequate, his toil was readily rewarded by good results and not nullified by unpredictable natural calamities. This happy state of affairs was due in the first place to the behaviour of the Nile, and secondly to the regular pattern of the climate of the country. Sunny, cloudless skies are common throughout the year; rainfall in Upper Egypt is negligible; at Cairo it rarely exceeds 5 cms a year and in the Delta it is rarely more than 20 cms. Such rain as does fall comes during the winter months. During the summer months the whole of Egypt is hot and dry; in the winter for the most part the weather remains dry and can be still very hot, especially in Upper Egypt. The prevailing wind throughout the country blows from the north (p. 21), but in Lower Egypt there is rather more variation than in Upper Egypt due to the nearness of the Mediterranean Sea.

The conditions of climate and the phenomenon of the inundation simplified the task of the Egyptian farmer but did not release him from the essential processes of ploughing, sowing, and reaping. Many of the tools used by the ancient farmer are exhibited in the Fourth Egyptian Room together with wooden models from tombs of the Old Kingdom–Middle Kingdom illustrating certain of the activities on the land (p. 207). The agricultural year began when the inundation subsided, leaving the earth soaked and overlaid with a thin layer of silt. The first tasks were the rehabilitation of the land and the planting of the crops before the ground dried out and became hard. Rehabilitation of the land included the clearing out of irrigation canals and ditches, the re-establishment of landmarks and the re-surveying of fields. The urgency of this work demanded special efforts, organized centrally no doubt, in each nome, with labour being conscripted as required. The recurrent character of these duties, and the constant endeavour to avoid being conscripted for them, led those who could afford to pay to appoint deputies who would perform the duties on their behalf. So fundamental for the continuance of Egyptian life were these duties that it was thought that they would be needed in the after-life. Consequently, from the early Middle Kingdom a man of means provided in his tomb a *shabti* (p. 169) who would carry out such duties on his behalf in the after-life. The earliest version of the *shabti*-formula (by which the figure is invoked to perform these duties) occurs on

Plate 6
Head from a granite
statue of an official

the outer wooden coffin of Gua (30839): 'If this Gua is assigned to royal field-works to the . . .(?) of the department, to re-establish(?) the dykes, to turn over the new fields of the reigning king, "Behold me", thou shalt say to any messenger who shall come concerning this Gua in his round. "Take up your mattocks, your hoes, your yokes and your baskets in your hands, as any man does for his master".'

The rehabilitation of the land was followed by the planting of the crops. There is some indication that canals and ditches were used to carry water from the Nile to fields after the inundation had ended, but in general crops were allowed to grow and ripen without further watering, as was the case in modern Egypt before the introduction of perennial irrigation. The harvesting of the various crops took place in the spring and was in a normal year completed by May. Land could then lie fallow for two months before the inundation again covered the fields. Gardens which were situated around villages, farms, and the country-houses of the rich had to be watered regularly both because they were usually laid out on high ground not reached by the flood and because of the type of crop grown. Such gardens remained in cultivation throughout the year and they were irrigated principally from canals from which water was raised by means of the *shaduf*, a well-sweep with a counterpoise. This primitive machine, which is still much used in Upper Egypt today, was adequate for light irrigation but not suitable for general field-irrigation. Marginal land which was not reached by the waters of the inundation was also irrigated in this way and could be used for summer cultivation. The crops raised on such land were, however, insignificant compared with the produce of the inundated area.

The principal crops sown after the inundation were corn and flax. Of corn emmer was the chief crop, followed by barley, which was designated either 'Upper Egyptian' or 'Lower Egyptian', and wheat. The last was grown only in small quantities until the Ptolemaic Period when it became the principal crop. Barley, in addition to its primary use for bread (ancient examples of which are on display) was largely employed in the manufacture of beer, the chief drink of the ancient Egyptians. Beer was made by fermenting barley-bread; the process of straining the mash made from this bread into the beer-vat is represented in a number of wooden models from tombs of the Old Kingdom–Middle Kingdom (e.g. 55728 from Sedment and 45196 from Asyut, fig. 5). The scenes and groups in which are depicted the preparation of bread together with the processes of grinding the corn, kneading the dough, and baking (e.g. 40915) are concerned, no doubt, as much with beer-

5 Wooden model of
a brewer

manufacture as with the making of food. The cultivation of
emmer, barley and flax dates back at least to Neolithic times.
During the historic period flax was a crop of great importance,
as is shown by the frequent representations of the flax-harvest
in tomb-scenes. It was used chiefly for the manufacture of linen,
which was the only fabric available to the ancient Egyptians
apart from woollen materials of which there is little evidence
until Hellenistic times. Ancient examples of linen garments in
the collection are on display.

The methods used for ploughing, sowing, and harvesting the
cereal crops and flax are well known. The tombs of all historic
periods contain scenes which illustrate these activities. Plate 2
reproduces part of a vignette from the papyrus containing the
Book of the Dead of Anhai, a priestess of Amun during the
Twentieth Dynasty (10472). In the vignette Anhai is shown

engaged in agricultural activities in the Egyptian equivalent of the Elysian Fields. The second register shows her ploughing with a team of two cows. The usual plough consisted of a share which was sometimes shod with bronze (as in the case of the exhibited example, 50705), fastened to a pole to which the team was harnessed. The handle was formed either by a backward continuation of the share, if there were no separate pole, or by an attachment to the pole. Tomb-scenes show that the activity of ploughing was carried on concurrently with sowing; sometimes the sower is shown casting the seed before the plough, in which case the plough served as a harrow; sometimes the seed is cast behind the plough into the furrow and then trodden in by flocks of sheep and goats that are driven over the furrows (as can be seen in one scene from the tomb of Ur-ir-en-Ptah, 718). Ground which was particularly hard was broken up by hoes of the kind seen in the top register of Plate 2. Three wooden groups are exhibited showing teams ploughing (51090, 51091, and 52947); another (63837), which includes a figure of a man using a hoe to dig earth for bricks, illustrates the use of this tool. There are also a single figure of a man wielding a hoe (45195) and several actual examples of hoes on exhibition (e.g. 22863).

The grain crops were cut with wooden sickles set with flint teeth (e.g. 52861) and only the tops of the stems bearing the ears were cut. These tops were collected in large panniers or sacks and carried away on donkey-back to the granary. The standing straw was, no doubt, pulled up afterwards and used for many purposes, such as bedding, thatching, brick-making, and sometimes in mummification. Flax was harvested by being pulled in bundles straight from the ground. The roots and tops were trimmed off and the bundles bound up and taken away. The middle register in the vignette from the papyrus of Anhai (Plate 2) shows on the left the harvest of flax (which is coloured green on the original) and of emmer (which is red).

The harvesting of emmer and barley was followed by threshing, winnowing, and storing of the grain. A reproduction of the harvest scenes from the tomb of Menna, exhibited in the corridor of the Third Egyptian Room, illustrates all these activities. Threshing was performed by cattle which were driven round the threshing floor while men forked away the spent ears. Wooden winnowing 'fans' (e.g. 18206) were used to toss the mixed grain and chaff into the air and the wind carried away the chaff. The clean grain was finally stored in granaries. Of the wooden tomb-models of granaries exhibited, one (2463) shows the owner of the farm seated on a platform above the store-chamber while a woman grinds corn in the court below; another (21804) has the names of the different grains written above the chambers of the granary; a third from a tomb at Beni Hasan (41573) contains some ancient grain.

The inevitable sequel to the harvest was the payment of taxes. Although the whole land of Egypt was in theory the property of the king, a kind of private ownership of land undoubtedly existed as early as the Old Kingdom. The practice of making grants to temples, nobles, and private persons (for mortuary estates) led to a position in which land was held as if by right, to be sold, bought, rented, and, consequently, to be worked privately and to be assessed officially for taxes. The details of the organization of tax-collection are not known. It is probable that the nome authority organized collection within each nome and that the great temples had their own private systems for the collection of taxes from the vast temple estates. While the crops were still standing the tax assessors visited the fields and took measurements, using the rope stretching methods illustrated in the Fourth Egyptian Room. On the basis of such measurements the tax assessment was made. Part of a scene of such an assessment (37982, Plate 3) comes from a Theban tomb of the Eighteenth Dynasty (probably that of Nebamun) and it includes a figure of a senior assessor who bends over a limestone stela marking the corner of a cornfield. He checks that the limits of the property are correctly defined before the assessment-survey begins. The text above his head gives the oath he swears: 'As the Great God who is in the heaven endures, the stela is correct, its (. . .?) stands up.' The title of the man who was originally represented walking behind him (only traces now remain) is also preserved; he is called 'Controller of the measuring of the granary'.

Two other important products of agriculture in ancient Egypt were oil and wine. Oil is frequently mentioned as an alternative to grain as a standard material for barter and its uses otherwise were many in cooking, lighting, cosmetics, ointments, and embalming. Many different kinds of oil are mentioned in texts but few are identified with certainty. Olives were not successfully grown in Egypt until the Ptolemaic Period; however, in earlier times olive-oil was imported. The fruit of the moringa tree was the only satisfactory alternative source of oil in quantity; other plants indigenous to the country which could produce suitable oil were the lettuce, the castor-oil plant, flax (for linseed oil), the *balanos* tree, the radish, saffron, and sesame.

Wine was produced from grapes and from dates, grape wine being the more highly regarded in antiquity. The best wine came from the Delta and from the oases of Kharga and Dakhla where viticulture was practised on a large scale. Vines were also cultivated to a lesser extent in small estates and gardens, and scenes of the vintage are common in tombs of the New Kingdom: the harvesting of grapes, their treading in large vats, and the storing of the juice in pottery jars. After fermentation the wine was sealed in jars and the jars marked with the place and year of vintage.

The culture of vines, as has already been mentioned, was practised in the gardens of estates in the New Kingdom. Most of the other vegetables and fruits grown in ancient Egypt were likewise cultivated in gardens where special arrangements were made for continuous irrigation. A garden was usually close to the farm or villa on ground raised above the level of the inundation, it had a pool to act as a reservoir, usually shaded by trees (as in the case of the garden shown in wall-painting 37983) and was intersected by ditches. These ditches and pools were filled by means of *shadufs* with water from canals leading from the Nile, and the irrigation of the gardens was effected either by directing water straight from a ditch on to a plot, or by means of water pots filled at the pool. Common garden-crops were beans, lentils, lettuce, onions, leeks, melons and other gourds, fruit (e.g. dates, figs, pomegranates), and flowers (much used for garlands at religious and secular festivals). A subsidiary product of Egyptian horticulture was honey, which was much prized as a sweetening agent.

Cattle- and poultry-breeding, the origins of which can be traced back to predynastic times (see, for example, the group of cows from El-Amra, 35506), were already highly developed in the Old Kingdom. Animals and birds were extensively reared not only for food but also for ritual purposes. The daily sacrifices at the temples and the provision of meat offerings in funerary services made great demands on the stock available and necessitated a high degree of skill in breeding and rearing. Oxen and sheep, much used as sacrifices, were the principal animals bred; goats, pigs, and donkeys were also kept for more general utilitarian purposes. In the Old Kingdom many desert animals like the antelope and oryx were captured and fattened, but it is not clear whether the Egyptians were successful in breeding them in captivity. There was usually sufficient rough grazing on the edge of the desert to raise herds of small cattle locally in Upper Egypt, but herds of cows were mostly pastured in the Delta.

Cattle were branded for identification purposes; a brand in the shape of horns (∪) is exhibited with other agricultural tools in the Fourth Egyptian Room (58817). His cattle were the pride of the farmer; thus many tombs contain scenes in which the deceased owner is shown viewing his herd or inspecting it at the time of census when taxes were assessed. Tomb painting 37976 is part of such a scene of cattle-inspection; it came from a Theban tomb of the Eighteenth Dynasty which was made for an official, a scribe and counter of grain, probably called Nebamun.

Another fragment from the same tomb (37978) bears part of a companion scene in which geese and other fowl are brought before the deceased owner. Geese were domesticated in remote antiquity and bred for the table and for ritual sacrifice. Other fowl are often shown in captivity, sometimes being forcibly fed. Wild fowl were captured in clap-nets in organized operations in the marshes and reared in the fowl-houses of estates and temples.

The marshes, which figure so largely in tomb scenes as the haunts of wild fowl and the places for hunting expeditions, were located in the Delta, round the lake in the Faiyum and in those depressions in the Nile Valley near the desert edge in which the flood-waters were trapped after the inundation. Organized hunting expeditions visited these marshes to catch birds and fish as a regular business. Private parties also went hunting in the marshes, women accompanying the men in their light boats. Fowling as a sport was practised with the throw-stick, cats being used to flush the birds. Wall painting 37977 (also from the tomb of Nebamun(?), Plate 4) illustrates such a fowling party and actual throw-sticks are exhibited in the Fourth Egyptian Room. With the throw-sticks are exhibited other instruments used in fishing and hunting—harpoons, a net (36886), bows and arrows, and an unusual bow-case with painted scenes of the chase on its sides (20648).

The resources of the land of Egypt

An account has been given of the agricultural riches of the land of Egypt; not only was the country exceptionally fertile for the raising of crops but it was also rich in its animal and bird life. Furthermore, the Nile teemed with fish and, although fish were held to be abhorrent to the gods, fishing was much practised both as an industry and as a sport. Dried fish, in particular, were used as food by ordinary people and many tombs contain scenes of fishing with nets together with the gutting and drying of the catch. A bowl of dried fish (36191) is shown in the Fourth Egyptian Room with other examples of food and fruits found mostly in Theban tombs of the New Kingdom.

Raw materials closely connected with the Nile, which will be dealt with more fully elsewhere, were papyrus (p. 92) and river-mud (pp. 206 ff.). The papyrus was a particularly useful plant of which scarcely any part was wasted. The flowers were used for decorative purposes, the stems, when complete, were employed as a primitive building material, and when separated into rind and pith were turned respectively into a fibre used for boxes, mats, ropes, and cord, and into a smooth, supple, thin writing material of great durability. Black Nile-mud was used for bricks and for pottery. Another type of mud, practically free from organic matter, found in certain valleys to the east of the Nile in Middle and Upper Egypt was also used in antiquity for producing a light grey-coloured ware with a greenish tinge.

For most domestic building and for many more formal structures sun-baked bricks were used, brick being the cheapest and easiest material to obtain and very easy to use (p. 206). The desire to construct buildings of greater size with the added advantages of imperviousness to water and durability led to the development of stone-construction at an early date in the historic period (p. 191). The Egyptian stone-mason was particularly fortunate in the materials available to him in the Nile Valley itself, or, more properly, in the cliffs and hills that edged the valley. From Cairo to Edfu the cliffs are mostly limestone; the quality varies considerably from place to place with the best stone being found not far to the south of Cairo at Tura and in parts of the Theban necropolis. South of Edfu the stone is mostly sandstone, the material that was used for most of the great temples from the Eighteenth Dynasty onwards. Finally, at Aswan in the region of the First Cataract there are great deposits of granite, both red and black.

Other stones used to a certain extent as building material were to be found in the immediate neighbourhood of the Nile Valley; chief among these were alabaster, the principal quarry of which was at Hatnub near El-Amarna in Middle Egypt; basalt, which is found in a number of places throughout the land and which was worked mostly in the Faiyum in the Old Kingdom, and quartzite, a very hard compact species of sandstone, most conveniently quarried in the Gebel Ahmar, to the north-east of Cairo.

Long before the time when the Egyptians first began to use stone for building they had worked it in small quantities to produce vases (p. 188). These vases were the great glory of Egyptian art in the Late Predynastic Period and during the Early Dynastic Period. Stones of all kinds were used and the Eastern Desert was scoured for its wealth of hard volcanic rocks. The stones mostly employed, in addition to those already mentioned as building materials, were breccia, diorite, dolerite, dolomite, various porphyritic rocks, schist, and serpentine. In the Eastern Desert also were found many semi-precious stones which were used to make jewellery; of these the most common were agate, amethyst, carnelian, chalcedony, felspar, garnet, jasper (red, yellow, and green), onyx, rock crystal, and turquoise. The precious stones such as emerald and beryl that existed in the Eastern Desert were not exploited until much later in the Graeco-Roman Period.

Two stones which played a great part in Egyptian economy throughout history, but which lacked the dignity of the great building stones, the beauty of the hard volcanic stones, and the charm of the semi-precious stones, were steatite and flint. The former, being soft and easy to work, was used for a variety of small objects; in particular the vast majority of Egyptian scarabs are made of steatite. As early as Badarian times the Egyptian learned how to glaze beads made of steatite (for glazing, see p. 213). This stone also is found in the Eastern Desert. Flint, on the other hand, is found freely throughout the valley of the Nile as nodules in the limestone or exposed on the surface where the surrounding limestone has been weathered away. From the very earliest times flint was used for tools and weapons, and even after the discovery of copper it continued in use for certain purposes: it seems to have acquired a ritual significance during the historic period for the knives used to slaughter and dismember sacrificial animals were usually made of flint. An admirable example of the 'ripple flaking' achieved during the manufacture of a flint blade is seen in the Pitt-Rivers knife (p. 40, fig. 9).

The wealth of stones found in Egypt satisfied most domestic needs and little had to be imported from abroad. Expeditions into the Nubian Desert for diorite and amethyst and to Sinai for turquoise were scarcely more than extensions of the exploration of the Eastern Desert. The only regular import of stone from elsewhere was that of lapis lazuli which probably came from Afghanistan via the Near Eastern trade routes: it was much used for jewellery and small figures and sometimes as an inlay. Obsidian, which was also used occasionally from predynastic times onwards for small objects like arrow-heads and amulets, and later for scarabs and small statuary, probably came from the coast of Ethiopia and may possibly have formed part of the trade with Punt (p. 36).

At an early period the Egyptians learned how to work metals and by the beginning of the Dynastic Age they had developed the techniques of mining and refining and were already seeking outside Egypt itself for additional sources of supply. The most important metal found in Egypt was gold; not only was it used lavishly in the arts and crafts of the country, but it became a powerful diplomatic weapon in the New Kingdom. The principal gold-bearing region was the Eastern Desert, and traces of ancient workings can be found in many places between the Nile and the Red Sea (p. 219); but much gold was obtained from Nubia where it was acquired by trading, as tribute, or from direct working by Egyptians when the country formed part of the Egyptian Empire. Gold came also as tribute from Asia, but probably in small quantities only. The wall paintings from the tomb of Sobkhotpe illustrate the manner in which gold arrived in Egypt from these places: two fragments show negroes bearing piles of gold ingots and gold rings (921 and 922, see Plate 5)–the unworked raw material; on a third fragment Asiatics are represented bearing articles of tribute, many of which are elaborately wrought vessels made of gold (37991). Silver, on the other hand, was not available in Egypt in a condition in which it could easily be mined and refined. In early times it was clearly rarer than gold and it was not until the Late New Kingdom that objects of silver equalled in number and value those of gold in important burials. Most of the silver probably had to be imported from Asia. Electrum, as used in Egypt, was probably always a natural alloy of silver and gold, the 'whiteness' of it depending on the proportions of the two metals. It was obtained from workings in the Eastern Desert.

The most common 'industrial' metal used in Egypt was copper, which was used in alloy with arsenic and, from the Middle Kingdom, with tin. Until recently it was thought that much of the copper used in ancient times was mined and smelted in Sinai. There is, however, very little evidence from antiquity to support this theory: it is certain, on the other hand, that copper was obtained from the Eastern Desert. Some copper also was imported, for the most part from Cyprus. In all probability arsenic and tin had to be imported from Asia. In consequence the general use of arsenical copper and bronze (the alloy of copper and tin) in Egypt developed later than elsewhere in the ancient Near East. In spite of their ability to master the most intractable materials and to develop advanced technical skills, the ancient Egyptians remained surprisingly backward in their use of metals (p. 218 ff.). Iron ores of various kinds exist in many parts of the Eastern Desert, but there is no evidence that they were mined and smelted until the Late Period, and not in any quantity until the Roman Period.

While Egypt was rich in stones of all kinds and in metals and other mineral resources, it was poor in timber. No large trees suitable for producing planks of good size grew in Egypt and there were very few small trees indigenous to the country which were of any use in carpentry or joinery. The acacia, sycomore-fig, dom-palm, and tamarisk were used to some extent in joinery and in small-scale carpentry and as the frameworks of boats; the date-palm was of no use in carpentry, but its trunk could be employed either whole or halved as roofing. From the earliest historic period and possibly even in the Late Predynastic Period, timber suitable for large-scale carpentry and for boat building was imported from the Levant. The most common source for this imported timber was the hinterland of the Syrian coast, the famous cedar wood of the mountains of Lebanon.

From the enumeration of materials available to the ancient Egyptians it will appear that in many respects the Nile Valley with its flanking deserts was able to satisfy most of the requirements of the Egyptian craftsmen. In addition to the general categories already dealt with, the raw materials for glaze and glass (the Sixth Room), for paints (e.g. 5547) and cosmetics (the Fourth Room), and for most of the preparations used in mummification were readily available in Egypt proper in antiquity. The needs of a civilized society were not, however, fully satisfied by the produce of the homeland, and trade-routes were developed to countries far afield. Western Asia could be approached by land and by sea, but the sea-route to the Syrian coast was most favoured from early times. Ships could carry large cargoes and they could move more quickly and reach any part of Egypt along the Nile. The port which handled most trade with Egypt was Byblos and the great sea-going ships used on the run to Byblos and elsewhere were called Byblos-ships. From Asia Minor came wood and wine, olive oil and metals, especially tin in later times. In the Mediterranean, sea-trade was also developed with Cyprus and, from the New Kingdom, with Crete, the Greek islands, and Greece. Sinai was reached by land via the isthmus of Suez. Land travel was laborious and dangerous, expeditions suffering much from shortage of water and attacks from desert tribes. Donkeys and asses were the only transport- and pack-animals available until the Eighteenth Dynasty. The route to Sinai was first opened up in the Early Dynastic Period and the chief prize there was, apparently, turquoise. Figure 6 (691) shows a fragment of a scene from Sinai in which Sanakhte, first king of the Third

6 Sanakhte smiting his enemies

Dynasty, smites the desert-dwellers: on the right of the fragment the word for 'turquoise' occurs, 𓄿 𓅱 𓏏 𓂝 ....

Many 'exotic' commodities were obtained from a region called Punt, the location of which has never been precisely established. It may have been part of the Somaliland coast. The first records of expeditions to Punt are preserved from the Fifth Dynasty. It is not known how often subsequent expeditions were sent but they were certainly dispatched from time to time until the reign of Ramesses III. Punt, also called 'God's Land', was the land of romance from which all kinds of strange, delightful things came —incense, gold, sandal-wood, ebony, giraffes, baboons, ivory, leopard-skins. The trade was carried on in sea-going ships from harbours on the Red Sea coast. The main route from the Nile Valley to the Red Sea coast passed through the Eastern Desert along the Wadi Hammamat, leaving the valley opposite Coptos and reaching the sea in the neighbourhood of old Quseir.

Trade with Nubia and countries to the south was conducted chiefly by land. Nubia was, for long periods, subjected to direct control by Egypt and was exploited accordingly. From the Middle Kingdom the principal commodity sought there was gold, but other materials were also obtained, such as diorite and amethyst. Through Nubia, too, came many of the products of equatorial Africa, some of which have already been mentioned as coming from Punt. The cast of the scene from the temple of Ramesses II at Beit el-Wali in Nubia, which is exhibited on the south wall of the Third Egyptian Room, shows clearly what the Egyptians were accustomed to get from Africa. The files of tribute-bearers bring leopard-skins, giraffe-tails, giraffes, monkeys, leopards, cattle, antelopes, gazelles, lions, ebony, ivory, ostrich-feathers and eggs, fans, bows, shields made of fine hides, and gold. African trade came into Egypt either through Aswan, where it was sub-jected to careful control, or by way of the line of oases running in a south-westerly direction from Kharga to Darfur in the Sudan. By this latter route some illicit trade was carried on. The only beast of burden available was the donkey; a pottery camel-figure found in the predynastic settlement at Abusir el-Melek is unique. Camel-figures otherwise do not occur until the Roman Period: a toy camel of this period is exhibited in the Fourth Egyptian Room (26664).

CHAPTER TWO

AN OUTLINE OF ANCIENT EGYPTIAN HISTORY

The terms used to describe the various periods of Egyptian history need some explanation. The first truly historical period is that which begins with the invention of writing and it is generally known as the Dynastic Period. It is a period extending from about 3100 BC to 332 BC and it derives its name from the thirty-one dynasties into which the successive kings of Egypt were divided in a scheme preserved in the work of Manetho, a priestly historian who lived during the reigns of the first two Ptolemies. The Dynastic Period is further divided into a number of relatively distinct shorter periods: the Early Dynastic Period (First and Second Dynasties, c. 3100–2686 BC), also known as the Archaic or Thinite Period, the Old Kingdom (Third to Sixth Dynasties, c. 2686–2181 BC), the First Intermediate Period (Seventh to Tenth Dynasties, c. 2181–2050 BC), the Middle Kingdom (Eleventh and Twelfth Dynasties, c. 2050–1750 BC), the Second Intermediate Period (Thirteenth to Seventeenth Dynasties, c. 1750–1567 BC; this period includes the Hyksos Period), the New Kingdom (Eighteenth to Twentieth Dynasties, c. 1567–1085 BC), the Late New Kingdom (Twenty-first to Twenty-fourth Dynasties, c. 1085–715 BC), the Late Period (a general term covering the whole period from the Twenty-third Dynasty to the Ptolemaic Period; it includes the Saite Period—the Twenty-sixth Dynasty). The Dynastic Period was followed by the Ptolemaic Period (332–30 BC) during which time Egypt was ruled by kings of Greek descent, and by the Roman Period (after 30 BC), when the country became a province of the Roman Empire.

The unlettered cultures which flourished in Egypt before the beginning of the Dynastic Period and which exhibit some of the characteristics which mark the earliest phases of Egyptian culture in the Dynastic Period are known as predynastic. The various stages of the predynastic cultures are discussed below. Such traces of human life as are found in the Nile Valley dating from before the Predynastic Period are usually described in the terms used for European Prehistory—Palaeolithic, Mesolithic and Neolithic.

The Prehistoric Period
The earliest remains of man's occupation of the Nile Valley and its neighbouring deserts are large, roughly shaped flint tools and

smaller flint scrapers, some of which are exhibited in the Sixth Egyptian Room. These primitive tools, made by the Palaeolithic inhabitants of Egypt, have been found principally on the desert hills and terraces bordering the Nile Valley in Upper Egypt. At this period North Africa was inhabitable throughout and Palaeolithic man ranged over the whole area, living the life of a nomad and hunter. The traces left by him in Egypt are no different from those left elsewhere in North Africa. In late Palaeolithic times the climate of the region changed markedly and pastures turned from grass to desert. Man withdrew from his old hunting-grounds to the neighbourhood of the Nile where traces of more settled occupation have been found in the shape of domestic refuse heaps near the sites of dried-up lakes and swamps. The use of flint was much developed by this time and smaller, finer tools for specialized purposes have been found, including arrow-heads and serrated blades which have been described as sickle-blades.

The possession of sickles presupposes the growing of cereal-crops, but there is no direct evidence in support of the view that such crops were cultivated in Egypt in late Palaeolithic times. The first positive evidence of such cultivation comes with the first remains of settlements in the Neolithic period. Occupation-sites of this period have been discovered on the western edge of the Delta, in the Faiyum, and in Middle Egypt. The inhabitants of these sites clearly lived a settled agricultural life growing crops of cereals and flax, making linen and baskets, crude pottery, and a wide variety of stone and flint tools. Objects from a particularly fruitful site on the northern edge of the Faiyum form the Museum's most important group of Egyptian Neolithic material: among these objects are a wooden sickle with flint blades still set in position (58701, fig. 7) and a finely woven fibre basket (58696).

The predynastic cultures

Little was known about the very early inhabitants of Egypt until the end of the nineteenth century when discoveries of predynastic cemeteries were made in Upper Egypt by Petrie and other excavators. The earliest discoveries were made at Naqada and consequently the principal predynastic cultures are distinguished as Naqada I (early) and Naqada II (late). The policy of naming the predynastic cultures after the sites of the first discoveries was continued in subsequent excavations, giving rise to the names Amratian (from the village of el-Amra), Gerzean (from el-Girza), and Semainean (from Semaina in Upper Egypt). These names are, however, best discarded, since

7 Wooden sickle with flint blades

they are merely duplicate terms for different stages of the Naqada I and Naqada II cultures. Amratian is essentially the same as Naqada I, Gerzean as Naqada II, and Semainean has been found to fall entirely in the early part of the First Dynasty. The earliest known predynastic culture, which was not discovered until the 1920s, is known by the separate name of Badarian, from the village of el-Badari. Guy Brunton, the excavator of this site, also proposed the existence of the Tasian culture (after Deir Tasa), which he believed to pre-date the Badarian period, but the evidence of the excavations suggests that Tasian is not to be regarded as independent but only as a phase of the Badarian culture. From graves of the Badarian Period the earliest copper objects found in Egypt have been recovered. Some small rings or beads are exhibited in the Sixth Egyptian Room. The use of copper was, however, still in its infancy and efficient smelting of ore had probably not yet begun. The pottery of the Badarian Period is particularly fine. Many different shapes were made and there developed a type of red-polished ware with blackened top which was to become very common in later periods. Much of the pottery is extremely thin and often decorated with delicate combed lines. Similarly, the uses of other materials like flint, ivory, bone, and stone were developed: a primitive form of glazing steatite beads was invented: for the first time the human figure was modelled (e.g. 59679, fig. 8). Among stone objects palettes of slate for grinding eye-paint are first found commonly in Badarian graves; stone vases may also have been first manufactured in the Badarian Period. It was in fact a period of great technical advance.

The Naqada I period, which succeeded the Badarian, is characterized by distinctive styles of pottery, including polished red ware, highly burnished, often with black, carbonized rims, or with white-painted incised decorations. This decoration may be in imitation of wickerwork or it may consist of simple scenes of animals and of hunting. Stone vessels are not common; those that have been found are mostly of basalt with decorative lug-handles and small conical bases. Slate palettes of simple shapes are commonly found in the graves of the period and disk-shaped mace-heads of granite and other hard stones may testify to the development of warlike tendencies although there is some reason to believe that these objects may have had a ritual purpose only. The large numbers of finely-cut flint arrow-heads, on the other hand, were no doubt used equally for fighting and for hunting. Flint was still the material mostly used for tools and weapons.

The bodies found in graves in the early predynastic cemeteries of Upper Egypt show that the typical Egyptian of the time was slimly built with long delicate features. From the rather crude

8 Terracotta figure of a Badarian woman

figures in clay and ivory found in their tombs it appears that the men of this Upper Egyptian race wore beards and long penis-sheaths, features which connect them ethnically with the Libyans.

Remains of the more advanced Naqada II culture occur at many sites throughout Egypt, often at places which have also yielded the earlier Naqada I artifacts, showing a continuity of occupation through these two consecutive phases of pre-dynastic culture. The Naqada II period was a time of considerable progress, as shown by the fine flint tools, copper implements, beads of hard stone, and of crude glazed composition which have been found in graves of that age. The graves themselves show improvement of design over the earlier simple pits, with reed matting and wood used to protect the burial. Slate palettes in animal form with eyes made of circular shell-beads are found in most graves, together with a distinctive style of buff pottery with decoration in purple paint. Hard stone was used for the manufacture of vases, which became more numerous than previously, and for pear-shaped mace-heads which superseded the disk-form of the Naqada I period. The occasional use of non-Egyptian materials like lapis lazuli shows that there was some trade contact at this early date between Egypt and Asia.

The progress achieved at this time led to further advances by the latter part of the Naqada II period, such as the introduction of brick-lined graves and refinements in the manufacture of implements, an excellent example of which is the Pitt-Rivers flint knife with an ivory handle, upon which are carved figures of animals in low relief (68512, fig. 9).

Nothing certain is known about the political organization in Upper and Lower Egypt during the Early Predynastic Period. It is generally thought that there existed two loose confederations made up of communities which corresponded to some extent with the later nomes. The political centres seem to have been Naqada (Nubt) in the south with Seth as the chief deity and Behdet in the north with the falcon-god Horus as chief deity.

In the Late Predynastic Period (i.e. the latter part of the Naqada II culture) the two confederations postulated above became more clearly defined and their leaders were already identified by their distinctive crowns which formed an important

9 Flint knife with a carved ivory handle

10 Slate palette decorated with the scene of a hunt

part of royal symbolism in historic times. The 'king' of Lower Egypt wore the red crown ( ) and the 'king' of Upper Egypt wore the white crown ( ). Two new capital cities were now established at Buto in the Delta and at Hierakonpolis in Upper Egypt. The period seems to have been one of continuous struggle and some of the individual events are known from the elaborately carved slate palettes which have been preserved. The Hunters' Palette and the Battlefield Palette exhibited in the Sixth Egyptian Room are two such monuments. The former (20790, fig. 10) shows the hunting of two lions and other wild animals; the scene contains possibly symbolic references to the national struggle. The latter (20791) on one side shows a lion, probably representing a king, seizing his enemies. The final conquest of the north by the south which led to the unification of the two kingdoms of Upper and Lower Egypt was effected by a king known to history as Menes. No contemporary monument bears a royal name that can with certainty be read as Menes, but he is generally identified with the king Narmer who is shown wearing both the red and the white crowns on a great palette now in Cairo. With the unification of the kingdoms begins the historic period in Egypt.

Early Dynastic Period (c.3100–2686 BC)

After the unification of the country a considerable administrative reorganization was effected. One of the few positive acts of this reorganization of which we know anything was the establishment of a new administrative capital at Memphis which lay at the junction of Upper and Lower Egypt. Tradition credits the legendary Menes with its foundation. Little is known about the history of Egypt during the first two dynasties. A Fifth Dynasty annalistic inscription, parts of which are preserved in Cairo (the Cairo Annals), Palermo (the Palermo Stone), and London

(University College), contains entries which are laconic and serve principally the purpose of identifying a year by some outstanding event. Most of these events are religious in character, such as the setting up of cult-statues, but occasionally an entry is more informative. Thus, one year of Djer, the third king of the First Dynasty, is designated by the phrase 'smiting of Sinai (?)', from which it may be reasonably deduced that punitive expeditions were sent beyond the limits of Egypt very soon after the establishment of the united kingdom. Similar grains of information can be gleaned from the texts found on the wooden and ivory labels used to identify the contents of boxes deposited in early tombs. One ivory label in the British Museum collection (55586, fig. 11) comes from Abydos and shows Den, the fifth king of the First Dynasty, braining a kneeling, bearded enemy;

the text of the scene reads 'the first time of smiting the East'. It has been thought that the event so commemorated was an early expedition into Sinai. Other tablets bear scenes of a religious and ritual character (e.g. 32650), and meagre though the evidence is, it does enable some evaluation to be made of the extraordinary advances in civilization made during this early period. Two cemeteries containing many important tombs of the Early Dynastic Period have been found at Abydos and Saqqara. There has recently been a great deal of dispute as to which of these two cemeteries contains the royal tombs of the period, but, when all the evidence is considered, there can hardly be any doubt that Abydos was the royal cemetery, and that the Saqqara tombs belonged to high officials. The tombs at both places have yielded many small objects which reveal the technical skill and artistic achievement of the Egyptians at the beginning of the historic period. In these tombs are found architectural elements in stone—the earliest in Egypt—and roofing timbers of such a size that the wood must have been imported from the coastal forests of western Asia. Small objects of materials not native to Egypt, such as lapis lazuli and ebony (?), further testify to the existence of trade connexions with Asia and tropical Africa.

11 Den striking an Asiatic chieftain

Unfortunately, the material remains of the two earliest dynasties do no more than provide tantalizing hints of what was happening politically in the country. It seems probable that the unification of Upper and Lower Egypt was a solution imposed by the successful conquerors from the south and that the tendency towards the dissolution of the union became stronger as the central authority weakened. This tendency was ever present in ancient Egypt and was due principally to the difficulty of ruling a country seven hundred miles long with only the Nile as the means of communication. Apparently some relaxation of the central authority occurred towards the end of the First Dynasty and from a period of political dissolution emerged the Second Dynasty, the first king of which was either Raneb or Hotepsekhemwy. The name of the latter, meaning 'the Two Powers are appeased', possibly preserves the memory of such an upheaval and the re-establishment of the single authority. The establishment and maintenance of the unity of the country had in these early times become a prime political aim and its significance for the kings of the earliest dynasties is evident in the entries that occur on the Palermo Stone to mark the beginning of each reign: 'Unification of Upper and Lower Egypt, Encircling of the Wall'. The wall here is the great white wall of the new capital Memphis and the reference is to one of the ceremonies of the coronation-festival. In the Sixth Egyptian Room is a small figure of a king dressed in the cloak characteristic of these ceremonies (37996). The statuette is of ivory and was excavated by Petrie at Abydos (fig. 54). It represents a king of the First or Second Dynasty, but there is no inscription to identify him precisely.

The largest object in the collection of the Museum from the Second Dynasty is a grey granite stela bearing the name of Peribsen, the sixth king of the dynasty (35597). The name is contained in a rectangular frame, known as a *serekh*, the lower part of which represents the façade of some great building, possibly a palace. This frame is surmounted by a figure of the Seth-animal, instead of the Horus-falcon which had been regularly used in this position by all kings from the beginning of the First Dynasty. In this substitution it is possible to detect some internal political change which prompted Peribsen to transfer the royal allegiance from Horus, traditionally the deity and ancestor of the king of unified Egypt, to Seth, his divine rival. The next king, who ascended to the throne with the name Khasekhem, 'the Power has appeared', reverted to the practice of writing the Horus-falcon over his name, but he later seems to have reconciled the theological dispute. He then changed his name to Khasekhemwy ('the two Powers have appeared'), written beneath both the Horus-falcon and the Seth-animal. At the same time he added to his name the phrase, 'the two Lords are content in him', which can only refer to the rival gods. The real reasons for these internal movements remain, unfortunately, obscure, but they may ultimately have led to the change which resulted in the establishment of the Third Dynasty.

The Old Kingdom (c.2686–2181 BC)

The Early Dynastic Period, in spite of the paucity of its material remains, was undoubtedly a great formative time in which the bases of Egyptian civilization were firmly established. By the end of the Second Dynasty artistic conventions had been evolved, hieroglyphic writing had advanced so far that it quickly became a flexible vehicle for the transmission of continuous narrative; techniques in craft and industries were highly developed. Egypt was in fact ready for an efflorescence of civilized activity which was to be marked by a sophistication strongly in contrast with the stiff archaic culture of the preceding period. The king whose reign ushered in this new epoch was Djoser and the chief agent in the transformation was Imhotep, the royal architect whose fame in later times was so great that he was ultimately venerated as a god and equated by the Greeks with Asklepios, their own god of healing (p. 133). The most striking monument of Djoser and Imhotep, and that which now characterizes the inauguration of the new epoch, was the Step Pyramid at Saqqara, with its great enclosure containing many buildings connected with the ritual ceremonies performed by the king. The complex, built of limestone, was faced with the fine white stone of Tura. Although stone had been used for some architectural features in tombs of earlier times, no building had previously been wholly constructed of stone; never before had such skill and mastery over material been shown. The architectural conception as a whole is, however, the outstanding feature of the monument which has, ever since its construction, remained a positive reminder that in Djoser's reign Egyptian civilization came of age. That the ancient Egyptians themselves thought so is shown not only by the evidence of later inscriptions scribbled on parts of the Step Pyramid buildings by visitors, and by the undoubted antiquarian interest taken in the pyramid in the Saite Period, but also by the fact that Djoser's reign is specially emphasized in the Turin King List of the Nineteenth Dynasty, by the unusual use of red ink. There is some doubt as to whether he was the first or second king of the Third Dynasty. His rival for this position is Sanakhte, a shadowy king of whom few monuments are known. Both Djoser and Sanakhte sent expeditions to Sinai in search of turquoise and possibly copper, and in the course of their expeditions the local Bedouin were subdued. Records were left in Sinai by both kings, and part of a relief of Sanakhte is now in the British Museum (691, fig. 6). It is also possible that during Djoser's reign the southern boundary of the kingdom was fixed at the First Cataract.

The expansion of power during the Fourth Dynasty is more adequately documented by the monuments and written records preserved from that time. During this dynasty pyramid-building reached its zenith. The culmination of the development may be seen in the Great Pyramid of Cheops, the second king of the dynasty. This structure, which dominates the desert plateau at Giza somewhat to the north of Memphis, on the west of the Nile, remains one of the most remarkable buildings ever erected by man. It is not, however, generally realized that in ground plan it is only a little larger than the northern pyramid built at Dahshur by Sneferu, the first king of the dynasty. Excavations have revealed the extent to which Egypt was highly organized from the early Fourth Dynasty with all departments of life and administration controlled from the royal residence at Memphis, where the king, the 'good god', was supreme. The king's pyramid was surrounded by the mastaba-tombs (p. 178) of the members of his family and of the great nobles who served him at court and at the provincial nome centres. From the inscriptions in the tombs of the nobles it is clear that the king was the focus of existence; to him all honour and duty were owed and from him all favours issued. The titles held by the nobles give some indication of the highly organized nature of administration. The false door stela of Kanefer, a son of Sneferu, now exhibited in the Egyptian Sculpture Gallery (1324) contains an enumeration of his titles which amount to 47, covering all departments of administration—priestly, civil, judicial, military, financial, and personal to the sovereign. Undoubtedly the holding of many of the titles was nominal but they presuppose that actual administrative functions were highly organized on well-defined departmental lines. The efficiency of administrative organization at this time is in nothing better exemplified than in the construction of the pyramids. The contention that these vast structures were built by slave labour is now generally discounted in favour of the view that the bulk of the building was carried out during the season of inundation when agricultural workers could not cultivate their fields. Only during this season was sufficient labour available. Furthermore when the Nile was in flood it was relatively easy to transport the quarried stone from the hills on the east of the Nile to the desert-plateau where the pyramids were erected. It is estimated that the Great Pyramid when complete contained about 2,300,000 blocks of stone of an average weight of $2\frac{1}{2}$ tons, the movement of which from quarry to site alone must have needed an organization of labour vast in extent. Cheops' successor, after the short intermediate reign of Radedef, was Chephren, who also built his pyramid at Giza; it is a little smaller than the Great Pyramid but from its situation on slightly higher ground it appears to be larger. Chephren also was probably the king whose likeness was preserved for posterity in the features of the great Sphinx which lies close to the Valley Temple of Chephren's pyramid. This great human-headed lion, carved out of a single knoll of rock, possibly represents the king as the sun-god, protecting the royal cemetery. Formidable though these building achievements of Sneferu, Cheops, and Chephren were, they undoubtedly put an excessively heavy strain on the economy of the country, for no attempt was ever made again to equal them. The pyramid of Mycerinus, a later king of the Fourth Dynasty, which completes the trio of large pyramids at Giza, is very much smaller in size, while Shepseskaf, the next king, built himself a large stone mastaba-tomb at Saqqara.

The history of the Fourth Dynasty is largely an account of its monuments, for very little is known about the activities of its kings in other respects. Inscriptions in Sinai and in the diorite quarries in Nubia show that expeditions were sent to obtain materials from these places and that these expeditions were commonly escorted by military contingents. From the Palermo Stone it is known that Sneferu sent a large punitive expedition into Nubia and another against the Libyans. Recent discoveries show that a copper-smelting factory was operating at the northern end of the Second Cataract during the Fourth Dynasty. The recording of the arrival of a number of sea-going ships laden with timber in Sneferu's reign further suggests the continuance of trade with western Asia through Byblos. During the Fifth Dynasty the sending of expeditions to Nubia, Sinai, and Libya is more fully recorded. There is also one mention of an expedition during the reign of Isesi, the eighth king of the dynasty, to the region of Punt. Knowledge of these enterprises comes largely from the biographical inscriptions set up in their tombs by the important nobles who acted as expedition commanders. One of the most interesting is that of Ptahshepses exhibited in the Egyptian Sculpture Gallery (682). Ptahshepses was born during the reign of Mycerinus, married a daughter of Shepseskaf, and continued in life and office at least until the reign of Nyuserre, the sixth king of the Fifth Dynasty. The increasing freedom of the nobles who were able thus not only to set up inscriptions celebrating their own personal achievements but even to marry members of the royal family is one indication of the relaxation of the strong personal authority that had characterized the rule of the Fourth Dynasty kings.

The concept of kingship also underwent modification during the Fifth Dynasty, partly because of the increased allegiance to the cult of the sun-god Re, worshipped at Heliopolis, partly owing to the growing influence of the myths of the Osiris legend (pp. 147 ff.). According to a story which was popular during the Middle Kingdom, the first three kings of the dynasty (Userkaf, Sahure, and Neferirkare) were the children of the wife of a priest of Re, the god Re himself being their father. From the early Fifth Dynasty every king called himself 'son of Re', a title which had been used previously only by a few fourth-dynasty kings. In honour of Re and in commemoration of the relationship between Re and the king, at least six of the Fifth Dynasty monarchs built elaborate sun-temples at Abu Gurab, some miles to the south of Giza. In addition to sun-temples they also built pyramids, some at Abu Sir and others at Saqqara, but these pyramids were very much smaller than the great structures of the early Fourth Dynasty. Nevertheless, they were greatly enhanced by extremely fine painted decorations in relief, and by the variety of architectural detail executed in fine hard stone as well as limestone, in the pyramid-temples and the ancillary buildings. A tall granite palm-tree column with a capital carved in the form of palm fronds bound together from the pyramid-temple of Unas, the last king of the dynasty, stands in the Sculpture Gallery (1385). The maintenance of the services connected with the cults of the successive dead kings was arranged by the establishment of foundations supported by grants of land freed from burdensome taxes and levies. In the Fifth Dynasty foundations of this kind were also set up for the maintenance of the sun-temples. Some of the documents relating to the temple of Neferirkare, compiled in the reign of a successor Djedkare Isesi, the eighth king of the dynasty, are preserved in the British Museum (10735). They form part of the earliest group of inscribed papyri yet discovered in Egypt (fig. 32).

An innovation of great importance was introduced into the pyramid of Unas: the walls of the vestibule and burial chamber were covered with religious texts concerned with the fortunes of the king after his death. These texts are now called the *Pyramid Texts*; they occur also in pyramids of the Sixth Dynasty (p. 178). The tombs of the nobles, which during the Fourth Dynasty were of modest size and were grouped closely around the royal pyramid, were, during the Fifth Dynasty, constructed on a far more ambitious scale and were less closely associated with the pyramid of the king. This development, which indicates a further diminution of the dependence of the noble on his monarch, was carried a stage further during the Sixth Dynasty when it became customary for the great noble to be buried in his nome, the local seat of his power, far away from the royal residence and the royal cemetery. The administration of affairs throughout Egypt became, during this dynasty, much decentralized and consequently the local officials became more important and more independent. This relaxation of central authority was to end in its complete dissolution, followed by a period of anarchy which is known as the First Intermediate Period. For the greater part of the Sixth Dynasty, however, the kings were sufficiently strong to maintain the unity of Egypt and to prosecute vigorous policies inside the country and abroad.

For this dynasty more than for any of the earlier dynasties the inscriptions from the tombs of high officials provide much information about the activities of the kings. From such sources the expanding nature of Egyptian foreign policy emerges. Under the kings Pepi I, Merenre, and Pepi II expeditions were sent deep into Nubia and Libya, into western Asia and Sinai, and to Punt. The descriptions of some of these expeditions show that the intention was frequently far more punitive than it had been in earlier times and that foreigners were recruited to supplement the slender domestic forces of the Egyptian army.

It was during the long reign of Pepi II, who is thought to have reigned about ninety-four years, that the central administration ultimately collapsed. The events which brought about the dissolution of central control are not known. Decentralization of administration and the consequent increase in power of provincial governors, especially in the case of the Governor of Upper Egypt, undoubtedly contributed to the process. In addition, the aged Pepi II in his last years could hardly have prosecuted the vigorous policies that had characterized the early part of his long reign. In ancient Egypt the relaxation of strong central government was almost always followed by political fragmentation of the country. Such appears to have happened either in the last years of or soon after the end of the reign of Pepi II, and brought about the downfall of the Old Kingdom.

The First Intermediate Period (c.2181–2050 BC)

The Sixth Dynasty, after the death of Pepi II, is credited with two or three shadowy rulers by the king lists. The time of political anarchy which followed the collapse of the central authority at the end of the Sixth Dynasty is known as the First Intermediate Period. The internal chaos in the country seems to have been intensified by the activities of groups of Bedouin who reached the Delta at about the same time. Very little is known about Egypt during this period, which lasted approximately one hundred and thirty years. Manetho's Seventh Dynasty may have been little more than a coalition of nobles centred on Memphis who tried to hold together the crumbling central authority. His Eighth Dynasty has a little more historical substance; its kings exercised some control from Memphis as far south at least as Coptos, where inscriptions bearing some of their names have been found. Otherwise Egypt was ruled locally by the nomarchs who, in the conditions of the time, became virtually regional princes. Inscriptions set up in their tombs reveal the extent to which these nomarchs were obliged to administer their territories as independent units, often engaging in petty warfare with their neighbours. The inevitable outcome of this inter-nome rivalry was the emergence of certain strong nomes with which weaker nomes became at first allied in confederacy and later bound in political dependence. The first nome to take a lead in this manner was the twentieth nome of Upper Egypt, the capital city of which was Heracleopolis. The rise of Heracleopolis (about 2160 BC) coincided with the decline of the Eighth Dynasty, and Achthoes the nomarch of Heracleopolis, to whom must be assigned the credit for establishing the new dynasty, claimed the kingdom of Egypt, assuming the throne-name of Meryibre. He pursued an active and (if the tradition preserved in Manetho is to be believed) ruthless policy of reducing Middle Egypt to his control, but he does not appear to have had any success in winning over the most southerly nomes of the country or the Delta. The Ninth and Tenth Dynasties were composed of nineteen kings ruling from Heracleopolis, several of whom bore the name Achthoes. While they never succeeded in gaining control of the whole of Egypt, they undoubtedly established a strong, stabilizing régime in the northern part of the country. In the Delta Asiatic influence was largely eradicated and trade with western Asia by the sea-route re-established, as is demonstrated by the use of Lebanese cedar wood for the large painted coffins which are so characteristic of the Heracleopolitan culture. Memphis again became the administrative capital of the northern part of Egypt and the kings were buried in the old royal cemetery at Saqqara. One of the kings named Achthoes, who had the prenomen Nebkaure, is chiefly famous as the king to whom a disgruntled Egyptian made a series of complaints in one of the most popular of Egyptian stories (p. 101).

Meanwhile, in southern Egypt a struggle for power had developed between changing confederacies of nomes among which those of Edfu (the second) and of Thebes (the fourth) were predominant. Thebes was a town that had only recently achieved prominence in its nome at the expense of Hermonthis, the old nome-capital. It was ruled by a family of nomarchs,

mostly called Inyotef, who followed a lively policy of aggrandize-
ment in southern Egypt. At first their efforts were principally
directed at securing hegemony in the south, but when this had
been achieved a clash with Heracleopolitan power in the north
was inevitable. The struggle between north and south acquired
a new significance when one of the Theban Inyotefs challenged
the position of his Heracleopolitan contemporary by assuming
the title 'King of Upper and Lower Egypt'. This 'king' Inyotef
Sehertowy ruled a 'kingdom' which remained the small
southern confederacy of nomes; but to future generations of
Egyptians he was regarded as the founder of the reunified
country and the first king of the Eleventh Dynasty. His successor
Inyotef Wahankh succeeded in extending his dominions as far
north as Aphroditopolis. The fine limestone stela of Tjetji
(614, fig. 12) records the limits of the kingdom at Elephantine
and This. Tjetji was a high official who held office under
Wahankh and his successor Inyotef Nakhtnebtepnefer. The
struggle between Thebes and Heracleopolis was resolved in the
reign of the next Theban king, Nebhepetre Mentuhotpe II, who
finally succeeded in reducing the northern power. After reuniting
the whole of Egypt under one authority he took the Horus-name
of Smatowy, 'He-who-unites-the-Two-Lands'. From this reunification (about 2050 BC) dates the beginning of the period now
called the Middle Kingdom.

The Middle Kingdom (c.2050–c.1786 BC)

The stages by which Nebhepetre Mentuhotpe completed the
reunification of Egypt are not known. What can be discovered
from contemporary inscriptions is that he pursued a very
energetic policy of consolidation and rehabilitation. The re-
establishment of a single administration for the whole country
was followed by campaigns in the north against the Libyans and
the Bedouin and in the south against the Nubians. The mines
and quarries were reopened and trade routes re-established. At
the end of his long reign of about fifty years Mentuhotpe II
could claim to his credit the formation of the Egyptian state
which achieved such great success politically and artistically
during the Middle Kingdom. His own tomb was constructed
according to a highly original plan in a bay in the cliffs at
Deir el-Bahri on the west bank of the Nile at Thebes. The reliefs
which decorated the associated temple were carved in a most
accomplished manner, far removed from that of the dispro-
portionate, awkward work of the First Intermediate Period,
and resuming much of what was best in late Old Kingdom
Memphite art. Fragments of these reliefs can be seen in the
Egyptian Sculpture Gallery.

12 Limestone stela of
Tjetji

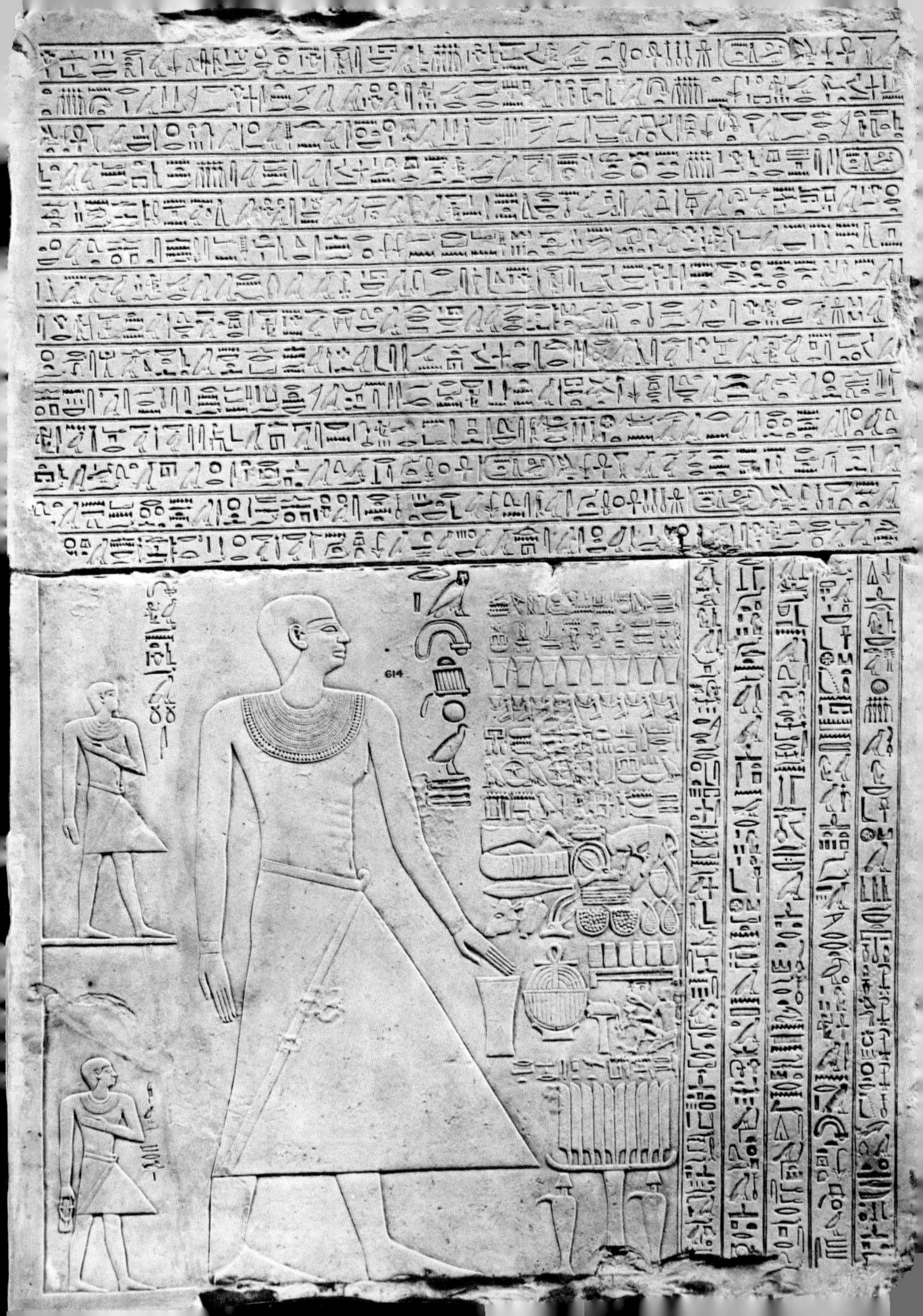
614

Among the activities which regularly indicated the revival of Egypt after a period of decline was the reinstitution of expeditions to Punt. The first expedition of the Middle Kingdom took place in the reign of Sankhkare Mentuhotpe III, the son and successor of Mentuhotpe II. It is recorded in an inscription carved in the Wadi Hammamat through which ran the road from the coast of the Red Sea to Coptos—the road along which the Punt expeditions travelled. Another inscription in the same place helps to make clear how the Eleventh Dynasty ended and the manner in which the ruling family was replaced by that of the Twelfth Dynasty. This second inscription records an expedition to the Wadi Hammamat in the reign of Nebtowyre Mentuhotpe IV, the last king of the Eleventh Dynasty. It was led by a vizier called Ammenemes and was remarkable for the occurrence of several incidents which were interpreted as significant omens. In about 1991 BC the government of Egypt was taken over by a certain Ammenemes who as king is now known as Ammenemes I. It is highly probable that he is to be identified with the Ammenemes of the Wadi Hammamat inscription and it is generally thought that he assumed control as king either when the government under Nebtowyre broke down, or on the death of that king.

Under the kings of the Twelfth Dynasty (c. 1991–1786 BC), of whom Ammenemes I was the first, Egypt once more became a highly organized, well-administered country with vigorously prosecuted policies in respect of Nubia, Libya, and western Asia. To ensure the strength and continuity of government it became the practice from the very beginning of the dynasty for the ruling king to accept, as a co-regent for the last years of his reign, his eldest son and intended successor. The wisdom of this arrangement was demonstrated at the end of the reign of Ammenemes I when that king was assassinated and his son, Sesostris I, was able to take over control immediately although he was on campaign in the Western Desert. An important move, designed to ensure a proper control over the whole country, was the transference of the seat of administration from Thebes in the south to a place at the entrance to the Faiyum in the north near the junction of Upper and Lower Egypt. This new capital was named Itj-towy, 'Seizer of the Two Lands', and in its neighbourhood the kings of the Twelfth Dynasty built their principal residences. They were subsequently buried in pyramids built at Itj-towy, at Dahshur (in part of the Old Kingdom royal necropolis), at Illahun, and at Hawara some miles to the south of Itj-towy.

One of the principal reasons for the political disintegration of Egypt during the First Intermediate Period was the increasing power and independence of the nomarchs. During the Twelfth

Dynasty steps were taken to ensure that their power was limited. From the inscriptions found in tombs of the nomarchs in Beni Hasan and elsewhere it emerges that Ammenemes II (1929–1895 BC) re-established nome-boundaries in some cases and that he, in other respects, reorganized the administration of the whole country so as to ensure greater central control and to curb the excessive power of the nomarchs. By the end of the dynasty the influence of these noble princes was completely broken and no longer are their tombs found in the provincial cemeteries. It has been suggested that the king responsible for this development was Sesostris III (1878–1843 BC), who may even have abolished the office of nomarch. Three statues of this king are shown in the Egyptian Sculpture Gallery (684, 685, 686; fig. 70).

In foreign affairs Egypt was particularly active during the Twelfth Dynasty, the pattern of activity being established by Ammenemes I. To keep out from the Delta the continuous waves of infiltrating Asiatics from the east, Ammenemes I constructed a fortification known as the Walls of the Prince. Very little is known of the actual warfare in western Asia during the dynasty apart from a foray by the General Nesymont in the joint reign of Ammenemes I and Sesostris I and an expedition by Sesostris III; it seems probable that the visibly active policy of the Egyptian kings was in itself sufficient to keep the migrant tribes of the area away from the borders of Egypt. The discovery of Egyptian objects of Twelfth Dynasty date in Syria and Palestine reveals, however, that there was considerable contact between Egypt and those countries, not least through the ancient port of Byblos. Two of the most interesting objects of the period in the British Museum were acquired in Beirut and probably came from Byblos: first is the diorite sphinx (58892) of Ammenemes IV (1798–1790 BC), exhibited in the Fifth Egyptian Room. The face of this sphinx was reworked in later times. The second is the gold plaque of the same king, exhibited in the Sixth Egyptian Room (59194, fig. 13). Throughout the Twelfth Dynasty Nubia presented a

13 Gold plaque of Ammenemes IV

great problem to the Egyptian kings. For many reasons it was found necessary to extend Egyptian control over the lands to the south of the First Cataract. Apart from the need to secure the southern boundaries of the kingdom, it was essential to ensure safe access to the mineral-bearing areas in Nubia and to establish the trade routes farther south into the heart of Africa. Under Ammenemes I Lower Nubia was annexed, and a fortress was established at the northern end of the Second Cataract at Buhen under his successor Sesostris I. Later in the Dynasty, most probably during the reign of Sesostris III, a series of fortresses was constructed in the districts of the First and Second Cataracts. The warlike temperament of the local tribes, particularly of those now called the C-group and Kerma peoples, forced the Egyptian kings to take vigorous precautions to prevent any sudden revolt against the occupying forces and to foil any attempts at infiltration over the southern boundary of Egypt established by Sesostris III at the southern entry to the Second Cataract, and protected by the fortresses of Semna and Kumma. To this end strict provisions were made regulating the movement of the native peoples living in the area of Egyptian influence and check-points were set up to regulate trade and immigration. The extent of effective Egyptian penetration southwards at this period has never been determined with certainty, although evidence of penetration south of the Second Cataract has been found in the form of various isolated inscriptions. Undoubtedly by the middle of the Twelfth Dynasty a large and permanent native settlement had been established at Kerma at the southern end of the Third Cataract, giving its name to the culture found there. The threat of aggression from Kush, the Egyptian name for this Nubian kingdom, is reflected in a group of despatches (a copy of which was deposited in Thebes), sent out from the fortress of Semna, and recording the movements of Nubians in that region. These documents, written early in the reign of Ammenemes III, admirably illustrate the well-organized administration developed by the Egyptians in Nubia (10752).

Much of the activity undertaken by the kings of the Twelfth Dynasty outside the narrow limits of the valley of the Nile was stimulated by the demands of the arts and crafts which flourished so vigorously during this time. As in the Old Kingdom, expeditions were regularly sent to exploit the quarries and mines in the Eastern Desert, Lower Nubia, and Sinai. Sea-borne expeditions visited Punt to obtain the exotic products of equatorial Africa, and Syria to obtain wood; it is possible that regular trade was established with Crete. Knowledge of the activities of Egyptian kings in foreign lands is preserved often only in the memorials set up in distant places by the officials concerned.

Ammenemes IV, who succeeded Ammenemes III, maintained the stability of the state and even prosecuted policies abroad in the tradition of his predecessors. He did not, however, equal them in energy, perhaps because he was already an old man when he was made co-regent with his father. The dynasty ended with Sobkneferu, his sister, of whom little is known.

Second Intermediate Period (c.1786–1567 BC)

The period between the end of the Twelfth Dynasty and the beginning of the Eighteenth Dynasty is generally called the Second Intermediate Period. Of the five dynasties allotted to this time by the late historian Manetho, three are native Egyptian and two are probably to be assigned to Hyksos rulers. The historical sequence of events has not yet been satisfactorily established and it appears that a certain amount of overlapping took place not only between the native and foreign dynasties but also within the limits of the individual dynasties. In brief the sequence seems to have been as follows: the centralized government of the whole country continued to function during the Thirteenth Dynasty until the increasing weakness of the central control gave opportunities to Asiatic settlers in the Delta to establish a separate kingdom in the north. These Asiatics are known as the Hyksos, a name derived from the Egyptian words *ḥekau-khasut*, 'princes of foreign countries'; they do not appear to have been an invading race but settlers who took advantage of chaotic conditions to seize power in the Delta, later extending their control farther south.

Manetho assigns sixty kings to the Thirteenth Dynasty and indeed the names of a large number of kings possibly belonging to the dynasty have been preserved on monuments and small objects. It is clear that the breakdown of central authority after the end of the Twelfth Dynasty was a gradual process and that the pattern of government was maintained both in the south and the north for many years. The credit for this state of affairs seems to rest more on the able viziers and other administrative officers of the time than on the kings who succeeded each other in rapid succession. The capital of the country remained in the north, friendly relations were maintained with Byblos and western Asia, and control was still exercised in Nubia. Some temple building was undertaken and there is much evidence of other activity within Egypt, indicative of a relatively settled political condition. Furthermore, artistic traditions were to a great extent maintained and the lamentable decline in style and technique so noticeable in the art of the First Intermediate Period was avoided. The statuette of Meryankhre Mentuhotpe in the Fifth Egyptian Room (65429, fig. 14) illustrates this maintenance of standards.

14 Schist statuette of Meryankhre Mentuhotpe

Nevertheless, the unstable position of the kings of the period, the precise reasons for which cannot now be determined, eventually led to such a weakening in government that Lower Egypt became progressively detached from the rule of the Thirteenth Dynasty kings. Of the Fourteenth Dynasty little is known except that it consisted of a large number of rulers (seventy-six according to Manetho) who seem to have controlled part of the western Delta from the town of Xois, capital of the sixth Lower Egyptian nome. It is possible that this region began to secede soon after the end of the Twelfth Dynasty and that the Thirteenth and Fourteenth Dynasties were largely contemporaneous.

No precise details are known of the rise to power of the Hyksos rulers in the eastern Delta. It is generally thought that Asiatic settlers, powerful locally, succeeded in about 1720 BC in establishing some sort of régime with its capital at Avaris and with Seth as its god. The line of rulers, forming the Fifteenth Dynasty, assumed control in about 1670 BC. The names of the minor Hyksos royalties of the Sixteenth Dynasty who apparently ruled concurrently with the Hyksos kings are preserved, for the most part, on scarabs. The Hyksos kings, on the other hand, can be identified as six in number, some of whom were rulers of great vigour and achievement. Their influence extended throughout Egypt although they did not apparently rule directly in the Theban area. Scarabs bearing their names have been found at Kerma in the Sudan and in Palestine. Antiquities found in Crete and western Asia testify to the widespread nature of their contacts. The granite lion (987), exhibited in the Fifth Egyptian Room, bears the name of Khyan, the third of the Hyksos kings; it was found in Baghdad. The tradition that the Hyksos were merciless tyrants who imposed a harsh rule on a resisting native population seems to have been deliberately fostered as early as the Eighteenth Dynasty, although indirect evidence from the period of their rule and from the early Eighteenth Dynasty itself in no way supports this tradition. On the contrary, the Hyksos seem in many ways to have ruled in the manner of native rulers, taking Egyptian names and fostering Egyptian culture. The great Rhind Mathematical Papyrus, part of which is exhibited in the Third Egyptian Room (10058, Plate 9), was written in the reign of Auserre Apophis I. This ruler, who occupied the throne for over forty years, apparently maintained good relations with Upper Egypt until comparatively late in his reign when a clash with a rising dynasty of Theban princes became inevitable.

One of the most interesting objects surviving from the Hyksos Period in the British Museum is the ivory figure of the forepart of a sphinx clutching an Egyptian by the ears (54678). The sphinx is thought to represent one of the Hyksos kings and the piece may have been made at the time when the Hyksos were establishing their suzerainty over Egypt. It was found in a tomb in a cemetery at Abydos containing some graves belonging to the Pan-grave people. These Pan-grave people were of Nubian stock who came to Egypt apparently to serve as professional soldiers. For some time during the Second Intermediate Period they preserved their native customs; their graves give evidence of a way of life different from that of the contemporary Egyptians (e.g. the black incised jar from Mostagedda, 63038). In later times they were more completely assimilated into Egyptian life, abandoning their old burial habits.

The movement which ended in the liberation of Egypt from the Hyksos domination began in Thebes. About 1650 BC the Thirteenth Dynasty was succeeded by a new family of rulers, known as the Seventeenth Dynasty. The members of this line, who affected the royal titles and attempted to preserve the culture and tradition of the Middle Kingdom, are divided into two groups. The earlier group consists of rulers who were seemingly content to confine their power to a small group of nomes in Upper Egypt. They probably acknowledged the suzerainty of the Hyksos and made no effort to improve their position politically.

A coffin in the Second Egyptian Room, made of wood overlaid with gold leaf, belonged probably to Nubkheperre Inyotef, the first king of the second group of Seventeenth Dynasty kings (6652). The kings of this second group asserted their claim to the throne of the whole of Egypt by prosecuting a policy which ultimately led to a violent clash with the Hyksos rulers. The struggle reached a peak under Kamose who not only penetrated Nubia at least as far as the Second Cataract, but also succeeded in carrying the war to the gates of Avaris itself. In the Fourth Egyptian Room there is an axe-head inscribed with Kamose's name (36772). The final defeat of the Hyksos and their expulsion from Egypt took place about 1567 BC under Kamose's successor, Amosis, the founder of the Eighteenth Dynasty.

New Kingdom (1567–1085 BC)

The character of the Eighteenth Dynasty as a whole was established by the policies of the early kings of the dynasty. These policies were in turn determined largely by the necessities of the situation that faced Amosis I when he became king of a united Upper and Lower Egypt after the capture of Avaris. The immediate steps that needed to be taken were the securing of the fortresses in the north, on the east and west of the Delta, the re-establishment of the central administration of the land of

Egypt, the consolidation of Egyptian control in Nubia and the reopening of trade routes to Africa and Asia. As at the beginning of the Middle Kingdom, a great upsurge of enthusiasm and activity followed the reunification of Egypt after the expulsion of the Hyksos. Amosis I followed up his successes in the Delta by besieging and reducing, after a three years' siege, the Hyksos stronghold of Sharuhen in southern Palestine. This new positive policy of aggression in Asia itself was followed by Amosis' immediate successors, especially Tuthmosis I, who penetrated as far as the Euphrates, defeating the strong kingdom of Mitanni and setting up a stela on the eastern bank of that river. The activities of the early kings of the Eighteenth Dynasty, were, however, devoted far more to the conquest of Nubia and the extension of Egyptian power southwards up the Nile. Amosis succeeded in recovering the country as far south as the Second Cataract, but further operations were hampered by subversive movements in Lower Nubia which had to be quelled. To promote Egyptian policy in Nubia, Amosis instituted the high office of viceroy, an office which remained of great importance throughout the New Kingdom. Amenophis I and Tuthmosis I extended the southern boundary well beyond the Third Cataract and continued the work of Amosis in rehabilitating the series of fortresses built during the Middle Kingdom. Similarly, these early Eighteenth Dynasty kings took firm steps to reconstitute the boundaries of Egypt on the west of the Delta, campaigning vigorously and successfully against the Libyans. Within Egypt itself the re-establishment of the united kingdom was marked by a great revival in temple building, especially at Karnak, and in a renaissance in art which derived its inspiration largely from the best work of the Middle Kingdom. Tuthmosis I was the first king to build his tomb in the Valley of the Kings. This valley on the west bank of the Nile at Thebes was chosen because of its remoteness and relative inaccessibility, and throughout the New Kingdom it was used as the burial place for the kings of Egypt.

Tuthmosis II, who succeeded Tuthmosis I in about 1512 BC, suffered apparently from poor health and was unable to continue the policies of his predecessors with equal vigour. He died at a comparatively young age, leaving as his heir and successor the boy Tuthmosis III. In view of the youth of the new king, his stepmother Hatshepsut assumed the position of regent and for a short time discharged this function with appropriate discretion. In the second year of the new reign, however, Hatshepsut either of her own volition, or at the instigation of a group of powerful officials, asserted her personal claim to the throne, secured her own coronation and successfully supplanted the young king,

15 Statuette in black
   granite of the
   steward Senenmut

ruling with apparently complete control over the whole of Egypt for about twenty years. Tuthmosis III was not deposed but was deprived of all effective power. Positive evidence of what happened during this time is lacking, but there is no reason to suppose that there was any deliberate lull in Egypt's aggressive foreign policy. The outstanding monument of the reign is the funerary temple of the queen at Deir el-Bahri which was built under the direction of her favoured steward Senenmut. Some of the scenes on the walls of this temple show an important trading expedition sent to the region of Punt. A granite statue (174) shows Senenmut nursing Neferure, the daughter of Hatshepsut, for whom he served as tutor (fig. 15).

In about 1482 BC Tuthmosis III succeeded in re-establishing himself as sole ruler, in the twenty-first year of his nominal reign. It is not certain whether his triumph followed the ousting of Hatshepsut or the death of that queen. The new régime was not at first openly hostile to the achievements and memory of its predecessor. Only towards the end of the reign of Tuthmosis III was positive hostility expressed in a campaign of destruction and mutilation designed to efface the memory of Hatshepsut. Her name was hammered out on monuments and buildings throughout the land. About the same time as the rehabilitation of Tuthmosis III a great revolt of subject princes occurred in Syria which resulted in the withdrawal of Egyptian garrisons to southern Palestine. It may in fact have been the revolt that enabled the king to recover his throne. He acted at once with great vigour and in 1481 BC inflicted a severe defeat on the rebelling princes at Megiddo. He did not, however, rest merely at re-establishing the *status quo* (from the Egyptian standpoint) in western Asia; in a series of well-planned, brilliantly executed campaigns he followed up his initial success by extending the limits of Egyptian control far to the east, across the Euphrates and to the north, to the boundaries of the Hittite Empire. Control over the conquered territories was exercised by local princes who could be trusted, their fidelity in most cases being stimulated by the presence of Egyptian envoys. In a similarly energetic manner he extended the southern limits of the Egyptian Empire beyond the Fourth Cataract in the Sudan, founding the important trading and garrison town of Napata in the region of that cataract. A positive and beneficial result of all this activity was a marked increase in Egypt's contacts with distant countries and a consequent development in trade and the exchanging of embassies. The prosperity of the country, combined with the stimulation received from foreign contacts, led to a dramatic increase in artistic activity in Egypt. New temples were built, great additions made to the existing national shrines; sculpture

16 Schist head from
a statue of a king
identified as
Tuthmosis III
(*opposite*)

17 Quartzite head
from a statue of
Amenophis III
(*above*)

and painting flourished and the minor arts profited from the
wealth of precious materials now available. Figure 16 shows
a life-size head in schist of a king who has been identified as
Tuthmosis III (986). The identification is, however, not certain.

The active policies of Tuthmosis III were continued by his
successors Amenophis II and Tuthmosis IV. The former, who was
unusually tall and strong for an Egyptian king, penetrated farther
south in the Sudan than any of his predecessors, but apparently
retained the effective boundary of the Egyptian empire at Napata.
He and Tuthmosis IV maintained Egyptian prestige in Asia, the
latter considerably strengthening the position by securing a
marriage with a daughter of the King of Mitanni, the powerful
buffer-state lying between the empires of Egypt and of the
Hittites. A fine bronze kneeling figure of Tuthmosis IV, present-
ing bowls of ointment to a god, is exhibited in the Fifth Egyptian
Room (64564); the granite model sacred bark of Mutemuia, his
Mitannian wife, is in the Egyptian Sculpture Gallery (43).

Amenophis III, the son and successor of Tuthmosis IV, became
king of Egypt when her fortunes had reached their zenith
(fig. 17). Abroad her empire was secure, its limits established at

Karoy in the Sudan and at Naharin in western Asia, as Amenophis III proclaimed in the text placed on one of a series of large scarabs which were issued by him to commemorate important happenings of his reign (examples of all the known commemorative scarabs are shown in the Sixth Egyptian Room). At home the country was settled and prosperous. No special effort was required of the new king to maintain the situation apart from a single punitive expedition to the Sudan in his fifth year, and possibly a few tours of western Asia in the early years of the reign. Foreign policy was otherwise restricted in the Sudan to the fostering of Egyptian ways and civilization accompanied by the extensive building of temples in some of which the king himself was worshipped as a god; in Asia to the development of friendly relations with the rulers of the subject principalities of the empire and of the countries bordering the empire. Some of the diplomatic correspondence from this reign and from that of Akhenaten written in Akkadian, the lingua franca of the period, was discovered at El-Amarna and part is preserved in the Department of Western Asiatic Antiquities of the Museum. Relations with several of the foreign kings were cemented by marriages between Amenophis III and daughters of the kings. The arrival in Egypt in year 10 of one of these princesses, Gilukhepa, daughter of King Shuttarna of Mitanni, was celebrated on one of the great commemorative scarabs.

Within Egypt prosperity and the attendant settled conditions enabled Amenophis III to devote himself to extensive building operations and to the fostering of the arts. Great temples were constructed, among which the temple of Luxor dedicated to Amen-Re, the god of the empire, was the most unusual in design and the most beautiful in appearance. Of several representations of the king in the British Museum, one of the most interesting is that on a small stela found at El-Amarna where the king is shown seated with his principal wife Tiy, a woman of non-royal birth whose strong personality left a considerable mark on the reign (57399, fig. 18). In this representation, which may have been carved after the death of the king, Amenophis III is shown as an old, obese man, slumping in his chair, an uncharacteristic pose for Egyptian kings and unlike the formal, conventional representations of the king found, for example, in the two colossal seated statues in the Egyptian Sculpture Gallery (4 and 5). It is a representation made when Egyptian art had developed strikingly realistic tendencies after the introduction of the worship of the Aten (p. 137). There is evidence that shows that the cult of the sun-disk already flourished during the reign of Tuthmosis IV (e.g. the scarab 65800 exhibited in the Sixth Egyptian Room which bears a text mentioning the Aten) and

18 Sandstone stela of Amenophis III and Queen Tiy

during the reign of Amenophis III it gained steadily in importance until it was formally adopted by his son. The precise order of events at the end of the reign of Amenophis III is uncertain; it is possible that for the last years of his reign he associated his son with himself on the throne and that this son, first as Amenophis IV and then as Akhenaten, took control of government. However, it is also possible that Akhenaten only came to the throne on his father's death. At first the centre of government remained at Thebes but the devotion of the young king to the cult of the Aten (for whom he constructed a temple at Karnak) brought him into conflict with the priesthood of Amun and its adherents. This conflict was resolved early in his reign by the proscription of the worship of Amun and other state gods and by the moving of the capital from Thebes to a site in Middle Egypt which was then named Akhetaten, 'the Horizon of the Aten' (now called El-Amarna). Here, with the support of his wife Nefertiti and of a party of faithful courtiers, he was able to devote himself to the promotion of the new religion (pp. 137–8). In the realm of foreign affairs Akhenaten did little to preserve the empire as he received it from his predecessors. His inactivity and lack of interest provided the opportunity for subversive movements

among the dependent princes and for successful incursions into friendly territories by hostile states. Many of the Amarna letters contain urgent appeals for assistance from loyal but hard-pressed vassal princes and provide a vivid picture of the gradual loss of Egyptian influence in Syria in the face of the growing power of the Hittites.

19 Fragment of a relief showing the head of Akhenaten

On his sculpture and reliefs Akhenaten is depicted as a person of unusual physical appearance; he is shown with an enlarged head, pronounced stoop, and heavy hips. It is not certain how much this appearance was due to his own physical peculiarities or to the artistic style of the period (fig. 19). He found little general support for his régime and towards the end of his reign of seventeen years suffered many set-backs which obliged him to modify his policies. Apart from the troubles in the empire his position was weakened by hostile movements within Egypt which eventually necessitated a *rapprochement* with the priesthood of Amun, though possibly not in his own lifetime. The agreement between the factions of Aten and Amun appears to have begun under Smenkhkare. He reigned as co-regent with Akhenaten for about two years and survived him by only a few months, being succeeded by Tutankhamun. In the reign of the last the return to the worship of Amun as the principal state god, and the abandonment of Akhetaten in favour of Thebes were finally accomplished. One of his chief advisers was General Horemheb who had a splendid tomb constructed for himself in the necropolis of Saqqara, panels from which can be found in the Museum's collection (550, 551, and 552, fig. 20).

Tutankhamun died while still a youth and he was succeeded for a short time by Ay, an elderly noble, who possibly reinforced his claim to the throne by marrying the widow of Tutankhamun, Ankhesenamun. With his reign it may be said that the interlude of the Amarna period came to an end. It is possible that Ay was made king by Horemheb to act as a transitional monarch until he himself was ready to take over the royal power. When Ay died in about 1348 BC Horemheb became king and a new era of positive government began for Egypt. His active policies were aimed at securing the internal stability of Egypt and her prestige abroad as they had existed before Akhenaten. Under the Nineteenth Dynasty the Amarna period was formally forgotten, the memory of Akhenaten eradicated from the records of the land, and his name hacked out of texts wherever it occurred; the town of Akhetaten and many buildings associated with Akhenaten were dismantled. Horemheb was credited with a reign that followed immediately that of Amenophis III.

The reign of Horemheb (who did not belong to the royal family of the Eighteenth Dynasty) served as a transition between the Eighteenth Dynasty and the Nineteenth Dynasty which was founded by Ramesses I in about 1320 BC. Ramesses I had clearly been groomed for the throne by Horemheb, who had made him his vizier in Lower Egypt. The family of Ramesses sprang from the Delta and one of the notable changes made later in the new dynasty was the moving of the royal residence from Thebes (which still remained the administrative capital) to Piramesse in the eastern Delta, a town occupying the site of Avaris, the ancient stronghold of the Hyksos. Ramesses I, who reigned for a short time only, and his son Sethos I continued the work of Horemheb in restoring the damaged pride of Egypt's temples and gods and in reasserting the authority of Egypt in Nubia and western Asia. Much work was done at Karnak in the national shrine of Amun, but the outstanding achievement in the field of temple-building was the new Osiris temple built by Sethos I at Abydos. In foreign affairs Sethos engaged in settling an insurrection in Nubia, in repulsing the Libyans from the western Delta and, principally, in pushing the limits of the Egyptian empire in Asia to the Orontes. The Hittites had by now become a major threat to the Egyptian Empire in Asia, and Sethos, after inflicting a defeat on them beyond the Orontes, eventually withdrew south of Qadesh.

Ramesses II, who succeeded his father in 1304 BC, after a period of association with him as co-regent, was eager to reopen the struggle. A preliminary campaign in his fourth year was followed in the subsequent year by a great attack which culminated in a battle at Qadesh on the Orontes. The Hittite and

20 Inscribed panel from the tomb of Horemheb

Egyptian records give divergent accounts of the outcome of this struggle, and it is probable that neither side could properly claim a victory. Ramesses, however, made out that a great triumph had been achieved through his own valour, and the battle was celebrated in a bombastic composition which was inscribed on the walls of a number of temples in Egypt and Nubia. Parts of two copies on papyrus are preserved in the British Museum and pages from both are exhibited in the Third Egyptian Room (10181 and 10683). In the years following the battle constant vigilance and frequent punitive expeditions were needed to preserve the security of the Asiatic Empire. Ultimately, in his twenty-first year, Ramesses II concluded a treaty with Khattushilish, king of the Hittites, the effect of which was subsequently cemented by a marriage between Ramesses and a daughter of Khattushilish. For the remainder of his long reign of sixty-seven years peace prevailed in the Egyptian Asiatic Empire.

The early years of Ramesses II's reign were in general devoted to settling external troubles. A campaign in Nubia was celebrated in reliefs carved on the walls of a rock-cut temple at Beit el-Wali; the large painted casts on the walls of the Third Egyptian Room reproduce the scenes. Early in the reign too there was a clash with sea-raiders known as the Sherden—a warning of much greater troubles that were to assail Egypt in future generations. Apart from the threat of trouble from the west of the Delta, which was countered by the construction of a series of fortified outposts, the greater part of Ramesses' reign was relatively free from warfare. The vigorous activity of the early years was consolidated by strong administration and firm diplomacy in Nubia and Asia and the king was enabled to devote his energies to building and to the development of his royal reputation as Egypt's greatest king. The tone of his work was set by the inscription which he set up in the Osiris temple of Sethos at Abydos which he completed. In this text he revealed himself as a ruler with a firm belief in his own ability to achieve great things; and in his reign he succeeded in fostering his reputation to such an extent that even in the Classical Period he was regarded as the great Egyptian king *par excellence*. This reputation was perpetuated largely by means of the great buildings erected throughout Egypt during his reign. One of his most remarkable monuments is the rock-temple of Abu Simbel in Nubia with its four immense seated figures of the king. In all the great centres in Egypt he built new temples or added considerably to existing buildings. Statues, large and small, glorified his person (e.g. 19, Plate 7) and many representations of earlier kings were usurped for Ramesses by the substitution of his names for theirs (e.g. 61).

Merneptah, one of Ramesses II's many sons, became king at an advanced age and was almost immediately faced with a crisis which had been developing for some years. Ethnic movements in northern Asia Minor and the Aegean resulted in attempts by migrant tribes to gain a foothold in the Delta. Ramesses II had repulsed such an attempt by the Sherden. Other tribes had been successful in establishing themselves to the west of the Delta. Forts erected by Ramesses II were not adequate to deal with more than local forays and in Merneptah's fifth year a considerable incursion was made into the Delta. A pitched battle was fought at Pi-yer, an unidentified place in the western Delta, Merneptah securing a decisive victory, which for some time relieved Egypt of pressure from Libya.

The later history of the Nineteenth Dynasty is hard to establish; even the sequence of the kings is uncertain. The historical summary in the Great Harris Papyrus (see below) declares that the country fell into decline and that for a time a Syrian named Arsu took control of Egypt. He is generally identified with the Chancellor Bay, an influential courtier at the end of the dynasty. The state of anarchy in this period has probably been exaggerated in order to extol a new-comer, called Sethnakhte, who established a new ruling line known as the Twentieth Dynasty. After a short reign he was succeeded by Ramesses III, the last great king of the New Kingdom, in whose reign Egypt both experienced a revival of glory and prosperity and suffered attacks which presaged her downfall as an imperial power. Three great campaigns were conducted by Ramesses III to repulse attacks made or threatened against the Delta. Two in years 5 and 11 were against the Libyans in coalition with various so-called Peoples of the Sea, among whom the Meshwesh were most prominent. In year 8 a serious attack came from the east, by land and sea, the invading forces again being composed of Peoples of the Sea (but not the Sherden, by then mercenaries in the Egyptian army). Ramesses III succeeded in gaining brilliant victories in all these crises and preserved the land of Egypt itself from invasion. Thereafter, Ramesses III undertook no further large-scale military operations, a few modest forays against insurgent tribes in southern Palestine being the extent of his activities abroad. With Egypt at peace for the greater part of his reign Ramesses III was able to foster trade and engage in extensive building works. The principal monument of his reign is his great mortuary temple at Medinet Habu (Plate 15), which became the administrative centre of the Theban necropolis during the late Twentieth Dynasty. Some idea of the prosperity of the land can be gained from the great lists of donations to temples recorded in the papyrus known as the Great Harris, now preserved in the

British Museum (fig. 34). This document, part of which is shown in the Third Egyptian Room, was prepared under Ramesses IV (fig. 21) to glorify the memory of his father. There is reason, however, to doubt that all was as well as it was painted in the Egypt of Ramesses III. Other documents record a strike of workers in the royal necropolis and a harim conspiracy directed at the life of the king himself towards the end of his reign. These subversive movements probably indicated a deterioration in

21 Kneeling figure of
Ramesses IV

prosperity and political stability which became more marked in the subsequent reigns. From the death of Ramesses III in about 1166 BC until the end of the Twentieth Dynasty about 1085 BC eight kings, all called Ramesses, occupied the throne. In this period Egypt finally lost the remnants of her Asiatic Empire and suffered serious economic consequences thereby. Towards the end of the dynasty it was discovered that the royal tombs at Thebes were suffering wholesale plundering. Many of the documents dealing with the investigation of the thefts and the legal action taken subsequently have been preserved and some are in the British Museum, such as the Abbott Papyrus (10221) and Papyrus 10053 which are exhibited in the Third Egyptian Room (p. 120 ff.).

During the last years of the reign of Ramesses XI power in Egypt was virtually divided between the High Priest of Amun at Thebes, named Herihor, who styled himself king at Thebes, and Smendes who governed Lower Egypt from Tanis. The king himself apparently withdrew to his Delta residence, and while recognized as monarch, he exercised no real authority. This division of the country, in which both parts existed apparently on amicable terms, continued for many generations.

Late Dynastic Period (1085–332 BC)

After the death of Ramesses XI the royal attributes were assumed by Smendes, who, relying probably on a connexion with the old ruling house, established a new dynasty, called the Twenty-first by Manetho, with its capital at Tanis in the Delta. Simultaneously the line of the High Priests of Amun, possibly descended from Herihor, assumed control in the south at Thebes. The members of the priestly dynasty did not claim for themselves the title of king of Upper and Lower Egypt and only rarely did they place their names in cartouches. Their efforts were aimed at developing the state of Amun in coexistence with the secular authority ruling from Tanis, and it seems that both sides were careful not to encroach on each other's prerogatives. One great task undertaken by the High Priests was the salvage of the old royal burials at Thebes, the plundering of which had caused such a scandal in the late Twentieth Dynasty. Those mummies which remained undamaged were in many instances rewrapped and they, together with such of their funerary equipment as had survived, were transferred to the tomb of Queen Inhapy at Deir el-Bahri and to the tomb of King Amenophis II in the Valley of the Kings. Here they remained, together with the burials of the High Priests of the Twenty-first Dynasty and their families, until the late nineteenth century. From these hiding-places came the *Book of the Dead* of Pinudjem, High Priest of Amun

under King Siamun, now in the British Museum (the Campbell Papyrus, 10793), the wooden *shabti*-board of Neskhons, the wife of Pinudjem (16672), exhibited in the Third Egyptian Room and the *Book of the Dead* of Herihor and Nodjmet (10541, fig. 22). The régime of the Tanite kings seems to have been without distinction and it was superseded apparently without any strife by that of the kings of the Twenty-second Dynasty, in about 945 BC.

During the Twentieth Dynasty colonies of Libyan (or Meshwesh) mercenaries had been established on Egyptian territory mostly in the Delta. Sheshonq I, the first king of the Twenty-second Dynasty, came from a Libyan military family in Bubastis and had previously served as a general under the last ruler of the Twenty-first Dynasty. He secured the allegiance of the High Priests of Amun by breaking the tradition of hereditary appointment that had lasted throughout the Twenty-first Dynasty, appointing his own son to the office. It is also known, from the Old Testament (1 Kings xiv. 25–26), that Sheshonq conducted at least one military campaign into Palestine in the course of which he carried off the treasures of the temple in Jerusalem; but it is not clear whether this campaign was prompted by simple aggressive intentions, or was launched in support of Jeroboam, pretender to the throne of Judah in the reign of Rehoboam (2 Chron. xii. 2–9). The scanty records of

22 Vignette from the *Book of the Dead* of Queen Nodjmet and Herihor

events which have been preserved from the Twenty-second Dynasty indicate that Egypt was in a very unsettled state. In spite of the move by Sheshonq I to attach Thebes more closely to the northern monarchy, the forces of separation in Thebes were continually exerted, especially when the High Priest of Amun, usually the son of the reigning king, did not have his residence at Thebes. During the reign of Osorkon II (*c.* 874–850 BC) one High Priest called Harsiese even assumed a royal titulary, but he was eventually replaced by the king's son. Part of a granite relief from Bubastis, exhibited in the Egyptian Sculpture Gallery, shows Osorkon II with his wife Karoma (1077, fig. 23). The state of the land during the dynasty may be deduced from the long inscription of the High Priest Osorkon, son of Takelothis II, in the temple of Karnak. From this text it is clear that there were many subversive groups active in different parts of the country and, in spite of the fairly close relations between Thebes and the king at this time, it was not easy to maintain peace throughout the land. In the succeeding reign of Sheshonq III (*c.* 825–773 BC) further troubles led to changes in the High Priesthood at Thebes and also to the establishment in the Delta of a parallel ruling line, the Twenty-third Dynasty, by a certain Petubastis, in about 818 BC. The lack of a strong central authority in Egypt always resulted in antiquity in the disintegration of the state into smaller units. Good relations between the kings of the Twenty-first and early Twenty-second Dynasties, ruling in the north, and the High priests of Amun, ruling at Thebes, went some way to keeping unity in the land; but when, from about 818 BC, even the outward forms of accord were absent, there was nothing to prevent the natural dichotomous tendency from developing. During the last reigns of the Twenty-second Dynasty and those of the concurrent Twenty-third Dynasty, further fragmentation took place and the process was halted only by the arrival in Egypt of a conqueror from the south.

For many years the town of Napata in the neighbourhood of the Fourth Cataract in the Sudan, after the withdrawal northwards of the Egyptians, had been ruled by a native Sudanese dynasty which preserved many Egyptian customs including the worship of the god Amun. The Napatan prince Kashta occupied the whole of Lower Nubia, but it was left to his successor Piankhi to make a decisive intervention in Egyptian affairs. His most determined opponent was Tefnakhte of Sais, a Delta ruler who seems to have attained considerable power in Lower Egypt, occupied Memphis, and was in the process of extending his influence southward. In about 727 BC Piankhi undertook a major campaign into Egypt to check his rival's advance. He took

advantage of the disunities in the country and advanced as far north as Memphis securing the submission of various local princes. Tefnakhte submitted ultimately to Piankhi, but was allowed to continue in power in Lower Egypt, founding the short-lived Twenty-fourth Dynasty. Piankhi himself withdrew to Napata, controlling Egypt from abroad and it was his brother Shabaka who effected the final conquest of the whole land, defeating and killing Bocchoris, Tefnakhte's successor, and setting himself up in Thebes as a full king of Upper and Lower Egypt. Under the kings of the Twenty-fifth Dynasty, of whom Piankhi is considered the first, signs of a marked revival in the artistic and cultural life of Egypt can be observed, well exemplified by the head 67969 (Plate 6). This revival reached its height in the subsequent Twenty-sixth Dynasty. Temples were restored and added to and the rituals received a necessary stimulus. The devotion of these kings to Amun was marked by the increase in importance given to the office of Divine Adoratrice of that god. This office was occupied usually by a royal princess and appointment to it was by adoption. During the Twenty-fifth Dynasty the Divine Adoratrice wielded real power in the Theban area, the first of that Dynasty being Amenirdis, daughter of Kashta and sister of Piankhi. A statuette of Amenirdis is exhibited in the Fifth Egyptian Room (46699). Devotion to Amun did not, however, prevent these Nubian kings from attending to the needs of the other national gods of Egypt. Evidence of the attention paid to the worship of Ptah at Memphis is provided by the copy of the ancient sacred dramatic composition recorded on a block of basalt at the order of Shabaka now exhibited in the Egyptian Sculpture Gallery (498, p. 146). Under Taharqa, a later king of the Dynasty, considerable building works were carried out in Egypt and the Sudan. At Kawa in Nubia, an old Egyptian town with an important sanctuary of Amun dating back to the Eighteenth Dynasty, Taharqa restored the old buildings and constructed a new temple, from which came the kneeling ram with a figure of the king between its front legs (1779, fig. 24).

The last years of his reign and the whole of the reign of his successor, Tanutamun, were troubled by attacks from the east where the Assyrians were in the ascendancy. The struggle came to a head in 671 BC when Esarhaddon the Assyrian King succeeded in penetrating into Egypt as far as Memphis, winning over many of the petty Delta rulers who seem once again to have secured a high degree of independence from the central authority. Shortly afterwards Taharqa succeeded in regaining Memphis, deposing the administration set up by Esarhaddon; but in 667 BC the Assyrians returned, this time under their new ruler Ashurbanipal, whose forces occupied Memphis and may have

23 Part of a relief
showing Osorkon II
and his wife Karoma

advanced as far as Thebes. He later carried off to Nineveh several of the Delta princes who were accused of conspiring against Assyrian rule. Among these captive princes was Necho of Sais, possibly a descendant of Bocchoris. Necho found favour with Ashurbanipal and was returned to Sais to be reinstated as local ruler. Necho's son Psammetichus was installed as prince of Athribis. Taharqa had fled to Nubia where he died in 664 BC. His successor Tanutamun embarked on a campaign of re-conquest, occupied Memphis after killing Necho of Sais, and won over the Delta dynasts; but his success was short-lived. In a second campaign Ashurbanipal again occupied Memphis and his forces sacked Thebes. Tanutamun withdrew to Nubia and Psammetichus I who had fled to the Assyrians on his father's death was appointed vassal ruler of Sais, Athribis, and Memphis. The administration of Lower Egypt and possibly most of Upper Egypt north of the Thebaid was now in the hands of local rulers—the period of the Dodekarchy, as the Greeks later called it—while Thebes was controlled by the Divine Adoratrice Shepenwepet II and a high priestly official called Mentuemhat (1643). Psammetichus, son of Necho, who was himself prince of Athribis, and who succeeded his father at Sais, campaigned with the help of Lydian and Carian mercenaries to reunite most of Lower and Middle Egypt under his rule, establishing himself as the first king of the Twenty-sixth Dynasty. He ultimately extended his control over the whole of Egypt in 656 BC by

24 Recumbent ram and figure of King Taharqa

securing the adoption of his daughter Nitocris by the Divine
Adoratrice, at Thebes, Shepenwepet II. He eventually felt strong
enough to discontinue tribute to Assyria and thus Assyrian
control over Egypt lapsed.

The Saite Period, a name commonly given to the Twenty-
sixth Dynasty, was a century of revived splendour for Egypt.
The artistic revival that had already begun in the Theban area
under the auspices of the Nubian kings now flowered abundantly,
much of its inspiration being derived from the ancient art of the
Old and Middle Kingdoms. In other ways too the period was one
of archaizing tendencies; in religious matters the Pyramid Texts
were studied and used again in private tombs; in administration
old titles and offices were revived. Egypt was now a country
much favoured by foreign immigrants, attracted by opportunities
of trade and of employment as mercenaries. In many parts of the
country large foreign colonies developed which contributed considerably to the prosperity of the land. The greatest of these
colonies was Naucratis in the Delta, founded probably in the
reign of Psammetichus II, which, later in the Dynasty, became
the sole town from which Greek traders could operate in Egypt.
The details of the many campaigns in which the Saite kings
engaged in Asia are not fully known. In the last years of
Psammetichus I the Assyrian kingdom was overcome by Babylon
under Nabopolassar and a new threat was offered to Egypt.
Some success by the Egyptians under Necho II in 609 BC when
Josiah, King of Judah, was slain at Megiddo (2 Kings xxiii.
29–35; 2 Chron. xxxv. 20–22; Jer. xlvi. 2) was followed by a
crushing defeat at Carchemish in 605 BC when the Babylonians
were commanded by Nebuchadrezzar. The reign of Psammetichus
II was relatively peaceful, apart from an expedition into Nubia,
apparently as far as Napata itself, possibly designed to thwart
a new attempt by the Nubian kings to assert their authority
in Egypt. The Nubian kingdom was subsequently transferred
to Meroe, although Napata continued to serve as a religious
centre. Thereafter contact with Nubia was spasmodic only,
although her rulers remained strongly influenced by Egyptian
culture. Within Egypt the Pharaoh Apries of the Twenty-
sixth Dynasty (589–570 BC) turned his attention to the north,
intervening on a number of occasions in the struggles being
fought out in Syria and Palestine. His downfall, however, was
brought about by a disastrous defeat suffered by the Egyptian
army which he sent to help the Libyans to eliminate the Greek
colony of Cyrene. In the aftermath of this defeat civil war
developed in the Delta and Apries was overthrown, being
replaced by Amosis II who was not apparently related to the
Saite ruling house. Of his long reign little is known apart from

what is written by Greek historians, but it seems that he devoted himself mostly to domestic affairs and to the promotion of good relations with Egypt's neighbours. During his reign the Divine Adoratrice of Amun at Thebes was Ankhnesneferibre, whose great sarcophagus is exhibited in the Egyptian Sculpture Gallery (32, fig. 25). Amosis died in 526 BC, thereby just escaping the doom which had threatened Egypt for many years since the rise of Persian power in the east. In 525 his successor Psammetichus III was defeated at Pelusium, Memphis was besieged and captured, and the whole of Egypt fell to Cambyses, who became the first king of the Twenty-seventh Dynasty.

Under the Persian kings of the Twenty-seventh Dynasty Egypt was reorganized as a satrapy of the Persian Empire. Greek tradition tells of the terrible sufferings of the land during this time, but contemporary evidence from Egypt does not confirm the tradition. Both Cambyses and his successor Darius I seem to have introduced administrative changes which greatly benefited the land; laws were codified; great public works undertaken, such as the completion of the canal begun in the reign of Necho II, connecting the Nile with the Red Sea; even new temples were built and old ones restored. In the years after the defeat of the Persians by the Greeks at Marathon (490 BC) an attempt was made in the Delta to throw off the foreign yoke. Xerxes, who succeeded Darius I in 486 BC, stamped out this revolt and is credited with having imposed a more severe administration on Egypt in consequence. Contemporary evidence of events in Egypt during the fifth century is very scanty and knowledge of what was happening there is derived principally from Greek writers. In 465 BC the accession of Artaxerxes I following the death of Xerxes was the signal for a new rising in the Delta, led by Inarus, a local prince, who was probably a descendant of the Saite royal family. At first the Egyptians had considerable success and gained control of most of the Delta. Unexpected help then arrived in the form of a considerable fleet sent by Athens in 459 BC, with which the Egyptians succeeded in capturing most of Memphis; but not the inner fortress to which the Persians had fled. For some time Inarus and the Athenians maintained their hold on Lower Egypt but ultimately they were unable to resist a well-planned counter-attack of the Persians under Megabyxus. In 454 BC the end came; Inarus was taken as a captive to Persia and slain, while the Athenians were almost wiped out. Resistance to the Persians continued in the north-western corner of the Delta under Amyrtaeus, a local prince, but no account of his activities has been preserved. His rebellion was soon crushed. The Egyptian tradition, as recounted by Manetho, ends the Twenty-seventh Dynasty with the death of

25 Figure of Ankhnesneferibre on the lid of her sarcophagus (see also fig. 59)

Darius II in 405 BC although documents dated to the early years of his successor Artaxerxes II are known from Elephantine.

The subsequent Twenty-eighth Dynasty is given only one king, named Amyrtaeus, possibly a descendant of the insurgent Amyrtaeus; of his reign little is known. He succeeded in expelling the Persians from Egypt and had secured control of Elephantine by his fifth year (400 BC). With his death came a change in the ruling house, the kings of the new Twenty-ninth Dynasty springing from Mendes in the Delta. The history of this dynasty and of that of its successor is, in so far as it is known, a long struggle to maintain the independence of Egypt against repeated attempts by the Persians to re-annex it as a satrapy. In their struggle the Egyptians relied heavily on Greek help. Nepherites I (398–393 BC), the first king of the Twenty-ninth Dynasty, contracted an alliance with Sparta which never in fact proved of much benefit; Achoris, a later king of the dynasty, engaged the services of Chabrias, a mercenary Athenian captain, who was, however, recalled to Athens on the complaint of Pharnabazus, the Persian satrap. In 373 BC a great attack was launched by Pharnabazus against Nectanebo I, then king of Egypt, the first ruler of the Thirtieth Dynasty which originated from Sebennytus in the Delta. The attack was, however, defeated by unexpected resistance and the arrival of the inundation. Further attacks were for the time averted by a revolt of satraps within the Persian Empire. Teos, the successor of Nectanebo I, felt himself strong enough in 360 BC to launch an attack on his own account against the Persians in Phoenicia. He enlisted the aid of the Spartans and Athenians but the expedition ended in a fiasco which resulted in Teos being supplanted by Nectanebo II, a young relative. Nectanebo II, like Nectanebo I before him, was a considerable builder and patron of the arts. His great granite sarcophagus is exhibited in the Egyptian Sculpture Gallery (10). The Persian king was now Artaxerxes Ochus and he determined to win back Egypt to the Persian Empire. After preliminary skirmishes the final assault was launched in 343 BC, and ended with the flight of Nectanebo II to Nubia. Once more Egypt became a satrapy of the Persian Empire and so she remained until 332 BC, the Persian kings being designated by some ancient writers as the Thirty-first Dynasty. Finally in 332 BC the Persian rule in Egypt was ended by the arrival of Alexander the Great who, although also a foreigner, was apparently welcomed as a deliverer. Alexander stayed for only a short time in Egypt but endeavoured to make himself acceptable to the native population by performing the necessary sacrifices to the gods of Memphis and by visiting the temple of Amun at Siwa. He was formally installed as Pharaoh and he reorganized the administration of the country. Before leaving Egypt to continue his campaign against the Persians he founded the city of Alexandria.

Ptolemaic Period (332–30 BC)

After its conquest by Alexander the Great, Egypt was organized as a province of the new Macedonian Empire. In 323 BC Alexander died suddenly and shortly afterwards Ptolemy Lagus was sent to Egypt as satrap by Philip Arrhidaeus. In the dissolution of the Macedonian Empire which occurred in the following years Ptolemy became more and more the master of an increasingly independent Egypt, but it was not until 305 BC that he finally became king of Egypt, taking the additional name of Soter ('Saviour') and establishing the so-called Ptolemaic Dynasty. Under the Ptolemies Egypt flourished and Egyptian civilization assumed a new appearance. In administration the country was organized on Greek lines with Greek becoming the official language; in art, new ideas were introduced from the Greek world, profoundly affecting the age-old traditions and conventions of Egyptian art (fig. 26); in military affairs the army

26 Schist head of a king

was fully reorganized on Macedonian lines and turned into an efficient fighting machine. In religious matters, however, the Ptolemies were careful not to offend the scruples of the native population and although many strange gods were introduced into Egypt during this time, both Greek and Asiatic, the principal deities of the Egyptian pantheon were sedulously cultivated. Some of the greatest temples were constructed during the Ptolemaic Period. In the reliefs in these temples the Ptolemies are regularly shown as kings in the ancient Egyptian manner and there is good reason to believe that they did in fact endeavour to behave as such; they adopted Egyptian royal titles and their names were written in cartouches. Their outlook, however, was very different and they paid particular attention to developing commerce; new ports were built and contacts with Asia and the classical lands developed. They were also enthusiastic patrons of learning and one of their finest memorials was the great library of Alexandria founded by Ptolemy I. Another enlightened ruler was Ptolemy V Epiphanes, who was an especial benefactor of the native temples; in his honour was passed the decree inscribed on the Rosetta Stone (24, fig. 28 and p. 82 f.). The rule of the Ptolemies did not, unfortunately, remain enlightened and energetic. By the early first century BC such empire as had been acquired in Asia was lost and internal control began to slacken. Dynastic squabbles increased the instability of the régime and the interest taken in Egyptian affairs by the Romans did not help to stabilize the situation. Under Ptolemy XII Auletes (80–51 BC), Roman intervention became actual and thereafter the Egyptian king was little more than a dependant on Rome. In 30 BC the Ptolemaic Dynasty ended with the death of Cleopatra VII and of Caesarion, and Egypt became formally a Roman province.

CHAPTER THREE

LANGUAGE, DECIPHERMENT AND WRITING MATERIALS

The ancient Egyptian language bears affinities to both the Semitic and the Hamitic groups of languages: at least 300 Semitic and 100 Hamitic words have been identified and, in addition, a number of words found in Egyptian seem to be shared by both groups. The following are some examples:

Egyptian	Semitic	Hamitic
m(w)t 'die'	*mwth* (Hebrew)	*emmet* (Berber)
nfr 'good'		*nefir* (Bedja)
djbᶜ 'finger'	*isbaᶜ* (Arabic)	*giba* (Bedja)
šms 'follow'		*šimiš* (Bedja)
gm 'find'		*egmi* (Touareg)
qfn 'bake'		*ekref* (Berber)
ḥsb 'count'	*ḥasaba* (Arabic)	

In order to account for these foreign elements the suggestion has been made that the language, as it is known to us, evolved independently after a fusion of races had taken place. Certainly the similarities appear to be too numerous to be explained as an outcome of commercial or other intercourse of infrequent or ephemeral kind. However, there is also reason to believe that ideas reached Egypt in very early times through occasional contacts with the inhabitants of other countries, even as far away as Mesopotamia, though by what channel is unknown. A number of inventions including the cylinder seal, stone mace-head of pear-shape and some distinctive artistic motifs, and architectural designs in brick, all of which were employed by Sumerians in Mesopotamia, were suddenly adopted in Egypt at the end of the period which preceded the foundation of the First Dynasty under Menes. Since no corresponding trace of Egyptian influence can be observed in the Sumerian products of the time (the so-called Jemdet Nasr and First Early Dynastic Period) it may be inferred that the movement was not in both directions. Egypt's debt to Sumer, however, does not seem to have been confined to the knowledge of a few artifacts and artistic conventions; certain words in the Egyptian language, particularly agricultural terms and the names of certain cereals, resemble very closely the corresponding terms in Sumerian and are almost certainly derived from the latter. Unquestionably the most important of Sumer's contributions must be counted the imparting of the principles of writing. It is true that the Sumerian

syllabic signs expressed both consonants and vowels, whereas
only the consonants were indicated in Egyptian hieroglyphs,
but the basic method of using a sign to express not only the
actual object which it represented but also other words or even
parts of words having a like sound (the rebus principle) is
common to both scripts. Furthermore, both scripts added sense-
signs—the so-called determinatives—to words in order to indicate
in a general way their meaning. The differences are of a kind
which would be expected to occur in systems which developed
independently; thus the determinative in Egyptian was placed
at the end of a word while in Sumerian it was prefixed. The
Egyptians alone employed signs representing single consonants
(alphabetic signs) and, whereas in Sumer picture writing soon
developed into the cuneiform script, the Egyptians retained the
hieroglyphic script for nearly 3,500 years, from about 3100 BC
until the end of the fourth century AD, the last known hieroglyphic inscription, on the Island of Philae, being dated to
AD 394. The latest hieroglyphic inscription in this collection is
dated to AD 296 in the reign of Diocletian (1696).

At about the turn of the third century AD the Egyptians began
to write their language in a script composed of the Greek
alphabet, to which were added seven characters derived ultimately from hieroglyphs. In this form the language came to be
known as Coptic (fig. 27), a word which is no doubt a corruption
of the Greek word *Aiguptios*. Knowledge of how to read and to
write the hieroglyphic script was lost probably soon after it had
been superseded and no key to its meaning was discovered until
1799 when some French soldiers in Napoleon's army working
under an officer named Bouchard found the Rosetta Stone
(fig. 28) while digging the foundations of an addition to a fort,

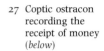

27 Coptic ostracon
recording the
receipt of money
(*below*)

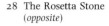

28 The Rosetta Stone
(*opposite*)

later called Fort Julien, near the town of Rashid (Rosetta) on the western arm of the Nile near the sea. The stone was ceded to the British under Article XVI of the Treaty of Alexandria in 1801. It reached this country in February 1802.

The immediate importance of the Rosetta Stone, as its discoverers realized, lay in the fact that the old Egyptian hiero-glyphic text was accompanied by a Greek translation which could be read. A third inscription on the stone was written in demotic, a cursive script developed late in Egyptian history and used, almost exclusively, for secular documents: the language of the demotic version was Egyptian. Thus the stone displayed three scripts but only two languages, Egyptian and Greek.

For twenty years after the stone had reached this country attempts were made by European scholars to decipher the hiero-glyphic and demotic texts. A Swedish diplomat named J. D. Åkerblad (1763–1819) was probably the first to achieve any substantial success when in 1802 he identified, by comparison with the Greek text, several proper names, e.g. Ptolemy, given in the demotic version; he also recognized, through knowing their Coptic equivalents, the words for 'Greeks' and 'temples' and the pronouns 'him' and 'his'. Dr. Thomas Young (1773–1829), the well-known physicist, was responsible in 1819 for the next important advance; among his contributions perhaps the most valuable was his demonstration of the correctness of a guess by the Abbé J. J. Barthélemy and C. J. de Guignes (1721–1800) that the groups of hieroglyphs written within oval rings (the so-called cartouches) on the Egyptian monuments gave the names of kings, and he was able to show that the name of Ptolemy, like-wise within a cartouche, occurred several times on the Rosetta Stone. He also succeeded in equating eighty-six groups of signs in the demotic version with Greek words, but the phonetic values which he gave to these demotic groups were mostly incorrect.

Young's achievement, considerable though it must be reckoned, cannot be compared with that of Jean François Champollion (1790–1832), who must be regarded as the real decipherer of the Egyptian hieroglyphic script. What had been for Young probably little more than a pastime was for Champollion a burning passion. Moreover, with his greater familiarity with languages, Champollion was better equipped than Young.

Champollion's triumph may be said to have begun in 1822 when he was able to reaffirm Young's reading of the cartouches of the Rosetta Stone containing the name of Ptolemy, and also to substantiate Young's deduction that the name of Cleopatra occurred in a cartouche on a fallen obelisk found at Philae by W. J. Bankes in 1815 and transported in 1819, together with its base-block, to his park at Kingston Lacy, Dorset. The base-block bore a Greek inscription which mentioned both Ptolemy (Ptolemaios) and Cleopatra and since the hieroglyphs in one of the cartouches on the obelisk agreed with the supposed writing of the name Ptolemy on the Rosetta Stone it was conceivable that the other cartouches concealed the name of Cleopatra. Three of the signs in the cartouches were identical with the signs read P, O, and L in the cartouche of Ptolemy and their sequence was correct; only the T was different; but Champollion was not perplexed by this discrepancy because both he and Young had recognized that different signs could have the same values by the principle of homophony.

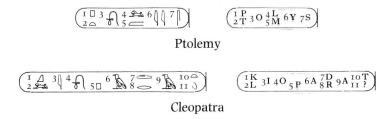

Ptolemy

Cleopatra

Champollion announced his discovery in September 1822 in a communication to the Académie des Inscriptions entitled *Lettre à Monsieur Dacier relative à l'alphabet des hiéroglyphes phonétiques.* Apart from Ptolemy and Cleopatra he was able to give the hiero-glyphic writings and transcriptions of the names of more than seventy rulers of Egypt from Alexander the Great (332–323 BC) to Antoninus Pius (138–161 AD). No further demonstration of the predominantly phonetic nature of the hieroglyphic script, as used in Hellenistic and Roman times, was necessary, but it still remained to be proved that the character of the script was the same in pharaonic times. Almost immediately after the publica-tion of his initial discoveries Champollion was able to decipher the cartouches of Ramesses and Tuthmosis, and by so doing to show that the principles underlying Egyptian hieroglyphs of the earlier period were not different from those which prevailed towards the end of their long history. Eighteen months later he published a book entitled *Précis du système hiéroglyphique* in which he gave, largely correctly, interpretations of not only a long list of royal names but also of words and phrases and even complete sentences. Before his death at the age of 42 on 4 March 1832, Champollion had made further substantial contributions to Egyptology including many additions to his repertoire of signs and words.

In order to appreciate the difficulties which confronted Champollion and the early decipherers it is necessary to bear in

mind that the hieroglyphic script consists not of a short alphabet
of the kind used by the Phoenicians and the Greeks in later times
but of a very large number of signs. Approximately 700 different
signs are now known and they can be divided into two main
classes: (a) ideograms (from the Greek *idea* 'form' and *gramma*
'written character') or sense signs, and (b) phonograms (from
the Greek *phone* 'sound' and *gramma* 'written character') or
sound-signs. An ideogram indicates the meaning of a word
pictorially without showing how it is to be read; thus the
ideogram ☉ representing the sun may signify the sun itself or
almost any word associated in meaning with the sun and its
characteristics, e.g. light, brightness, day, to rise, to shine, etc.
Similarly the ideogram ⛵ may signify several kinds of boat, ship,
or vessel and also the verbs expressing sailing. Phonograms
indicate the consonantal spelling of words, but not the vowels.
They are of three kinds: (1) alphabetic signs representing a single
consonant, e.g. ⌒ (the mouth) *r*, ⬭ (the hand) *d*, ∥ (a piece of
cloth) *s*; (2) biliteral signs representing two consonants, e.g. ⌑
(a house) *pr*, ▽ (a basket) *nb*, 🐇 (hare) *wn*; (3) triliteral signs
representing three consonants, e.g. ⌓ (a loaf on a mat) *ḥtp*,
♁ (heart and windpipe) *nfr*.

The Alphabet

Sign	Transcription	Sound-value
𓄿	(vulture) *ꜣ*	Glottal stop (as in 'bottle' when pronounced by a Cockney)
𓇋	(flowering reed) *i*	I
𓏭𓏭	(two flowering reeds) *y*	Y
\\	(oblique strokes) *y*	Y
𓂝	(forearm and hand) *ꜥ*	Ayin of the Semitic languages
𓅱	(quail chick) *w*	W
𓏲	(cursive development of 𓅱) *w*	W
𓃀	(foot) *b*	B
𓊪	(stool) *p*	P
𓆑	(horned viper) *f*	F
𓅓	(owl) *m*	M
𓈖	(water) *n*	N
⌒	(mouth) *r*	R
𓉔	(reed shelter) *h*	H
𓎛	(wick of twisted flax) *ḥ*	slightly guttural *h*
𓐍	(placenta?) *ḫ*	CH (as in loch)
𓄡	(animal's belly) *ẖ*	slightly softer than *ḫ*

Sign	Transcription	Sound-value
(door bolt) s	S
(folded cloth) s	S
(pool) š	SH
(hill) ḳ	Q
(basket with handle) k	K
(jar-stand) g	G (as in goat)
(loaf) t	T
(tethering rope) ṯ	Tj
(hand) d	D
(snake) ḏ	Dj

All these letters are consonants, even though the weak 𓄿, 𓇌, and 𓅱 at the end of a syllable were probably assimilated to a preceding a, i, and u. Vowels were not written by the ancient Egyptians; it is therefore difficult, and often impossible, to ascertain the pronunciation of words, but it may be sometimes deduced from the Coptic derivatives. As a mere aid to pronunciation Egyptologists insert a short *e* between consonants, e.g. *ḥetep* 'rest', *per* 'house', using *a* for ꜣ and ꜥ, and *u* for w.

When writing a word the Egyptian scribe could, in most cases, adopt one of several different methods. He could write simply the ideogram, accompanied as a rule by a vertical stroke, e.g. 𓉐 (*per*) 'house', 𓇳 (*rꜥ*) 'sun'. More frequently, however, he would use phonograms followed by an ideogram which would convey the general meaning of the word (the ideogram in this position being called a determinative by modern grammarians), e.g. (*depet*) 'boat', (*weben*) 'rise', 'shine'. When a suitable biliteral or triliteral phonogram existed he would generally use it and frequently he would add some alphabetic signs, even if they were already included in the phonogram, e.g. (*ḥetep*) 'rest', which consists of the triliteral phonogram (*ḥtp*) plus t and p; (*mer*) 'pyramid' is composed of the biliteral sign (*mr*) plus m and r followed by a picture of a pyramid used as a determinative. So cumbrous and illogical does this multiplicity of signs seem that it is hard to understand the process of thought by which it was evolved, and even more difficult to imagine why it should have continued with so little development over so long a period of time.

To discover the significance of a hieroglyphic sign, and even to be able to read a royal name, though vital as preliminaries to further progress, would have been but barren achievements if it had not been possible also to translate the texts in which they occurred. That the decipherment of the script and the translation

of words were able to proceed side by side and to assist each other
was due, in the main, to the good fortune which allowed Coptic
to survive until the sixteenth century as the language of the
Christian population of Egypt. Even at the present day it is still
read, though not understood, in the Coptic churches. Its vocabulary consists of Egyptian words supplemented by a considerable
number of words borrowed directly from Greek. The following
are examples of some Egyptian words and their Coptic equivalents:

(rȝ) mouth	ⲣⲟ (ro)
(pt) heaven	ⲡⲉ (pe)
(kmt) Egypt	ⲕⲏⲙⲉ (keme)
(bin) bad	ϩⲱⲱⲛ (boon)

   Champollion realized the importance of Coptic and, at an early
age, acquired a mastery of it. As a result, he was able to translate
words in the Greek version of the Rosetta Stone into Coptic and,
when he had discovered the principles of the hieroglyphic script,
to search in the appropriate places in the hieroglyphic version for
words which corresponded in spelling with those of his Coptic
translations. His task was made more difficult because the hieroglyphic text was written, in accordance with the regular practice,
without any division between the words. As the number of signs
deciphered increased he was able to apply the same method in
reverse and to translate into Coptic characters words which he
could read in hieroglyphic texts and thus obtain the meaning.
This method had, however, its limitations both because the
Egyptian words which had been preserved in Coptic were few in
comparison with the immense hieroglyphic vocabulary and
because many words in Coptic had developed so far from their
forms in earlier times as to be difficult to recognize as derivatives.
When Coptic could offer no assistance in interpreting a word it
was necessary to resort either to deduction, chiefly based on
several occurrences of the same word in different contexts, or
Hebrew in which were preserved many words from the common
Semitic stock which had become incorporated into the Egyptian
language. By these means scholars have succeeded in determining the reading of nearly all the hieroglyphic signs and the
meaning of a very high proportion of the vocabulary.
   In addition to hieroglyphic, Egyptians employed two other
scripts, both of which were descendants of the hieroglyphic script,
one directly and the other indirectly. The names given to these
scripts are hieratic (from the Greek hieratikos 'priestly') and
demotic (Greek demotikos 'popular'), sometimes called enchorial
(Greek enkhorios 'native'), which has already been mentioned in

connexion with the Rosetta Stone. They were thus named because in Greek times hieratic was used only for religious texts (although in earlier times it was also used for literary, business, and other secular documents), whereas demotic was reserved exclusively for secular purposes. In contrast with the hieroglyphic script, which could be written in either direction, hieratic and demotic were always written from right to left. They were usually written in ink on papyrus (fig. 29), potsherds, or flakes of limestone (fig. 30); only rarely and at a late date were they carved on stone (fig. 31).

Hieratic, in its earliest form, differs from hieroglyphic to no greater extent than would naturally happen as a result of using a rush pen instead of a pointed tool; the angular signs are more rounded and are drawn with less detail. Sporadic examples on stone dating from the First to the Third Dynasties are known, but the earliest considerable body of hieratic texts is a group of late Fifth Dynasty papyri from Abu Sir (fig. 32). By the Eleventh Dynasty it had developed into a much more distinctive and cursive script; in certain cases, two or more signs were joined to form a ligature. Texts were usually written in vertical columns, as often in hieroglyphic inscriptions, the signs being arranged so that when two or more stood side by side in a column they would

29 Hieratic letter of the Eleventh Dynasty (*left*)

30 Hieratic ostracon recording arrears of water for necropolis workers (*right*)

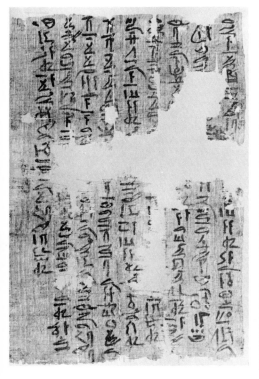

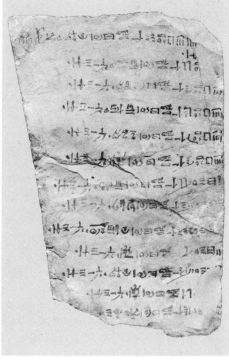

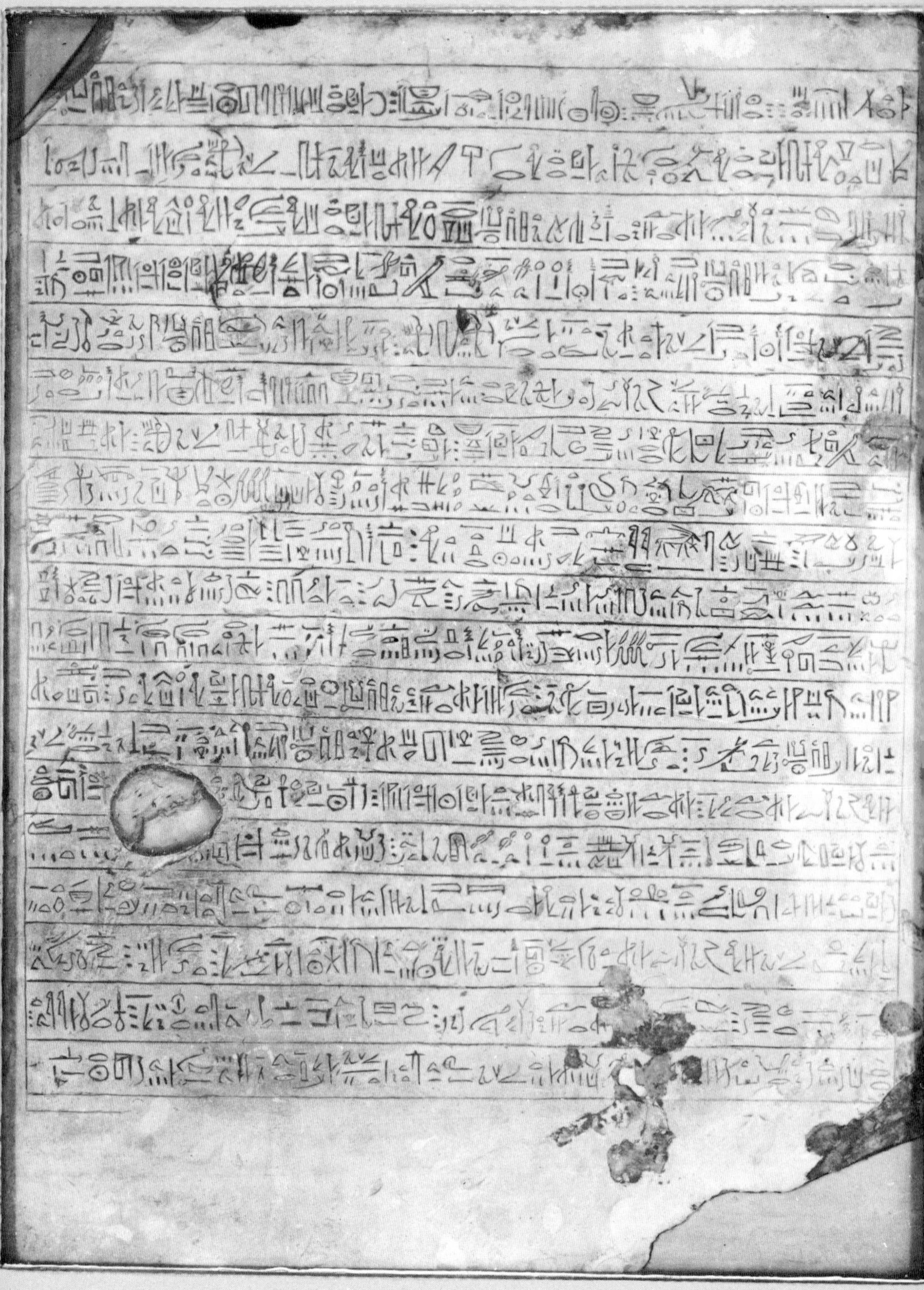

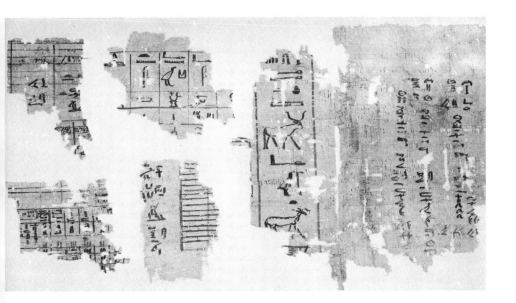

31 Twenty-first Dynasty hieratic copy of the decree establishing the *ka*-chapel of Amenhotpe, son of Hapu (*opposite*)

32 Old Kingdom temple accounts written in hieratic (*above*)

be read from right to left (fig. 32). In the Twelfth Dynasty this method was gradually discontinued and, instead, the Egyptian scribes began to write their texts in horizontal lines, a practice which not only was continued to the end of Egypt's history but also influenced the development of the script by allowing the writer to adopt a more cursive hand than would have been possible if he had been writing in vertical columns. This natural tendency was further aided by the avoidance of signs representing elaborate hieroglyphs, or by the substitution for such a sign of an oblique stroke, and by the introduction of some new signs, though these innovations were few in number. By the Eighteenth Dynasty a clear distinction existed between the well-formed hieratic used for literary purposes and the more cursive hieratic employed for business documents. So quickly did the divergence progress that long before the end of the New Kingdom the two scripts might not have been thought to be derived from a common ancestor. Moreover, two even more cursive scripts, namely demotic and the so-called abnormal hieratic, developed out of the business hieratic of the late New Kingdom. Not more than about forty-five documents written in abnormal hieratic have been identified (of which one long text is in this Museum, 10798). One of the earliest, dealing with the sale of a collection of *shabtis* (10800), dates probably to the Twenty-second Dynasty and so clearly belongs to the formative period of the script. In its fully developed form abnormal hieratic does not occur until the reign of Piankhi (Twenty-fifth Dynasty); the latest document dates to the first half of the reign of Amosis II (Twenty-sixth Dynasty).

Demotic documents (fig. 33), which are numbered in hundreds, extend over a period of a thousand years from the twenty-first year of Psammetichus I (Twenty-sixth Dynasty) to the middle of the fifth century AD. From the evidence available at present it seems that demotic originated in Lower Egypt, spread southwards in Saite times and quickly superseded abnormal hieratic, itself a product of Upper Egypt. Examples of hieratic and demotic dating from many different periods are shown in the Third and Fourth Egyptian Rooms.

Of the various materials, apart from stone, on which the ancient Egyptians wrote their documents, the most important was certainly papyrus. The derivation of the Greek word *papyros*, first found in the writings of the philosopher and natural historian Theophrastus (fourth–third centuries BC), is unknown. It is, however, most probably a word representing *pa-per-aa* 'that of a king', so called because in Greek times the production of papyrus may have been a royal monopoly. It is used with reference both to the plant *Cyperus papyrus* (which in ancient times grew in abundance in the marshes and pools of Egypt, but it is not now found in the Nile Valley north of Khartum) and to the writing material made from the stems of the plant. Satisfactory results have been obtained in practical experiments in manufacturing the writing material in this Museum by the following method: The long stems were first cut into pieces, each about 30 cms in length. After peeling off the rind, the pith was cut lengthwise into fairly thin slices which were placed side by side. A second layer of slices was then laid above the first and at right-angles to it. The two layers were then either pressed or beaten until they became welded together. No adhesive of any kind was used apart from the natural starch in the juice which was discharged from the slices during pressing or beating. When this method was used on mature stems a tendency to blotchiness, which had occurred with young stems, was absent and a smooth white surface was produced. Probably even greater smoothness could have been achieved by burnishing the papyrus with a stone or wooden polisher when it was thoroughly dry. The finished sheet possessed an upper surface with horizontal fibres (known as 'recto') and an under surface with vertical fibres ('verso').

Papyrus was made in sheets which never exceeded about 48 cms in height and about 43 cms in width. Several of the sheets might be joined by pasting the edges together so that the fibres ran in the same direction in all the sheets, and the long strip thus produced would be rolled with the horizontal fibres on the inside, until it was required for use. Specimens of both the widest and the longest papyri at present known are exhibited in the Third Egyptian Room. The widest, a Book of the Dead, named after its

33 Upper part of a demotic document dated 270 BC

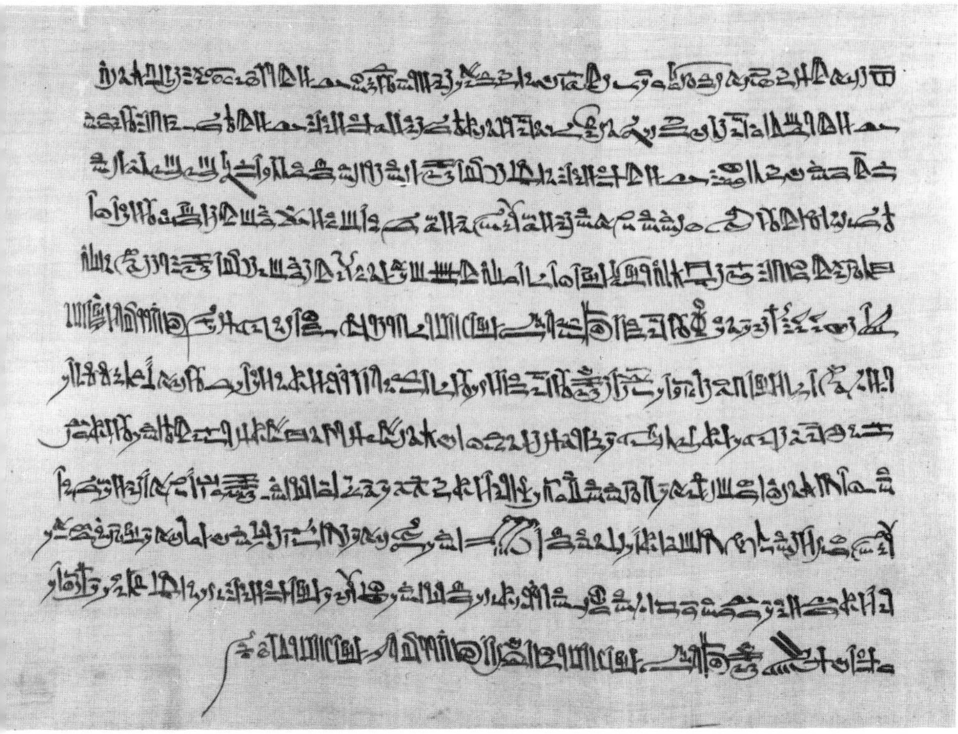

34 The Great Harris
Papyrus

donor the Greenfield Papyrus (10554), measures 49·5 cms in
width; the longest, the so-called Great Harris Papyrus (9999,
fig. 34), is 41 metres in length. As an invention papyrus seems to
be as old as the hieroglyphic script, for an uninscribed roll was
identified in the mastaba of a First Dynasty noble named
Hemaka at Saqqara. The earliest written examples are the fragmentary temple account books of the late Fifth Dynasty from
Abu Sir, most of which are now in this collection (10735, fig. 32).

As a rule, a scribe, holding the roll in his left hand, wrote first
on the side which had horizontal fibres, the 'recto'. When writing
in vertical columns he began at the outer end of the roll and
added column on to column, unrolling the papyrus as he pro-
gressed, until he had either reached the inner end or completed
what he had to write. A different method was necessary when
writing in horizontal lines; the scribe would write a top line of
whatever length he wished and then write successive lines of
the same length until he had reached the bottom of the page,
when he would unroll more of the papyrus and write a further
'page' in the same way but not necessarily of the same width.
Blank spaces between the pages varied from document to document but they were generally not less than about 1·5 cms or
more than about 2·5 cms. The action of 'writing' with a rush pen

resembled painting, the hand being held away from the written surface and not resting upon it. There was, therefore, no danger of smudging what had been written.

35 Hieratic ostracon with an excerpt from an inquiry into the ownership of a tomb

Other materials used by scribes were flakes of white limestone and potsherds (both of which are called ostraca by Egyptologists) and wooden boards, frequently overlaid with gesso. In contrast with papyri, documents written on these materials were generally of an ephemeral character, e.g. school exercises, drafts of contracts, deeds and letters, records of attendance at work, inventories, magical texts, oracles (fig. 35), etc.; these materials were also used for plans and sketches (41228, 8506–8, and 5601). The wooden boards covered with gesso painted white were probably used in schools for hieratic texts intended as models for students to copy; each board has a small hole bored in it, probably to hold a leather thong on which it could be suspended from a peg when not in use. The text on a board could be washed off, and, if necessary, the board could be repainted or resurfaced with gesso and used many times for different texts. A selection of the Museum's collection of more than 8,000 ostraca and of writing boards is exhibited in the Fourth Egyptian Room. Dressed leather and vellum were sometimes used for documents of a kind more often written on papyrus, e.g. a series of additions of fractions written on leather which a scribe probably used as a mathematical table (10250, *c.* 1700 BC) and the Book of the Dead of the late Eighteenth Dynasty scribe Nakht (10471 and 10473) written partly on vellum and partly on papyrus. Ivory, clay, and linen were also used and, at least in late times, even bronze, as is shown by two Ptolemaic-Roman tablets inscribed in demotic and hieroglyphs (57371 and 57372).

The trade-mark of the Egyptian scribe was his palette. As a rule it was made of a rectangular piece of wood, from 20–43 cms long, from 5–8 cms in width, and about 1·5 cms in thickness. At one end were two, and sometimes several, cavities for holding black, red, and other inks in the form of solid cakes. Black ink was made of carbon and red ink consisted of finely ground red ochre: both were mixed with a weak solution of gum so that they congealed when they dried. In order to dissolve the ink again it was only necessary for the scribe to dip his brush in water and rub it on the surface of the cake, as would be done with modern water-colour paint. The brush itself was made of the stem of a rush, *Juncus maritimus*, which was shortened to about 15–25 cms in length, the tip being first cut on a slant and then chewed by the scribe to break up the fibres. Brushes were kept in a slot carved out of the middle of the palette (fig. 36). In the later examples the slot is sometimes partly covered by a sliding lid. Pens made of a reed, *Phragmites*

36 Wooden scribal palettes

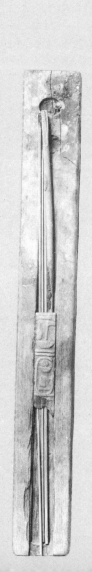

communis, cut to a point and split in two at the tip were first used by Greeks residing in Egypt in the third century BC. A series of palettes ranging in date from the Sixth Dynasty to the New Kingdom is exhibited in the Fourth Egyptian Room. Many of the examples show hieratic inscriptions in ink, some of which appear to be notes scribbled by the scribe, e.g. measurements and records of sacks delivered (5524), names (12783), accounts (5518), etc. The hieroglyphic inscriptions are generally invocations to Thoth, the god of writing, and in consequence they may indicate that the palettes were part of their owners' funerary equipment.

Proficiency in the art of writing was not easily acquired. Pupils in the scribal schools were first set to copy excerpts from well-known literary works, one of the most common apparently being the so-called *Book of Kemit* (e.g. ostracon 5640), a didactic composition which is devoted partly to enunciating moral principles and partly to extolling the profession of the scribe. Ostraca inscribed with excerpts from this book invariably date from the New Kingdom: they are, however, written in a large hand and the text is arranged in vertical columns so that they resemble the hieratic documents of the Middle Kingdom. These anomalies are probably to be explained as evidence that pupils were taught to write in the bold script of the Middle Kingdom before they developed their own style of handwriting. As their skill advanced the pupils copied not only the classics of Egyptian literature but also model letters, mathematical exercises and lists of technical words, place-names, etc. (e.g. the Hood Papyrus, 10202, and a leather strip, 10379). Their copies were often imperfect but the fact that so much has been preserved of what the ancient Egyptians regarded as their most important literary and educational productions is due mainly to their schoolboys.

Scribes enjoyed certain privileges, including relief from taxation. Their profession was frequently contrasted favourably with other occupations in compositions which pupils in schools were set to copy (e.g. Anastasi Papyrus II–V, 10243, 10246, 10249, and 10244; Papyrus Sallier I, 10185 and Papyrus Lansing, 9994). Nowhere, however, is their profession more highly evaluated than in the Chester Beatty Papyrus IV (10684):

As for those learned scribes from the time of the successors of the gods, (even) those who foretold the future, it has come to pass that their names endure forever, although they themselves are gone, having completed their lifespan and all their kindred are forgotten.

They did not make for themselves pyramids of copper or stelae of iron. They could not leave children as heirs to pronounce their names; they made as heirs for themselves the writings and books of instruction which they had compiled.[1]

[1] For the whole text, see Gardiner (1935), 38–9.

CHAPTER FOUR

EGYPTIAN LITERARY AND OTHER WRITINGS

Egyptian writings are generally classified both according to their subject-matter and according to the phase of the language to which they belong. Three main phases are distinguishable to which grammarians have given the following names: Old Egyptian (First–Eighth Dynasties, *c.* 3100–2160 BC), Middle Egyptian (Ninth–Mid-Eighteenth Dynasties, *c.* 2160–1380 BC) and Late Egyptian (Mid-Eighteenth–Twenty-fourth Dynasties, *c.* 1380–715 BC). It was the second of these phases, Middle Egyptian, which the Egyptians themselves regarded as the classical phase, the writings of which served as models in schools in later times; it was also Middle Egyptian which the scribes of the Twenty-fifth and Twenty-sixth Dynasties (*c.* 747–525 BC) adopted in their literary compositions. Late Egyptian became common in documents of the Amarna Period, apparently owing to a deliberate attempt by Akhenaten to break away from the traditional literary style in order to bring the written language into line with the vernacular. Unlike his artistic innovations it survived the collapse of his revolution and continued in use for many generations thereafter; indeed some of the best-known literary works in Late Egyptian date from the Nineteenth and Twentieth Dynasties.

Even without taking historical records into account (see Chapter 2) the variety of subject displayed in Egyptian literature is surprisingly wide. Among the different branches, most of which are represented in the Museum's collection, the following are perhaps the most interesting:

Wisdom literature

The texts in this category deal chiefly with practical wisdom. As their Egyptian title 'Instructions' would suggest, they are didactic works composed of maxims and precepts. One of the earliest examples is the *Instruction of Ptahhotep*, a vizier of the Fifth-dynasty king Djedkare Isesi (*c.* 2380 BC), who complains to the king that he has grown old and wishes to make way for his son. The king tells him to instruct his son in behaviour appropriate in a high official for 'there is no one born wise'. The instruction begins with these words: 'Do not be arrogant because you are learned; do not be over-confident because you are well-informed. Consult the ignorant man as well as the wise one.' More than forty maxims follow and the discourse ends with the assurance that if the young man reaches his father's position sound in body and the king is contented with his work then he shall enjoy a long life. One of the earliest known copies of these instructions is contained in papyrus 10371, written about 2000 BC.[1]

An indication of the popularity of another didactic work, *The Instruction of Ammenemes I,* is the fact that part of it is preserved in no fewer than four papyri (of which one is Papyrus Sallier I, 10185, verso 8), a leather roll, now in the Louvre, three wooden tablets and about fifty ostraca (e.g. 5623, 5638). One papyrus only (Papyrus Sallier II, 10182) contains the entire work, but it is far from accurate. All these texts date from the New Kingdom. In content this composition differs from the other wisdom literature in so far as it is more biographical. Like the earlier *Instruction to Merikare,* which is preserved on an Eighteenth Dynasty papyrus at Leningrad, it consists of advice given by a king to his son and heir. In the case of Ammenemes I, the first king of the Twelfth Dynasty, the alleged reason for issuing the 'Instruction' was an attempt on his life which may have been caused by a harim conspiracy. Apart from describing the attack and giving his son advice, the aged king narrates some of his achievements and confirms that he has chosen as his successor his son Sesostris I who had already been co-regent for ten years.[2] Some authorities, who believe that the assassination took place, regard this 'Instruction' as a work composed after the event, the author being a scribe named Achthoes of Sebennytus about whom another papyrus in the collection (Papyrus Chester Beatty IV, 10684) says: 'It was he who made a book as the (?) Instruction of King Sehetepibre' (i.e. Ammenemes I). This same Achthoes, the son of Duauf, was certainly the author of a well-known 'Book of Instruction' (also part of Papyrus Sallier II, 10182, and Papyrus Anastasi VII, 10222; extracts are given in Papyrus Chester Beatty XIX, 10699 and on an ostracon 29550). In the introduction he states that he composed it for his son Pepi 'as he sailed south to the Residence, to place him in the school for scribes, among the children of magistrates, the foremost of the Residence'. Commonly known as the *Satire of the Trades,* this work glorifies the profession of the scribe by enumerating the hardships associated with other occupations. Its main theme is expressed in the words 'See, there is no occupation free from directors except for that of the scribe: he is his own director'.[3]

Because they contain many ideas which are also expressed in the Old Testament Book of Proverbs, the thirty chapters of the *Teaching of Amenemope, son of Kanakht* (10474, fig. 37),[4] have attracted much attention both from Egyptologists and from

[1] Translations of the whole text: Erman (1927), 54–66; Pritchard (1955), 412–14; Simpson (1972), 159–76; Lichtheim (1973), 61–83. Papyri 10371, 10435, and 10509.

[2] Translations: Erman (1927), 72–4; Pritchard (1955), 418–19; Simpson (1972), 193–7; Lichtheim (1973), 135–9.

[3] Translations: Erman (1927), 67–72; Pritchard (1955), 432–4; Lichtheim (1973), 184–92.

[4] Translations: Pritchard (1955), 421–5; Simpson (1972), 241–65.

37 Part of a papyrus containing *The Teaching of Amenemope, son of Kanakht*

Biblical scholars. An almost verbal parallel occurs, for example, in the opening lines of the first chapter: 'Give your ears, listen to the words which are spoken, give your mind to interpreting them. It is profitable to put them in your heart' (cf. Proverbs xxii. 17). Although some authorities have suggested that it was Amenemope who made use of an earlier Hebrew compilation of proverbs, most critics have argued that the loan was in the other direction. The text, which is completely preserved in the papyrus, was probably copied in the Twenty-first Dynasty (*c.* 1000 BC), but the composition is believed to be from a work which is considerably older.

Only two books of instruction which were actually composed in the New Kingdom have yet come to light. The more famous, known as the *Maxims of Ani*, is preserved on a papyrus (Papyrus Boulaq IV) in the Cairo Museum, but two extracts are included in the Chester Beatty Papyrus V (10685). The author of the second book, the fullest version of which is found on an ostracon in this collection (41541) bore the name Amennakht. Both these authors were sacerdotal scribes, Ani in the funerary temple of Queen Nefertari and Amennakht in the so-called 'House of Life'—an institution associated with several temples in Egypt where religious and secular works were composed and copied. In this respect, at least, the books differed from the older wisdom literature, some of which was produced by kings and the rest by officials in the royal circle.[1]

A book of instruction contained in a demotic papyrus (10508, fig. 38), dating to the late Ptolemaic Period, *c.* 100 BC, is named after its writer *The Instructions of Onkhsheshonqy*. In the Introduction Onkhsheshonqy son of Tchainefer relates how he was imprisoned for complicity in a plot against Pharaoh and wrote

[1] Translations of the *Maxims of Ani*: Erman (1927), 234–42; Pritchard (1955), 420–1; French translation only of the *Instructions of Amennakht*: *RdʾE* 10 (1955), 61–72.

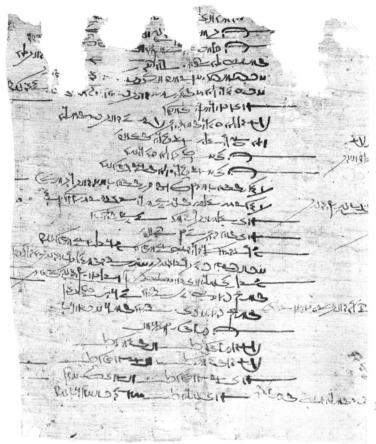

38 Part of a papyrus
containing *The
Instructions of
Onkhsheshonqy*

39 Part of the *Story of
the Eloquent Peasant*

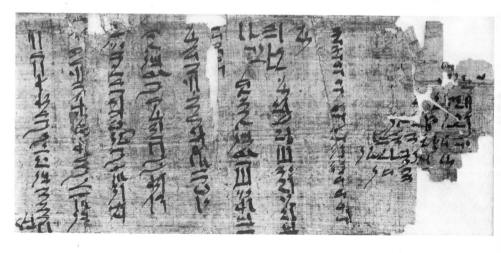

the instructions for his son from prison. The insistence on practical instruction is close to that embodied in the *Maxims of Ani*: 'Do not long for your home when you are at work', 'Do not drink at a merchant's house, he will charge you for it' and 'Do not acquire wealth until you have a strong-room'; the high moral tone of Amenemope is lacking. There is a likelihood that Onkhsheshonqy's collection of proverbs was first compiled only a few centuries before their commital to papyrus: there does not seem to be a Middle Kingdom original at their root.[1]

The *Story of the Eloquent Peasant* (partly preserved in the Butler Papyrus of the Twelfth Dynasty, 10274, fig. 39), although generally classed as a narrative, may also be regarded as a treatise on equity with a narrative background.[2] In the course of a journey to Egypt to sell the products of his plot of land, a peasant of Wadi Natrun, by a trick, is robbed of his asses by an Egyptian landowner. Having failed to persuade the landowner to return the asses, he goes to the high steward, who tries to help him by bringing an action against the landowner before the local magistrates but is unsuccessful. The peasant again appeals to the high steward to use his influence on his behalf. So greatly is the high steward impressed by the peasant's eloquence that he goes to tell the king about it. The king instructs the high steward to provide the peasant with food and to detain him so that he may go on speaking, and tells the high steward to write down what he says. Nine petitions were then recorded on papyrus and sent to the king who, when he had read them, was so impressed that he ordered the high steward to give judgement himself in favour of the peasant and to reward him with not only the restoration of his own asses and their loads, but also the possessions of the unjust landowner. Another Twelfth Dynasty papyrus (10754) preserves fragments of a somewhat similar work containing the moral sayings of a scribe named Sisobk, who was imprisoned but eventually released upon a petition of a dancer.

Meditations and pessimistic literature

The years of political unrest and social and economic instability which followed the Old Kingdom (pp. 48 ff.) furnished the setting for a class of literature which was invariably pessimistic and sometimes prophetic in character. At least one of the works in this category, the *Admonitions of Ipuwer*,[3] which is preserved on a papyrus dating from the New Kingdom in the Leiden Museum, may well have been composed before the end of this troubled period. Another work, which seems to be of the same date, is a remarkable *Dialogue of a Pessimist with his Soul*[4] (Berlin Museum, 3024) in which a man contemplates suicide

[1] Translation: Glanville (1955).

[2] Translations: Erman (1927), 116–31; Pritchard (1955), 407–10; Simpson (1972), 31–49; Lichtheim (1973), 169–84.

[3] Translations: Gardiner (1909); Erman (1927), 92–108; Simpson (1972), 210–29; Lichtheim (1973), 149–63.

[4] Translations: Erman (1927), 86–92; Pritchard (1955), 405–7; Goedicke (1970), 211–17; Simpson (1972), 201–9; Lichtheim (1973), 163–9.

but is dissuaded by his soul. As a piece of literature it belongs to the same *genre* as the Book of Job, but it is far inferior in spiritual content.

With its setting in the court of Sneferu, the first king of the Fourth Dynasty, the *Prophecy of the Great Lector Priest Neferty* (completely preserved only in Leningrad Papyrus 1116B, but an excerpt is inscribed on a writing-board of the Eighteenth Dynasty in this collection, 5647, verso) presents a dismal account of conditions in the future from which the country would ultimately be saved by the advent of a king from the south named Ameny who would build the 'Walls of the Prince' in the eastern Delta and thereby prevent the incursions of marauding bands of Asiatics.[1] Since Ameny is almost certainly to be identified with Ammenemes I, the first king of the Twelfth Dynasty, it may be conjectured that the 'prophecy' was composed during his reign to bolster his claim to the throne. The wickedness of men and the corruption of society are the main theme of another well-known pessimistic work attributed to a priest of Heliopolis, Khakheperreseneb, found on an Eighteenth Dynasty writing-board (5645 and fig. 40). It is clear from the name of the writer, which embodies the prenomen of Sesostris II, that these *Meditations of Khakheperreseneb*[2] cannot date from earlier than the second half of the Twelfth Dynasty but there can be little doubt that the conditions to which they refer were those which prevailed in the First Intermediate Period. Pessimism of a different kind is reflected in the so-called *Song of the Harper* (Papyrus Harris 500, 10060): the transitoriness of life and scepticism

40 Eighteenth Dynasty writing board containing the *Meditations of Khakheperreseneb*

[1] Translations: Erman (1927), 110–15; Pritchard (1955), 444–6; Simpson (1972), 234–40; Lichtheim (1973), 139–45.

[2] Translations: Gardiner (1909), 95–112; Erman (1927), 108–10; Simpson (1972), 230–3; Lichtheim (1973), 145–9.

concerning the next life are the subjects with which it deals: 'Those who built chapels, their places are no more ... their walls are destroyed . . . as though they had never been'—and it recommends a hedonistic attitude towards the present life:

> Be glad therefore; forgetfulness is profitable to you.
>
> Follow your desire as long as you live. Put myrrh on your head, clothe yourself in fine linen. . . .
>
> Do things (while) you are on earth. Do not be upset until that day of lamentation comes to you. . . .
>
> Make holiday and do not weary of it. See, no-one is allowed to take his goods with him and no-one who has gone comes back again.[1]

The preface to this song states that it was inscribed in front of the figure of a harpist in the tomb of one of the kings called Inyotef— very probably one of the Inyotefs of the Eleventh Dynasty—but the extant copies all date from the New Kingdom.

A similar theme is expressed in an inscription on a stela of Late Ptolemaic date (147) in which a deceased woman named Taimuthes addresses her husband from her tomb. She says:

> O my brother, my kinsman, my friend, the Greatest of the Master-Craftsmen (i.e. High Priest of Ptah), cease not to drink, to eat, to get drunk and to make love. Make holiday, pursue your desire day and night. Do not allow anxiety in your heart. How many are our years upon earth? As for the West [the land of the dead] it is a land of sleep and darkness, a burdensome place for those who dwell in it. The glorious ones sleep in their god-like forms; they cannot awake to see their brothers; they cannot look upon their fathers and mothers; they lack wives and children. . . . Would that I had flowing water (to drink). . . . Would that my face were turned towards the north wind on the river bank. . . .

Poetry, lyrics, and hymns

Vowels not being represented in writing it is impossible to discover any strict metre in Egyptian poetical compositions. What can be detected is a strophic arrangement generally consisting of three or four lines, each strophe often beginning with the same word. Parallelism of construction and of meaning, alliteration, and even word-play were also devices employed in poetry but so far no trace of rhyme has been found. The excerpt from the *Song of the Harper* already quoted demonstrates both that a standard comparable with the level of some of the poetical passages in the Old Testament was sometimes attained, and also that strict metre was not a necessary element in the structure of Egyptian lyrics. In every probability each line consisted of a certain number of accented syllables separated by a number of unaccented, or only weakly accented, syllables as in Coptic poetry of Christian times.

[1] Translations: Erman (1927), 132–4; Pritchard (1955), 467; Simpson (1972), 306–7; Lichtheim (1973), 194–7.

Music and singing were regular concomitants of daily occupations and religious festivals in Egypt. Workers in the fields sang
simple folk songs as they laboured, guests at dinner-parties were
entertained by songs and dances while they ate and drank, and
the gods were worshipped by laudatory hymns often sung to the
accompaniment of the harp. No recognizable musical notation
seems to have been devised so that the tunes played are lost, but
the words of many songs and hymns have been preserved. A song,
which accompanies a threshing scene in the beautifully
decorated tomb of an Eighteenth Dynasty nobleman named
Pahery at El-Kab, is put in the mouth of a herdsman as he drives
the oxen pulling the threshing sledge:

Thresh for yourselves, thresh for yourselves, you oxen.
Thresh for yourselves, thresh for yourselves.
Straw for (you) to eat, corn for your masters.
Let not your hearts grow weary; there is refreshment (?).

A painting from the tomb of a Theban nobleman named
Nebamun (37984, Plate 9), who lived in the middle of the
Eighteenth Dynasty, reproduces a banqueting scene in which
the guests are entertained by dancers, a woman playing two
reed-pipes and three singers who also beat time by clapping
their hands. Part of their song, written in the spaces between
the musicians and the dancers, reads as follows:

[Flowers of sweet] scents which Ptah sends and Geb makes to grow.
His beauty is in every body.
Ptah has done this with his own hands to gladden (?) his heart.
The pools are filled anew with water.
The earth is flooded with his love.

Love songs no doubt originated as simple spontaneous
utterances, but by the time they were committed to writing in
the Nineteenth Dynasty they had become rather artificial and
studied; they had ceased to be intimate exchanges and had
developed into songs sung at banquets. Among three cycles of
such songs in the Papyrus Harris 500 (10060) is one in which
a maiden describes the flowers in her garden, the names of which
bring to her mind some fresh thought about her lover:

There are *saamu*-flowers in it before which we are glorified. I am
your foremost sister. I am yours as is the acre of land which I made to
flourish with flowers and all manner of sweet-scented herbs. Pleasant
is the channel in it which you dug with your own hand for our refreshment in the north wind, a beautiful place for walking hand in hand. My
body is satisfied and my heart rejoicing at our going together. Hearing
your voice is pomegranate wine: I live when I hear it. If ever I see you
it is better for me than eating and drinking.

In the first cycle of songs in this papyrus, containing many references to the Memphite region, a young man outlines the way in which he will trick his love into visiting him:

> I shall lie down inside and feign sickness.
> My neighbours shall come in to see me
> and my girl will come and put the physicians to shame
> For she knows my disease.[1]

The Chester Beatty Papyrus I, which is not in the collection, has a cycle of seven songs each with its own title. In the first song the lover describes his mistress as

> One alone, a mistress without equal, more beautiful than mortal man . . . her excellence shines bright, her skin gleams, her eyes are beautiful when she gazes, sweet her lips when she speaks. . . . She steals my heart in her embrace. She turns the head of every man, captivating him at sight.[2]

A papyrus of the Second Intermediate Period, or slightly later, now in the Moscow Museum, preserves a group of hymns which date back to the Old Kingdom. By the time when the papyrus was written, the hymns had been adapted to the cult of the crocodile-god Sobk (to whom a hymn on a Twelfth Dynasty papyrus from the Ramesseum, 10759, is also dedicated), but originally they were intended for the veneration of the royal crowns and the king himself. They depend mainly on parallelism for their effect and are rather monotonous, but they show that even in the third millennium BC the Egyptians had gained some appreciation of literary form. Far better, both in imagery and in their use of metaphor, are some hymns to King Sesostris III of the Twelfth Dynasty (c. 1878–1843 BC):

> How great is the lord for his city: he is a refuge which rescues one in fear from his enemy.
> How great is the lord for his city: he is a cool and refreshing shade in summertime.
> How great is the lord for his city: he is a warm dry corner in wintertime.
> How great is the lord for his city: he is a mountain which shuts out the storm when heaven rages.[3]

[1] Translations: Simpson (1972), 297–306, 308–15.

[2] Translation: Simpson (1972), 315–25.

[3] Translations: Simpson (1972), 279–84; Lichtheim (1973), 198–201.

Several Pharaohs of the New Kingdom from Tuthmosis II onwards were the subjects of *Victory Hymns*, generally inscribed on stelae which were set up in their temples. Tuthmosis III's victory hymn, carved on a stela from Karnak now in the Cairo Museum, is partly written in prose, but the middle portion is clearly poetical and is divided into ten stanzas, each beginning with the words 'I have come'. The speaker is none less than the god Amun himself.

I have come
That I may grant to you to trample on the chiefs of Phoenicia,
That I may strew them beneath your feet throughout their lands;
That I may cause them to see your majesty as Lord of Rays
  When you shine in their faces in my image.
I have come
That I may grant to you to trample on those who are in Asia
  And smite the heads of the Asiatics of Syria;
That I may cause them to see your majesty equipped with your panoply,
  When you take up the weapons of war in the chariot.[1]

Ramesses II in his hymn on a stela at the temple of Abu Simbel adopted a less repetitive mode of presentation and also employed a much more graphic style as the following excerpt will show:

> . . . A jackal swift of foot seeking his attacker, traversing the circuit of the earth in a moment of time . . . who puts to flight the Asiatics, fighting upon the battlefield. They break their bows and are given over to the fire. His might has power over them, as when a flame seizes hold of scrubland, and a storm-wind is behind it; like a fierce flame when it has tasted the heat of the blaze and all within it scream as they are destroyed. King of Upper and Lower Egypt, Ramesses.
> Ruler mighty in destroying those who know not his name; like a hurricane howling loudly (?) over the ocean and its waves are like mountains and none can approach it; but all that are in it are sunk in the Underworld. King of Upper and Lower Egypt, Ramesses.

The bold images of this piece are not typical of Ramesside style. A more representative example of court poetry of the period is the Battle of Qadesh poem which Ramesses had recorded on the walls of many of his temples. Part of this poem is contained in two papyri, Chester Beatty III (10683) and Sallier III (10181). In the latter:

> His majesty appeared like Montu. He put on his panoply of war, he donned his armour. He was like Baal in his might . . . Their hearts become faint in their bodies; their arms grow weak and they cannot shoot their arrows. (His majesty) plunged them into the water as crocodiles plunge.

The Nile and many of the gods were worshipped in hymns which often display deep religious feeling. *The Hymn to the Nile* (Papyrus Sallier II, Papyrus Anastasi VII, and Papyrus Chester Beatty V, 10182, 10222, and 10685) is thought to have been composed in the Middle Kingdom but the earliest extant copies, all very corrupt, date from the Nineteenth Dynasty (c. 1250 BC).

Hail O Nile, who issues forth from the earth, who comes to give life to
  the people of Egypt. Secret of movement, a darkness in daylight.
Praised by his followers whose fields you water.
Created by Re to give life to all who thirst.

Who lets the desert drink with streams descending from heaven.
Beloved of the earth-god, controller of the corn-god, who causes the
    workshops of Ptah to flourish.
Lord of fish who causes the water-fowl to sail upstream . . .
Who makes barley and creates wheat so that temples celebrate . . .
When the Nile overflows, offerings are made to you, cattle are slaughtered
    for you, a great oblation is made to you, birds are fattened for you,
    desert lions are trapped for you that your goodness be repaid.[1]

Hymns to the sun-god date back to the royal Pyramid Texts of
the Fifth and Sixth Dynasties. By the time of the Eighteenth
Dynasty they were often inscribed on the walls of private tombs
and on the funerary stelae of private persons. At that time also
they began to represent the sun-god, Amen-Re, as the universal
creator, a conception which is well exemplified in a sun-hymn
carved on a stela of two architects named Suty and Hor, who
lived in the reign of Amenophis III (826, fig. 52).

> Creator are you, fashioner of your own limbs;
> One who brings into being, himself unborn;
> Unique in his qualities, traversing eternity
> Upon roads with millions under his guidance.

In this same hymn the unique position of the sun-god and his
authority over all lands and peoples is unequivocally stated:

> Sole lord taking captive all lands every day,
> As one beholding those that walk therein.

Only a few years after this text had been carved, Amenophis III's
son, Akhenaten, composed his famous *Hymn to Aten*, the sun's
disk, which has often been compared with Psalm 104 and which
is the first truly monotheistic composition in the literature of the
world. Its key-note is the all-embracing love of Aten for the works
which he has created:

    . . . At dawn when you rise in the horizon, when you shine as the
Aten by day, you dispel darkness and give forth your rays. The Two
Lands are in festival, they wake up and stand on their feet for you have
raised them up. They cleanse their bodies and put on their clothes, their
arms are raised in praise at your appearance. The whole land performs
its work. All beasts are content with their pasturage. Trees and plants
grow green. The birds fly from their nests, their wings (stretched) in
praise of your spirit. All small beasts skip upon their feet, all that fly
and alight live because you have arisen. Boats sail north and south likewise; all roads open at your appearance. The fish in the river leap before
you; your rays are in the depths of the ocean.
    Creator of the foetus in women, maker of seed in men, who creates
life in the son in the womb of his mother, soothing him that he may not
weep; nurse in the womb who gives breath that all may live whom he
has made. . . .

[1] Translation:
Lichtheim (1973),
204–10.

How countless are your works! But they are concealed from sight. O unique god like whom there is no other. You created the earth according to your desire when you were alone: all men, all creatures great and small which are upon earth going on their feet and that which is aloft flying upon wings; the foreign lands too, Syria, Nubia and Egypt herself. You set each man in his place and provide their requirements; everyone has his sustenance and his lifespan is reckoned. Their tongues are distinguished in speech and their natures likewise. Their complexions are different. You have distinguished foreign peoples. . . .[1]

The hymn ends with lines in which Akhenaten expresses his belief that he alone on earth has true knowledge of the Aten and his intentions towards mankind. It was probably part of the ritual performed by Akhenaten in the temple of Aten at Amarna. Clear evidence that hymns were sung in temple services is afforded by a papyrus (Chester Beatty IX, recto, 10689) which includes hymns to be sung by the whole congregation.

In addition to hymns glorifying the principal deities, Egyptian religious literature includes a few examples of poetical compositions of a very different kind. They are more intimate and in many respects they resemble the penitential psalms of the Old Testament. Some are written on papyrus, e.g. a prayer to Amun by a poor litigant in court (Papyrus Anastasi II, 10243, recto viii. 5–ix. 1), but the majority are carved on the stelae of humble workmen of the Nineteenth Dynasty, who dwelt at Deir el-Medina and whose lives were spent carving and painting the tombs of the kings and nobles at Thebes. A member of that community named Neferabu, who had been stricken with blindness for swearing falsely by the god Ptah, has left the following message to posterity on his stela (589):

I am a man who swore falsely by Ptah, Lord of Truth; and he caused
    me to see darkness in daylight.
I shall proclaim his power to the one who does not know him, and the
    one who does,
To the small and the great.
Beware of Ptah, Lord of Truth!
He will not overlook the deed of any man.
Beware of uttering the name of Ptah falsely;
Lo, he who utters it falsely,
He is cast down.
He caused me to be as the dogs of the streets,
When I was in his hand;
He caused men and gods to take note of me,
I, a man who had done an abomination against his lord.
Just was Ptah, Lord of Truth, towards me
When he punished me.
Pardon me; look upon me that you may pardon me.

[1] Translations: Pritchard (1955), 370–1; Simpson (1972), 289–95.

Magic

Magic in its various forms enters into a very large body of Egyptian literature. Besides such Books of Magic as the *Harris Magical Papyrus* (10042) and the *Salt Magical Papyrus* (10051), which include hymns as well as incantations, there are many collections of spells against diseases and other misfortunes (e.g. Chester Beatty Papyrus VII, 10687). Every day of the year was believed to possess some magical significance, which rendered it good, bad, or partly good and partly bad, and *Calendars of Lucky and Unlucky Days* (e.g. Sallier IV, 10184 recto) were compiled for purposes of reference. One papyrus (Chester Beatty III, 10683) gives a list of dreams and their interpretations, each dream beginning with the words 'If a man see himself in a dream'; then follows a short description of the dream, a bald statement that it is good or bad, and finally its interpretation:

If a man sees himself in a dream
    eating donkey flesh, good, it means his promotion;
    seating himself upon a tree, good, it means the destruction of all his ills;
    looking into a deep well, bad, it means being put in prison;
    eating an egg, bad, it means the seizure of his possessions beyond repair.

Problems of many kinds might be solved by consulting an oracle. The highest offices in the land, even the kingship, were occasionally filled by oracular revelation. Disputes which arose over matters of property could be settled by reference to an oracle: ostracon 5624 (fig. 35) for instance, describes how the deified king Amenophis I decided the ownership of a tomb in favour of a workman in the Theban necropolis named Amenemope; another ostracon (5625) mentions a dispute concerning the occupation of a house at Thebes which the same deity was asked to settle. A Twentieth Dynasty papyrus (10335) narrates the oracular proceedings which led to the identification of a thief who had stolen five garments from a certain Amenemwiya, a keeper of a store-house. At one period in the end of the New Kingdom children wore long cylindrical amulets often of metal (a Middle Kingdom example is in the Sixth Egyptian Room) containing narrow rolls of papyrus inscribed with long oracular texts promising divine protection against all kinds of misadventures. The following quotation from a papyrus of this kind (10083) gives the declarations attributed to three deities:

We shall keep her safe from Sakhmet and her son.
We shall keep her safe from the collapse of a wall and from the fall of a thunderbolt.
We shall keep her safe from leprosy, from blindness . . . throughout her whole lifetime.

The pharaonic tradition of magic continued well after Egypt was absorbed into the Roman Empire: Papyrus Anastasi 1072 (10070) contains a collection of magical spells and recipes written in demotic with glosses in Greek, dated to the third century AD.

Egyptian stories

These often included a description of some incident involving magic, none more entertainingly than the *Story of Cheops and the Magicians* recounted in the Westcar Papyrus[1] a document in Berlin which dates from Hyksos times. After listening to some stories of wonders performed by magicians in the days of his predecessors, Cheops sent for a magician named Dedi, who succeeded in joining the severed heads of a goose, a duck, and an ox, so that the birds were again able to cackle and quack and the ox to low. The story continues with an account of the miraculous birth of triplets sired by the sun god himself upon the wife of one of his priests. Dedi forecasts that these three children will grow up to become the first kings of a new dynasty. The papyrus breaks off just when it seems that the children's whereabouts are about to be betrayed to Cheops. In spite of the king's Herod-like intentions we must assume that he was thwarted for the first three kings of the succeeding Fifth Dynasty bore the same names as the three children.

At least in some details, the adventures of Sindbad and the *Story of the Shipwrecked Sailor*[2] (written on a Middle Kingdom papyrus in Leningrad) have something in common. The sole survivor of the wreck, the sailor was cast up on an enchanted island where he was befriended and encouraged by a serpent of fabulous appearance: 'He was thirty cubits long, and his beard was more than two cubits long. His body was plated with gold, his eyebrows were of real lapis lazuli.' Eventually, as the serpent had foretold, he was rescued by another ship and taken safely back to Egypt.

In the *Story of the Two Brothers* (D'Orbiney Papyrus, 10183), elements which in origin belonged to folk-tale and mythology have been woven into a continuous narrative.[3] It begins with an account of life on a farm in which Bata helps his elder brother, Inpu, i.e. Anubis, in his agricultural work. Inpu's wife, however, makes amorous overtures to Bata and, having failed to achieve her aim, falsely alleges to Inpu that Bata has ill-treated her after she refused his advances. Inpu then lies in wait behind the door of the byre ready to kill his brother when he returns with his cattle at sunset; as the first cow enters her stall she warns Bata of his danger and he flees, pursued by his brother armed with a spear. The sun-god intervenes, creating a stretch

[1] Translations: Erman (1927), 36–47; Simpson (1972), 15–30; Lichtheim (1973), 215–22.

[2] Translations: Erman (1927), 29–35; Simpson (1972), 50–6; Lichtheim (1973), 211–15.

[3] Translations: Erman (1927), 150–61; Pritchard (1955), 23–5; Simpson (1972), 92–107.

of water full of crocodiles between the brothers. Bata, thus protected, as a sign of good faith mutilates himself and is able to convince his brother of his innocence. Inpu returns to his house, slays his wife, and throws her to the dogs.

Bata tells his brother that he will go to the Valley of the Cedar and will place his heart on top of the flower of the cedar. Having reached the valley and having built a castle for himself, Bata takes to himself a wife, who 'was more beautiful than any woman in all the world', specially created by the gods to relieve his loneliness. Eventually a lock of her hair is carried by the sea to the Pharaoh and its perfume induces him to send soldiers to carry her off. Having reached his court she persuades the king to have the flower on the cedar containing Bata's heart cut down. The heart of Bata falls with the flower and he himself dies.

Inpu learns of Bata's death by a previously arranged magic sign and immediately sets forth to the Valley of the Cedar where, after a long search, he finds his brother's heart in the form of a fruit and brings him back to life. Bata, revivified, takes on the form of a bull and carries Inpu home to Egypt on his back. Inpu becomes Pharaoh's favourite; Bata reveals himself to his one-time wife who persuades the king against his will to slaughter the bull, but two drops of his blood fall to the ground outside the palace and grow into two persea trees in which Bata continues to live. Again he reveals himself to his wife and again she attempts to be rid of him by inducing the king to cut down the trees so that they can be made into furniture. While the carpenters are fashioning the furniture the woman comes to see them and swallows a splinter which has flown into her mouth. As a result she becomes pregnant and gives birth to a child who is none other than Bata. When he grows up the king makes him crown prince and at length he succeeds to the throne of Egypt. His one-time wife is denounced and put to death (presumably) and his faithful elder brother Inpu is made his heir.

The Blinding of Truth by Falsehood (Chester Beatty II, 10682) belongs to the same class of allegorical literature as the *Story of the Two Brothers* and is also of Ramesside date. Unfortunately the beginning of the papyrus is missing, but the plot may be deduced from what follows.[1] A knife which Falsehood had entrusted to his brother, Truth, had somehow been lost or damaged. When Truth offered to replace it, Falsehood claimed it was impossible because of its size and value. Acting on False-hood's demand the tribunal of the gods condemned Truth to be blinded and to become Falsehood's door-keeper. After some further adventures Truth begat a son who, when he grew up, determined to avenge his father. Having picked a quarrel with

[1] Translations: Gardiner (1935), 4–6; Simpson (1972), 127–32.

Falsehood over the possession of an ox, the boy took him to the divine tribunal and by a trick obtained the verdict. As a punishment Falsehood was beaten and blinded and made to serve as Truth's door-keeper.

A simple but touching narrative of Ramesside date, which is preserved in the Harris Papyrus 500 (10060), is the *Story of the Foredoomed Prince*.[1] When the goddesses of fate, called the Seven Hathors, came to visit the prince on the day of his birth they decreed that he should die by a crocodile, a snake, or a dog. His father, the king, in order to protect him from exposure to these hazards, built a castle for the prince and kept him within its walls. At length the boy persuaded his father to let him have a dog as a pet and subsequently to leave the castle and go to Syria, accompanied by his dog. When he arrived there he found the young nobles competing for the beautiful daughter of the local chief, her father having promised her hand in marriage to the youth who would first succeed in climbing to her window, seventy cubits above the ground. The prince joined in the contest and won, the daughter becoming his devoted wife. By her watchfulness he was saved from an attack by a snake. The end of the papyrus is very damaged but it seems that when his own dog threatened him the prince sought refuge in the sea where a crocodile caught him. The papyrus breaks off just after the crocodile offers escape if the prince will kill an enemy for him. It has been supposed, however, that the story had a happy ending.

Another story written on the same papyrus (10060) is an historical romance known as the *Capture of Joppa*. Its beginning is missing, but it clearly refers to the Palestinian campaign of Tuthmosis III.[2] Having failed to take Joppa by direct assault, his general Djehuty achieved victory by a stratagem involving the introduction into the city of two hundred soldiers hidden in baskets pretending to have been captured by Joppa's prince.

The *Story of King Apophis and Seqenenre* (Sallier I, 10185) has sometimes been regarded as an historical romance.[3] The Hyksos king Apophis sent a messenger to Seqenenre (c. 1600 BC) complaining that the hippopotami in the hippopotamus pool at Thebes were disturbing his sleep. Since the residence of Apophis lay at Avaris in the Delta, more than five hundred miles distant from Thebes, the complaint was clearly without substance. In every probability, as Sir Gaston Maspero observed (*Les Contes populaires de l'Égypte ancienne*, 4th ed., pp. xxvi–xxvii), the story was 'simply the local variant of a theme popular throughout the entire East. The kings of those times were wont to send one another problems to be solved on all sorts of matters, the condition being that they should pay one another a kind of

[1] Translations: Erman (1927), 161–5; Simpson (1972), 85–91.

[2] Translations: Erman (1927), 167–9; Pritchard (1955), 22–3; Simpson (1972), 81–4.

[3] Translations: Erman (1927), 165–7; Pritchard (1955), 231–2; Simpson (1972), 77–80.

41 Demotic papyrus containing the story of Setne-Khaemwese and the prince of Nubia

tribute or fine according as they should answer well or ill to the questions put to them.' Unfortunately the young scribe Pentawer, who copied this story in the time of King Merneptah (c. 1236–1223 BC) never completed his work and Seqenenre's answer is not recorded. It used to be assumed that Amen-Re came to the assistance of the Egyptian king and the story ended with the outwitting of Apophis and Sutekh his god. However, the mummy of Seqenenre (probably the hero of the story) preserved in the Cairo Museum bears such frightful wounds that he must have fallen in battle, and there are indications that he did not die victorious. Nevertheless it was one of his sons who finally drove the Hyksos from Egypt (p. 57).

Four great demotic historical romances have survived from the Late Period, two from the Petubastis cycle and two from the Setne-Khaemwese cycle (fig. 41). The first of the stories concerning king Petubastis has been called the *High Emprise for the Cuirass* and is contained in the Papyrus Krall dated to the end of the second century AD.[1] It purports to be a history of events written down during the reign of a king Petubastis, possibly based on the Twenty-third Dynasty king of that name. Petubastis reigns at Tanis in the Delta but has powerful equals in Inaros, ruler of Heliopolis, and another Delta king called apparently Wer-tep-Amen-Niwt. Inaros has a cuirass which on his death is seized by Wer-tep-Amen-Niwt. Petubastis tries to console Inaros' son Pamay by ordering a great funeral for his father but

[1] Translation: Maspero (1915), 217–42.

Pamay still demands the return of the cuirass which Wer-tep-Amen-Niwt refuses to do even when summoned before Petubastis. War threatens: Wer-tep-Amen-Niwt calls up his forces and Pamay and the Great Chief of the East, Pakell, call up theirs. After Pamay with his advance guard are caught by Wer-tep-Amen-Niwt, only the arrival of reinforcements saves him from defeat; then Petubastis arrives and a fight between picked champions of the two armies is arranged. It turns into a full-scale battle with Montubaal, another son of Inaros, spreading such slaughter that Petubastis is forced to ask him to stop in return for the cuirass. However, when they find Pamay he is about to kill Wer-tep-Amen-Niwt and then Petubastis has to intervene to prevent his own son Ankhhor being slain. Meanwhile Minirmy seizes the cuirass by force and returns it to Heliopolis; Petubastis is commanded to write down the history of the events.

The second story of the Petubastis cycle is on a papyrus in Strasbourg which dates to the first half of the first century AD.[1] It has been entitled the *High Emprise for the Throne* and is basically the same story as that involving the cuirass except that the object of contention is now the throne of Amun and the events clearly take place some years after those just described. The throne, held by the High Priest of Amun, on his death is seized by Petubastis' son Ankhhor. In reprisal Amun's sacred bark is carried off by the High Priest's son. Neither will return the stolen objects so armies are drawn up but the High Priest's son captures Ankhhor, Petubastis' son, and the royal champion Wer-tep-Amen-Niwt and keeps them in the stolen bark. Amun himself is continually participating to give advice in person. Meanwhile Minirmy, son of Inaros, does combat with one of the priests which lasts for days without result, then royal reinforcements arrive. Presumably Petubastis won eventually and the throne stayed with his son. Scraps of other stories from the cycle are also in existence.

The Adventure of Setne-Khaemwese and the Mummies is contained in two fragmentary papyri in Cairo dated to the Ptolemaic period.[2] The hero Setne is based on prince Khaemwese, a historical son of Ramesses II who had a reputation as a wise man and scholar. By the time the cycle was composed Setne has become a magician. The story takes place at Memphis where the real Khaemwese must have spent much of his life as High Priest of Ptah. Setne is tempted by the dead magician Naneferkaptah to steal from his tomb the Book of Thoth which gives its possessor the power to charm heaven and earth, night, the mountains and water; to understand the language of birds and reptiles, to see to the depths of the sea, and, greatest spell of all, to resurrect the

[1] Translation: Maspero (1915), 243–62.

[2] Translations: Maspero (1915), 115–44; Griffith (1900), 16–40.

dead from the tomb. After a search in the Memphite necropolis Setne finds and enters Naneferkaptah's tomb where he meets the dead magician, his wife Ihwery and son Merib. Ihwery recounts her marriage with her brother, his recovery of the Book of Thoth from Coptos, the subsequent drowning of her son and herself and their burial at Coptos. Naneferkaptah himself was drowned shortly afterwards but managed to keep the Book of Thoth with him so although buried at Memphis was able to use its powers to keep the ghosts of his wife and son with him. Setne plays him at *senet* for the book and is losing badly until his brother uses amulets to rescue him and the book. Against Pharaoh's advice Setne refuses to return it to Naneferkaptah so the succubus Tabubu seduces him into transferring all his property to her and even agreeing to the slaying of his own children and then vanishes. On awaking Setne returns the book to Naneferkaptah who asks that the bodies of his wife and son be reburied with him at Memphis. Their bodies, hidden at Coptos, are found with magic aid and then taken to Memphis for reburial with Naneferkaptah.

The True Story of Setne-Khaemwese and his Son Si-Wsir is contained in papyrus 10822 which has on its reverse a land register written in Greek dating to the first century AD.[1] In this story Setne's wife Mekhweskhet is childless but after incubation in the Temple of Ptah receives advice and accordingly after following it becomes pregnant. The child, called Si-Wsir after a dream of his father's, is a prodigy. One day he and Setne witness the funeral of a rich man and a beggar but when Setne expresses the wish that his burial may be as sumptuous as the rich man's, Si-Wsir wishes him the beggar's funeral. Setne is distraught until his son takes him by magic to see the treatment of rich and poor in the Other World. There a splendidly-clad man is revealed as the beggar; the rich man is in hell with a door pivot in his eye.

A new episode begins with the arrival of a man termed the Prince of Nubia bringing a sealed letter which must be read unopened or Egypt must admit Nubia's supremacy. Setne becomes ill with worry because he cannot do the feat but Si-Wsir succeeds. The letter is about a man called Hor who is encouraged by the King of Nubia to use magic to transport Pharaoh to Nubia for a beating. An Egyptian also called Hor uses the Book of Thoth to protect Pharaoh on subsequent occasions then reverses the process so that the Nubian king is carried to Egypt three times and beaten. The Nubian Hor enlists his mother's aid before going to Egypt to seek out his namesake. The two compete at magic, the Nubian is beaten and about to be killed when his mother intervenes. The two promise never to return and are allowed to go. Si-Wsir then unmasks the

[1] Translations: Maspero (1915), 144–70; Griffith (1900), 42–66.

messenger as the Nubian Hor and reveals himself as the Egyptian Hor reincarnated. The Prince of Nubia is consumed by fire and Si-Wsir vanishes. Setne is desolate but then his wife conceives another son. . . .

Travel

This is represented by the *Story of Sinuhe* and the *Adventures of Wenamun*. In all, five papyri and more than twenty ostraca (e.g. 5629) inscribed with excerpts from Sinuhe's narrative are known; so large a number of copies would not have been preserved if the tale had not been exceptionally popular.[1] The story begins with a reference to the death of Ammenemes I, the first king of the Twelfth Dynasty (*c.* 1991–1962 BC). Sinuhe, when he heard the news, was returning with the king's co-regent, Sesostris I, from a military expedition against the Libyans. For reasons which are nowhere fully explained, but were somehow connected with a conversation which he overheard between the king's sons, Sinuhe felt that his life was in danger and decided to flee from Egypt. Since Ammenemes I, the dead king, may well have died as the result of a conspiracy Sinuhe could have been implicated either as an enemy of the new king or as his ally. A graphic account is given of his flight to Palestine, where eventually Amunenshi, king of the Upper Retjenu, befriended him, gave him his eldest daughter in marriage and made him head of a tribe and commander of his army. The royal favours led to jealousy and a local warrior challenged him to a duel which Sinuhe describes in a lively passage. After many years during which he accumulated great wealth, Sinuhe, being advanced in age, felt the urge to return to the land of his birth. Sesostris I, who had heard of Sinuhe's successes, invited him back and promised him a lavish burial when his days were over. The story ends with a description of his ceremonial return to Egypt and his regal reception.

The *Adventures of Wenamun* may represent the actual report of an ill-fated journey from Thebes to Byblos:[2] if so it would explain why no copies of the text have come to light to supplement an incomplete papyrus in Moscow. Wenamun was an emissary sent by Herihor to the Lebanon in order to obtain cedarwood needed for the state-barge of Amun at Thebes. After being robbed of his money, Wenamun suffered misfortunes and indignities in the ports of Palestine and Syria, but eventually the prince of Byblos allowed him to leave for Egypt in one of his own ships. His troubles were, however, not at an end, for when the narrative breaks off Wenamun had been cast by a storm on the shores of Cyprus and is pleading for his life and the lives of the crew of the prince of Byblos.

[1] Translations: Erman (1927), 14–29; Pritchard (1955), 18–22; Simpson (1972), 57–74; Lichtheim (1973), 222–35.

[2] Translations: Erman (1927), 174–85; Pritchard (1955), 25–9; Simpson (1972), 142–55; Goedicke (1975), 149–58.

In a somewhat different category from the two works previously mentioned must be placed a famous satirical letter of the Nine-teenth Dynasty (Papyrus Anastasi I, 10247). The letter was written by a scribe named Hori, who held a position in the royal stables, to another scribe and army commander named Amenemope.[1] In an earlier letter Amenemope had claimed the title of Maher, a word of uncertain derivation which was apparently applied to someone who had travelled in Palestine and Syria. Hori replies by naming many localities which he believes Amenemope has not seen and by describing some of the hazards of a Maher's life. A long cross-examination follows on various towns, mountains, streams, roads, beginning with Byblos and ending in the Delta. Earlier in the letter Hori had propounded a number of mathematical problems which he claimed Amenemope would not be able to solve. Teachers at scribal schools often chose excerpts from this letter (e.g. ostracon 50724) for their students to copy, probably because it gave them practice in spelling foreign words and place-names.

Letters

In his letter, Hori jeers at Amenemope for having written an unintelligible letter, a taunt which could not fail to provoke resentment, for Egyptian scribes were carefully trained at school in the technique of letter-writing. No doubt much of their time, not only at school but also after completing their training, was thus occupied, if the number of letters preserved may be regarded as indicative. Many of those which have survived were certainly models, intended for instruction, but actual communications are also numerous. The oldest letter known, written on papyrus, dates from the Sixth Dynasty (c. 2250 BC) and is now in the Cairo Museum. It contains a protest by a military commander, whose troops are working in the Tura quarries, because six days were required for providing his men with new clothing when one day should have been sufficient. Several Middle Kingdom letters have survived: one Eleventh Dynasty example (10549, fig. 29), also from an army commander, whose name was Nehsi, complains that a female member of his household named Senet is short of provisions although he had sent grain to a certain Kay, her father; the commander believes that it is Kay's wife, whose character is like that of his stepmother, who is trying to starve the girl. A papyrus found at the Ramesseum in Thebes (10752) gives copies of a series of letters received from an official stationed in the Second Cataract fortress of Semna in the reign of Ammenemes III of the Twelfth Dynasty (c. 1842–1797 BC); they deal with the movements of the Nubians and their visits to the fortress to sell their wares. Of the numerous letters which

[1] Translations: Erman (1927), 214–34; Pritchard (1955), 475–9.

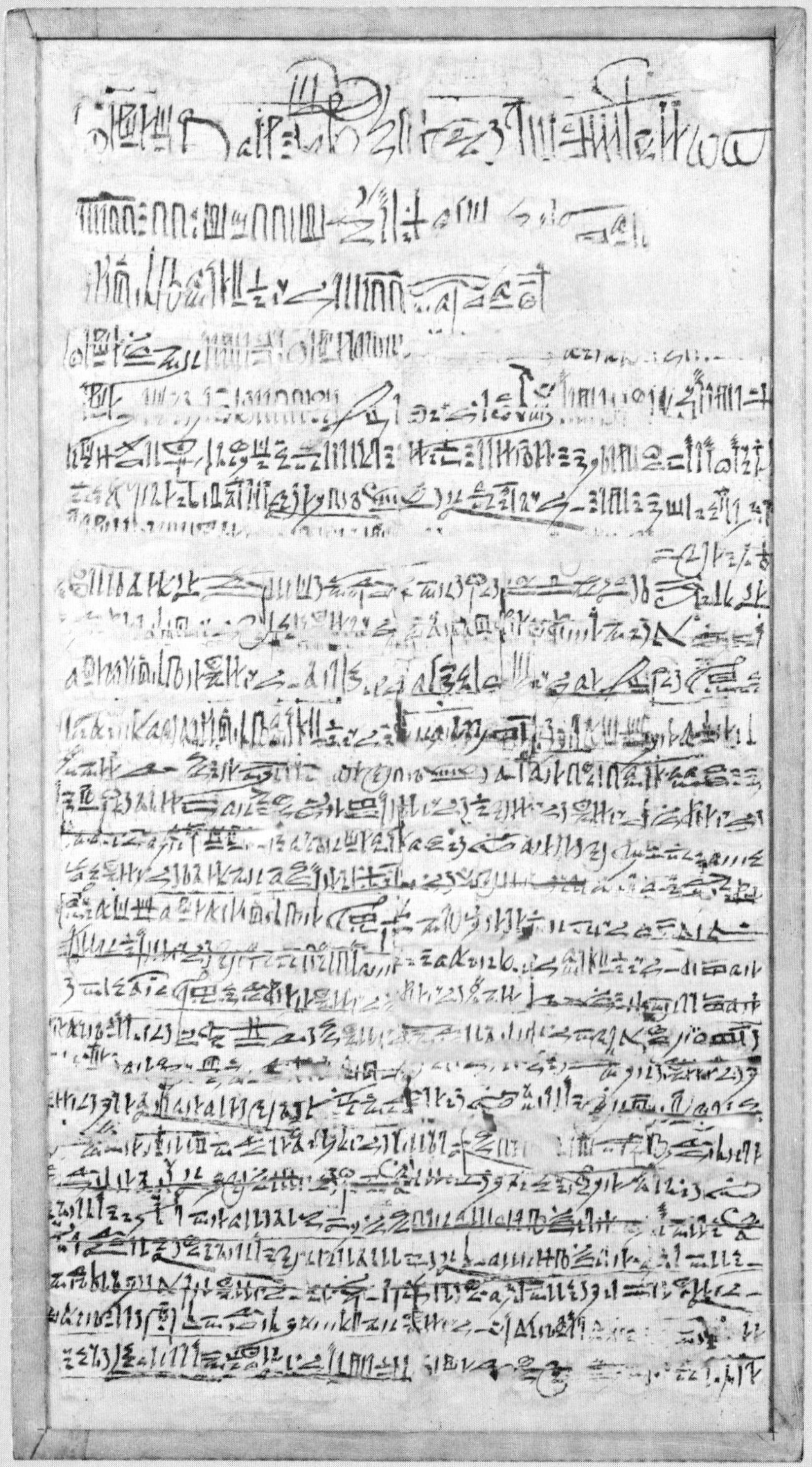

date from the New Kingdom, some of the most interesting are those which have come from Deir el-Medina, the Theban village occupied by the artists and craftsmen who constructed the Ramesside royal tombs (e.g. nos. 10100, 10284, 10300, 10326, 10375, 10412, 10417, 10430, 10433). These letters occasionally mention incidents in the lives of members of this community which can be confirmed from other documents. A letter addressed to Paankh, son of the priest-king Herihor, is written in the fluent hand of one of the best-known scribes in the community, Butehamun (10375, fig. 42).

Letters were sometimes written to friends and relations who had died. As a rule they were written on bowls containing food-offerings so that they would be seen by the intended recipients when they visited their tombs to partake of the offerings. Such letters were not prompted by a desire to remain in communication with a dead friend; their purpose was to seek the aid of the deceased person in some way, generally to bring to an end some undesirable interference in the affairs of the writer or his household. A dead friend might, for instance, be asked to prosecute a troublesome departed spirit before the divine tribunal in the Next World. Extant examples of such letters, which are not numerous, date from the Sixth to the Nineteenth Dynasties (c. 2345–c. 1200 BC).

Undoubtedly stemming from these letters to the dead are documents in the demotic script written to various deities imploring their aid, often in situations for which there can be no legal redress. In one such papyrus (10845) dated to the first century BC, Pasherdjehuty and Naneferher, the children of their father's first marriage, complain that as soon as their mother died they were cast out by their father who took another wife. Their prayer is addressed to the Ibis, the Hawk and the Baboon, three gods of the Memphite necropolis. A typical pastoral letter written in Coptic by a bishop to his congregation is recorded on ostracon 32782 (fig. 43).

42 Letter addressed to the General Paankh by the scribe Butehamun (*opposite*)

43 Coptic ostracon recording a letter from a bishop to his congregation (*right*)

Business and legal records

These frequently shed most valuable light on the economic and social conditions of their times. In many cases these texts, especially those on ostraca, deal with trifling transactions and matters which were purely ephemeral: lists of objects given in exchange for a bed (5636 and 5644) or for a bull (5649), quantities of water conveyed by various water-carriers (5638), objects lent by one woman to another (29560), etc. One ostracon (5634) dated to the fortieth year of the reign of Ramesses II (c. 1264 BC) contains a register of the names of some workmen engaged on the royal tomb, each name being followed by a note of the days on which the man was absent from work and the reason for his absence; among the reasons given are sickness, caring for another workman who was sick (and mentioned as 'sick' in his own record), brewing beer and domestic hindrances. From this document it is apparent that every tenth day was a rest day. Legal documents deal with a wide range of subjects, from private contracts and trials for petty larceny to state trials for participation in conspiracies against the king or acts of robbery committed in the royal tombs at Thebes. The writer of an ostracon (5631) which dates from the Nineteenth–Twentieth Dynasties (c. 1200 BC) mentions that he had been condemned to a term of forced labour for embezzlement, but his father had appealed to the king and had obtained his release. Papyrus Salt 124 (10055) describes a series of charges laid before the Vizier (who was also the Chief Justice) by a certain Amennakht against a chief foreman of the workmen in the royal tomb named Peneb (the owner of stelae 272–3). Among the charges are accusations of having stolen objects from the tomb of King Sethos II (c. 1216–1210 BC), allegations of offences against the wives of fellow workmen, and other irregularities which included abuse of privilege. The papyrus does not unfortunately record the outcome of Amennakht's complaint, and the fate of Peneb remains unknown. More informative are some papyri which deal with judicial inquiries conducted at Thebes in the sixteenth and seventeenth years of Ramesses IX (c. 1142–1123 BC) and the nineteenth and twentieth years of Ramesses XI (c. 1114–1085 BC) into robberies which had occurred in the Theban necropolis. Seven of the twelve known papyri in the group are in the collection of the Museum (10052, 10053, 10054, 10068, 10221, 10383, and 10403). From one of these documents, the Abbott Papyrus (10221), it is clear that both the mayor of the city of Thebes, Paser, and the mayor of Western Thebes, Paweraa, had reported that several tombs, among them those of kings and queens, had been violated and their contents plundered. Investigation carried out in the necropolis during the inquiry

Plate 7
Upper part of a colossus of Ramesses II

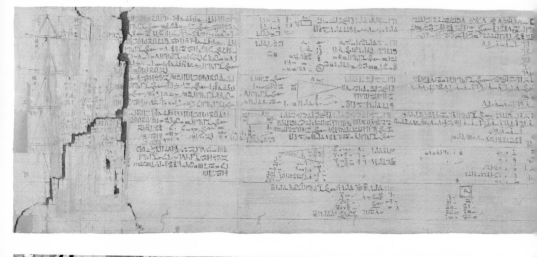

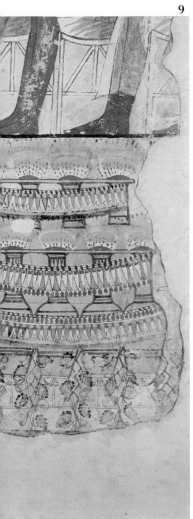

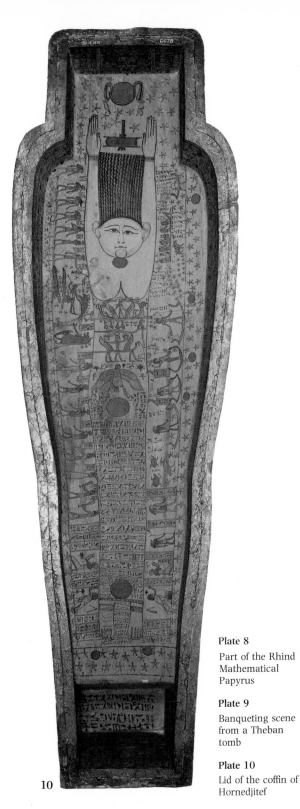

8

9

10

Plate 8

Part of the Rhind
Mathematical
Papyrus

Plate 9

Banqueting scene
from a Theban
tomb

Plate 10

Lid of the coffin of
Hornedjitef

showed that the charges made by Paser were greatly exaggerated and it is hard to believe that, in making his report, he was not trying to discredit his colleague on the west bank. Nevertheless serious robberies had been committed, including the plundering of the tomb of King Sobkemsaf (c. 1650 BC) and his wife Nubkhaas, and the tomb of Isis, wife of King Ramesses III (c. 1198–1166 BC), from whose temple at Medinet Habu a gilded portable shrine had also been stolen. In the main the papyri are devoted to recording the evidence given by the accused, some of whom were acquitted, and lists of the objects found in the possession of the guilty parties.

Very many of the demotic papyri which have survived are concerned with business transactions and throw much light on social life in Egypt during the last three centuries BC. One of the longest known demotic papyri (10026, fig. 44), contains the cession of certain property at Thebes by the woman Nes-Khons to her eldest son Pana with four witness copies. The date is December 265 BC. Although there is a good deal of variation in detail in such cessions and their accompanying bills of sale (in this case not present because the cession is really a will) the general contents are stable. A bill of sale usually runs:

(1) date (sometimes with the names of eponymous priests and priestesses);

(2) names of the contracting parties in the form X says to Y;

(3) the payment involved: 'You have made me content with the price of my (e.g. house)' then details of the property;

(4) a clause of surrender: 'I give to you my (e.g. house)';

(5) a possession clause: 'Yours is my (e.g. house)';

(6) receipt of payment: 'I have received the price of my (e.g. house) from your hand';

(7) a clause excluding the former owner from further rights: 'I have no claim against you in its name';

(8) security from others' claims: 'No man has legal rights against you in my name, in anyone's name from this day forth';

(9) a deed clause: 'Yours are its deeds and records';

(10) an oath to carry out the promises;

(11) closing formula: 'There are no legal claims against you' or the confirmation of the transaction by a third party, usually a relative of the first party;

(12) the scribe's signature.

The deed of cession has many identical clauses but instead of clause (3) there is a clause of surrender: 'I renounce all claim on your (e.g. house)'; there is no clause (6) and after clause (10)

Plate 11
Queen Ahmes-Nefertari

44 Demotic papyrus containing details of a cession of property by the woman Nes-Khons

is a closing pledge: 'I have made the deed of cession for you in the matter of my (e.g. house)'. The witnesses of the transaction, usually 16 in number, sign their names and filiation on the verso of the papyrus. Sometimes, as in this case, up to four of the witnesses were required to copy out the document in their own hand on the recto.

Scientific literature

Egyptian writings of a scientific nature are limited to the fields of mathematics, astronomy, and medicine. At what date the study of mathematics began is not known, but it was certainly long before the earliest extant mathematical documents were written. These documents are not sets of rules but lists of problems and their solutions. The Rhind Mathematical Papyrus (10057 and 10058, Plate 8) begins with a long table of the division of 2 by odd numbers from 3 to 101 and continues with eighty-four problems of an arithmetical kind which include mensuration, the calculation of areas, and the measurement of angles of slopes. The following are examples of these problems:

(*a*) Divide 2 by 97.

(*b*) A circular container of 9 cubits in its height and 6 in its breadth. What is the amount that will go into it in corn?

(*c*) Method of reckoning a circular piece of land of diameter 9 *khet*. What is its area in land?

(*d*) A pyramid 140 (units) in length of side, and 5 palms and a finger in its slope. What is the vertical height thereof?

Three lines of partly mutilated text, which serve as a preface, state that the papyrus was copied from 'a writing of antiquity' by a scribe named Ahmose who lived in the time of the Hyksos king Auserre Apophis (*c.* 1575 BC). To about the same date may be ascribed a list in duplicate of twenty-six sums in the addition of fractions written on a strip of leather (10250). In every probability this list was intended as a kind of ready-reckoner.

The Egyptians adopted a decimal notation, the highest unit employed being 1,000,000. Addition and subtraction of whole numbers presented no difficulties. Multiplication, except for the most simple cases in which a number had either to be doubled or to be multiplied by ten, involved a somewhat laborious process of doubling and adding. Thus in order to multiply 77 by 7 they wrote out the following table:

$$1 \times 77 = 77$$
$$2 \times 77 = 154$$
$$4 \times 77 = 308$$

The multipliers 1, 2, and 4 were first added together, giving a total of 7, and then the corresponding products (i.e. 77, 154, and 308), thereby obtaining 539 as the quotient. Division was achieved by reversing the process:

$$1 \times 7 = 7$$
$$2 \times 7 = 14$$
$$4 \times 7 = 28$$
$$8 \times 7 = 56$$

In this case they added the products, the sum of which amounts to 77 (i.e. 7+14+56), then by adding the corresponding multipliers (i.e. 1, 2, and 8) they obtained the desired result of 11.

Apart from $\frac{2}{3}$ and (rarely) $\frac{3}{4}$ no fractions were written with numerators higher than unity. Thus, instead of writing $\frac{2}{11}$ the Egyptians wrote $\frac{1}{6}+\frac{1}{66}$. No doubt tables of the kind shown on the strip of leather (10250) and in the first section of the Rhind Mathematical Papyrus were kept at hand to save the necessity of working out complex fractions. Multiplication and division of fractions were achieved by the same process as was employed in multiplying and dividing whole numbers.

Two measures of capacity were, at least from the Middle Kingdom onwards, normally in use: the *heqat*-measure, approximately a bushel, and the *hin*-measure, about $\frac{1}{2}$ litre. The *heqat* was divided in fractional parts $\frac{1}{2}$, $\frac{1}{4}$, $\frac{1}{8}$, $\frac{1}{16}$, $\frac{1}{32}$, and $\frac{1}{64}$, and 16 *heqat* might be expressed as a sack (*khar*). Other liquid measures are known, but their sizes have not been determined.

Linear measurement was usually expressed in terms of cubits. Two cubits of different length were in use: the royal cubit (52·3 cms), which was employed as a measurement in building, being equal to 7 palms (of the hand) or 28 fingers, and the short cubit (about 45 cms) being equal to 6 palms or 24 fingers. For long measurements another unit, the 'river-measure' corresponding with the Greek *schoinos* (roughly 10·5 km or 20,000 cubits) was used.

Area and weight were likewise measured in specialized units and fractions of units, the most common being the *setjat* (100 cubits squared, roughly $\frac{2}{3}$ acre) and the *deben* (about 91 grammes).

Time was measured in terms of years and subdivisions of a year, each year consisting of 12 months of 30 days (i.e. three 10-day weeks), to which were added 5 intercalary days giving a total of 365 days. For purposes of dating, the year was divided into three seasons, each of 4 months: 'inundation', 'winter', and 'summer'. The day was further divided into 24 hours, 12 hours of day and 12 hours of night; the length of the hour varied according to the season. Both water-clocks and shadow-clocks (933 and 938) were used to measure hours; a different calibration for each month was sometimes marked on the water-clocks (*clepsydrae*) in order to allow for the varying length of the day (fig. 45).

45 Fragment of a water-clock dated to the reign of Alexander the Great

Astronomical observation

A systematic kind of astronomical observation certainly began in very early times. The most ancient astronomical texts at present known are found on the lids of wooden coffins dating from the Ninth Dynasty (c. 2150 BC). These texts, the so-called 'diagonal calendars' or 'diagonal star clocks', give the names of the decans (stars which rose at ten-day intervals at the same time as the sun), of which there were thirty-six. The purpose of these charts was to enable the deceased to tell the time of the night or the date in the calendar. Star charts of essentially the same kind, but more elaborate, were reproduced in the New Kingdom on the ceiling of the tomb of Senenmut, Queen Hatshepsut's architect, and on the ceiling of the cenotaph of Sethos I at Abydos. In the tombs of Ramesses IV, VII, and IX, a figure of a seated man is shown together with a net of stars. The accompanying inscriptions, which relate to the first and the sixteenth day of each month, give the position occupied by a star at each of the twelve hours of the night in relation to the seated figure: 'over the left ear', 'over the right ear', etc. The signs of the zodiac were not introduced into Egyptian astronomy until Ptolemaic and Roman times, when they were sometimes represented on the ceilings of temples and the lids of coffins (6705 and 6678; Plate 10). Although there is no evidence that the Egyptian civil calendar possessed an astronomical basis, proof is available that a careful check was kept on the occurrence of at least one sidereal event in relation to the civil calendar. This event was the annual rising of the dog-star, Sirius, at the same time as the sun (i.e. heliacally), approximately on 19 July of the Julian calendar. Since the civil calendar of 365 days made no allowance for leap years it gained one day in every four years on the astronomical calendar (which was used for agriculture and for determining the dates of religious festivals), with the result that the two calendars became progressively out of step until at the end of 120 years the civil year would be a month ahead of the astronomical year. Eventually at the end of 1,460 years the two calendars would again coincide, but only for four days. Censorinus mentions that a heliacal rising of Sirius on the first day of the civil year occurred in AD 139, from which it has been calculated that a similar coincidence must have occurred in the pharaonic period in 1321–1317 BC and 2781–2773 BC. By a fortunate chance three texts have been preserved which record the date, in the civil year, on which Sirius rose heliacally: (a) 11th month, day 28, of an unspecified year of Tuthmosis III; (b) 11th month, day 9, of the ninth year of Amenophis I, and (c) 7th month, day 25, of the seventh year of Sesostris III. Translated into terms of the Julian calendar these three dates become approximately 1469, 1537, and 1872 BC.

Invaluable as these three dates are for pin-pointing the reigns in question, little progress in reconstructing Egyptian chronology could have been made without help from other sources. The

documents which afford the greatest information are the fragmentary Royal Annals (the so-called Palermo Stone and its
congeners in Cairo and University College London) which, however, record with many lacunae only kings and the principal
event in each year of their reigns down to the Fifth Dynasty; the
mutilated Royal Canon of the Turin Museum, compiled in the
Nineteenth Dynasty, which gives the names of the kings in
chronological order, the length of their reigns, and the total
number of years occupied by each dynasty; the History of
Manetho (written in Greek in the third century BC and preserved
only incompletely in the works of other writers) which follows
the same pattern as the Royal Canon of Turin; and lastly the
innumerable inscriptions and papyri dated to such and such
a year of a named king. In spite of many gaps and, especially in
Manetho, copyists' errors, these four sources provide an
immense amount of information about the length of individual
reigns and the duration of many dynasties. Second to them only
in importance are the lists of kings arranged in chronological
order found in the temples of Abydos and Karnak, and in a tomb
at Saqqara. Though far from complete, these lists (one of which
was found in the temple of Ramesses II at Abydos and is now in
this Museum, 117) contain many names which are missing
from the documents previously mentioned, but they lack details
of the length of reigns and corruptions sometimes occur. By far
the most complete and the best preserved is the famous list of
king Sethos I which still stands in his temple at Abydos.

Medical works

These are relatively numerous. In this Museum there are eight
examples: three, dating from the Twelfth Dynasty, were found
in the Ramesseum (10756–8) and are among the earliest
medical papyri known; 10758 is actually written in cursive
hieroglyphs rather than hieratic, which indicates that it was
composed much earlier. It deals with stiffness in the limbs;
10757 contains spells and prescriptions for pregnant women
and newly-born children. The London Medical Papyrus (10059)
dating from the late Eighteenth Dynasty contains sixty-three
recipes but just over a third are medical, the remainder being
purely magical. One spell claims to have been found at night
in the sanctuary of the Temple of Isis at Coptos by a lector-
priest: 'The earth was in darkness but the moon shone on this
papyrus scroll on every side and it was brought as a marvel to
the majesty of king Khufu'. The Chester Beatty Medical Papyrus VI
(10686, fig. 46) and three further papyri of lesser importance,
Chester Beatty X dealing with aphrodisiacs, XV and XVIII
(10690, 10695 and 10698), date to the Nineteenth Dynasty.

16 The Chester Beatty Medical Papyrus VI

Since many ailments were thought to be caused by evil demons, magic was considered the most effective method of treatment; spells suitable for use in such cases were therefore interspersed with prescriptions of drugs and were intended to be recited while the drugs were being administered. Alternative prescriptions are often given for a disease, so that if one remedy failed to effect the cure another remedy could be tried. The ingredients of the prescriptions were generally the fat or blood of animals, plants and vegetables, honey, and all the common liquids. Ointments were generally mixed with honey or animal fat including goose-grease. Surgery was practised by the Egyptians, but mainly in cases of injury. A papyrus in the possession of the New York Academy of Medicine, known as the Edwin Smith Papyrus, lists the appropriate surgical treatment for wounds of the head and thorax. The Ebers Papyrus in Leipzig and a Twelfth-dynasty papyrus from Illahun in the Petrie collection also contain information about surgical treatment, the former in connexion with boils and cysts and the latter with reference to gynaecological conditions.

CHAPTER FIVE

RELIGIOUS BELIEFS

General considerations and origins

An account will be given in the next chapter of the funerary
beliefs and customs of the Ancient Egyptians. Here it is only
necessary to say that the interest shown by the Egyptians in their
fate after death and the elaborate preparations made by them for
their burial arose in part from their passionate interest in life
itself. The vast majority of religious texts which have survived
are mainly funerary in intent, but they provide valuable information about the general religious beliefs of the Egyptians, or at
least of certain classes of Egyptians. The complexity of these
beliefs and the great number of their gods suggest that Egyptian
thinking in religious matters was haphazard and confused. Much
of the apparent confusion is, however, understandable when it
is realized that by the time of the Late New Kingdom, two
thousand years of development had taken place; simple, primitive beliefs had been turned into complicated theological systems.
Much of this development resulted from the additions contributed by successive generations to what they had inherited;
much of the confusion sprang from the unwillingness of the
Egyptians to discard outmoded or contradictory beliefs; much
of the proliferation of gods was prompted by political reasons.

Written texts from which substantial information about
religious beliefs can be extracted do not occur before the Fifth
Dynasty (the *Pyramid Texts*, p. 171), but their subject-matter is
to a large extent derived from earlier compositions, some
elements undoubtedly dating from very primitive times. Useful
evidence from the Predynastic Period is largely confined to what
may be deduced from burial customs, but some additional
information on the nature of the gods at this early time can be
extracted from the decoration of painted vases and from the
objects placed in tombs. Many predynastic burials contain small
female figurines of pottery, ivory, and other materials, and it is
thought that these may represent a primitive fertility- or
mother-goddess. Buff-coloured Late Predynastic pottery with
painted designs also carry representations of a large female
figure which has similarly been identified as a fertility-goddess.
Examples of female figurines (fig. 47) and of the painted pottery
can be seen in the Sixth Egyptian Room and of the former also
in the Fifth Egyptian Room. Many of the small animal figures
found in predynastic burials may in the same manner represent

47 Ivory figure of a
Badarian woman

gods, and the early slate palettes in the forms of animals, birds, fishes, and other creatures may also possess religious or amuletic properties connected with primitive deities associated with these creatures. It is possible, for example, that in the small hippopotamus-figures and palettes in the form of hippopotami, examples of which can be seen in the Sixth Egyptian Room, the later hippopotamus-goddess Thoeris may be distinguished, but it is impossible to be certain that such an identification is correct. Further, the correspondence in form between predynastic animal-shaped objects and theriomorphic deities of the historic period may not indicate any certain continuity of cults between the two periods. That continuity in the case of some cults did take place, however, is shown by the appearance on predynastic objects of distinctive cult-signs which were used during the historic period. The slate palette 35501 (fig. 48) bears in low relief a sign which has been identified as a rudimentary form of the cult-object of Min, a god whose antiquity is otherwise attested by large primitive stone figures found at Coptos, the cult-centre. This sign and others of a similar kind are also found, shown mounted on poles, in the painted scenes on buff-coloured pots of the Late Predynastic Period. These signs are thought to be the crests or banners of the predynastic nomes or their equivalents. Their presence, so represented, on pots, further confirms the great antiquity of some of the later cults of Egypt. Apart from the Min-sign, the distinctive crossed arrows of the goddess Neith have been identified. Standards of a more elaborate type, similar to those used in the writing of nome-signs in later times, are found on a few of the proto-dynastic slate palettes, and further testify to the antiquity of some deities. The Hunters' Palette (20790, fig. 10) carries three representations of standards, two with falcons and feathers and one consisting of what has been described as an elaborately decorated spear. These signs are similar to those which are later used to write 'west' and 'east' in hieroglyphs, and it is probable that they here stand for the district standards of western and eastern regions, possibly of the Delta. Falcon-deities in later times had cult-centres in the western Delta. The decorated spear likewise was probably a district cult-sign. The inference to be drawn from these and other representations is that in predynastic Egypt each district had its own deity or cult-object. Of the nature of the individual cults nothing is known, but it may be assumed that they consisted mostly of simple primitive beliefs of local importance. Their significance increased or diminished, however, according to the political fortunes of the districts and this phenomenon was to become a special characteristic of the religious history of Egypt in later times.

48 Schist palette with the emblem of Min

With the unification of Egypt and the beginning of the Historic or Dynastic Period, the gods of the small districts of the land encountered a crisis from which some emerged as national gods, while others remained only locally worshipped. The order of events leading up to the unification is not fully known; neither are the political groupings in the final conflict known. It is possible that the Upper Egyptian and Lower Egyptian coalitions of states both revered the falcon Horus as their principal god. There is some evidence to suggest that Horus was originally a Lower Egyptian god, but it seems certain that he eventually became the great state god of a unified Egypt from his position as the principal deity worshipped by the conquerors from Hierakonpolis who ultimately subdued Lower Egypt and founded Memphis. Among the Upper Egyptian local gods who profited from this victory were Seth of Ombos and Thoth of Hermopolis. Of these two, the former developed an essentially malevolent character, being later regarded as the arch-enemy of Horus; the latter was held to be the scribe of the gods. At the same time other gods achieved prominence, for political reasons principally, and among those who retained their importance throughout the Dynastic Period were Ptah and Re. Ptah was the local god of Memphis, while Re, the sun-god, was worshipped at Heliopolis, a short distance to the north of Memphis. This process by which local deities were elevated to become national gods was repeated from time to time throughout Egyptian history. Thus, during the First Intermediate Period the ascendancy of Heracleopolis brought with it the temporary elevation of Arsaphes, the ram-headed deity of that city. At about the same time the Theban god Month became the principal deity of the southern confederacy of nomes which ultimately won control of the whole of Egypt. After this triumph, for reasons that are not fully understood, Amun, an obscure god, became in the Middle Kingdom the great state god. His claim to this position was reinforced at the beginning of the New Kingdom inasmuch as he was the principal god of the Theban kings who had driven out the Hyksos, and with his enhanced status he became the god of the Egyptian empire. Neith, the goddess of Sais, whose cult-sign, the crossed arrows, is found on predynastic objects, achieved special prominence during the Twenty-sixth Dynasty, the kings of which came from Sais.

To a great extent the fortunes of any local cult in Egypt depended on political developments, but the elevation of parti-cular deities rarely affected the local status of the majority of gods. Over the years most of these local deities were assimilated into the Egyptian pantheon, fulfilled their minor roles in the general myths, and contributed their particular elements to the

49 Bronze figure of an Apis bull dedicated by Peteesi

amalgam of religious beliefs. As a result, the gods who played some part in the daily religious life of the Egyptians were very varied in character and infinitely various in form. In many of the important religious centres for political reasons the principal god was associated with two other local deities to form a divine family, known as a triad. At Memphis Ptah had Sakhmet as his consort and Nefertum as his son; at Thebes the triad consisted of Amun, Mut, and Khons; at Elephantine it consisted of Khnum, Anukis, and Satis. Numerically the Egyptian pantheon was immense. In early times most gods were worshipped in the forms of animals and inanimate objects (p. 129). At some point, probably early in the historic period, the idea of anthropo-morphism had gained currency and the gods were represented with at least human bodies. The theriomorphic conception still persisted, however, to a limited extent, and many gods were shown with human bodies and animal or other shaped heads. In official religion, as opposed to private and personal religion, this unusual mixture of anthropomorphism and theriomorphism seems to have had no more than a representational significance. It is probable, however, that locally the old cults retained a close attachment to the original forms of the gods; but this allegiance to gods in animal and other forms does not become strikingly apparent until the Late Period when the cults of gods in animal forms were widely revived. Most of the figures of gods in animal forms date from this time (fig. 49) and the large Late Period

animal-cemeteries in the cult-centres testify to the popularity of
this type of worship (p. 161). Figures of gods, in animal, human,
and mixed form are exhibited in the Fifth Egyptian Room and
brief descriptions of the principal gods are given below (pp. 149 ff.).

Private religion

Any discussion of religion in ancient Egypt is complicated by the
necessity to distinguish between official religion and private
religion, and one of the principal problems is to determine
whether the Egyptians recognized the existence of divinity as
an abstract element or considered it only as an aspect common
to a vast number of particular deities. Most of the religious texts
are concerned with official religion or with the various funerary
cults, and while much is known about what the Egyptian
(especially in the highest ranks of society) thought in connexion
with his fate after death, little is known about the way in which
religion affected him while he was alive. The complicated
theologies developed at places like Heliopolis and Hermopolis
(pp. 146 f.), and which undoubtedly existed in a lesser degree at
most of the cult-centres, were the fabrications of priests, kept
exclusive, and made unapproachable for ordinary folk. High
theology at Heliopolis and Thebes affected the conception of the
kingship, but the subtle myths of creation and of the behaviour
of the gods (pp. 147 f.) could have had little appeal to most
people. Some knowledge of the great gods inevitably percolated
down to the lower classes, but the evidence provided by the
occasional prayers of simple workmen which have been preserved shows that this knowledge was superficial and usually
confined to a few simple ideas about the basic characteristics of
the god invoked (p. 108). This state of affairs is hardly surprising
when it is realized that the great temples were not built for
public worship but for the regular private practice of the cults
by the priests, with only occasional public festivals. In these
festivals the people participated more probably for the splendour
of the pageantry and the concomitant 'fun of the fair' than for
reasons of piety. Some idea of the excitement generated on the
occasion of a great festival is conveyed by the account given by
Ikhernofret, the chief treasurer of Sesostris III, who was sent to
Abydos to conduct the festival of the 'Going-forth of Wepwawet';
the events of the festival included a ceremonial procession to the
legendary tomb of Osiris and a dramatic re-enactment of the
revenging of Osiris' death by Wepwawet. The well-preserved
texts in the Temple of Horus at Edfu provide abundant information about the private and public festivals celebrated at Edfu
throughout the year, and again it is clear that participation by
the people took place only in those festivals which involved

processions, such as that of the sacred marriage of Horus of Edfu with Hathor of Dendera. The so-called Ramesseum Dramatic Papyrus (10610) preserves part of the ritual drama enacted by priests representing characters in the Osiris legend at the time of the enthronement of King Sesostris I of the Twelfth Dynasty.

It is unlikely that Egyptian religion, as represented by the great cults, was ever a vital influence on the religious beliefs of the ordinary people. The presence of the great temples no doubt inspired feelings of awe and mystery; in addition they engendered subsidiary cults of great popular appeal, often attached to architectural features of the buildings. At Memphis, for example, there was the cult of Horus 'on the corner of the southern door'. In Thebes many of the royal mortuary temples developed in time secondary cults more acceptable to the humble people. Popular cults also evolved out of the posthumous reputations of famous men. The worship of Imhotep in the Late Period arose from his long-established reputation as a physician and a sage. In the Theban necropolis the craftsmen who worked on the tombs especially revered the memory of Amenophis I and his mother Ahmes-Nefertari, who were held to be the patron deities of the necropolis (Plate 11). Other gods who achieved considerable popular followings in the New Kingdom and later were foreign deities introduced into Egypt by soldiers returning from the Asiatic wars, by foreign prisoners, and by foreign craftsmen. These gods no doubt appealed to the humble Egyptian because they were in no way connected with the overpowering state-cults, from full participation in which he was prevented by social considerations. Deities like Anat, Astarte, and Qadesh were worshipped in a private manner from Tanis in the north to Thebes in the south (fig. 50); particular allegiance to such cults existed in those quarters of Memphis inhabited largely by foreigners and also in the community of workmen, already mentioned, who lived in the Theban necropolis and worked on the royal tombs. Many of these workmen were of foreign origin or in contact with foreigners. From their village at Deir el-Medina has come much material providing valuable information about private religion during the New Kingdom. One interesting fact which has emerged from discoveries at Deir el-Medina is that ancestor-cults flourished in the Theban area (and possibly elsewhere) at this period. Formalized busts were kept in niches in the houses and were undoubtedly the object of worship. Examples of such busts are exhibited in the Fifth Egyptian Room (270, 49735, 61083).

Apart from the formal attachment to specific cults, the ordinary Egyptian's religion seems to have consisted largely of magical

practices and the invocation of those deities who might protect him from the dangers of daily life. One of the most popular deities in this respect was Bes, a dwarf with leonine features, who not only brought happiness to the home, but also protected it in general ways. His image was represented on beds, head-rests, mirror-handles, and other domestic articles. Amulets for the living, carved from hippopotamus ivory, often bear figures of a creature like Bes (p. 160 and fig. 51); their purpose was to keep away snakes and other harmful creatures, some of which were, to judge from the forms carved on the amulets, the imaginary inhabitants of the desert. In the Theban area during the New Kingdom the goddess Meresger provided protection against

50 Stela depicting the goddess Qadesh standing on a lion (*opposite*)

51 Amuletic wand in ivory (*above*)

serpents, and another deity whose figure was worn as an amulet against snakes and scorpions was Shed (65842). In later times Shed became identified with a form of Horus-the-Child, represented standing on crocodiles and holding in his hands snakes, scorpions, and gazelles (thought to possess a special malevolence). Small stelae, called Cippi of Horus, incorporate the god so represented (sometimes also with a head of Bes above the figure of Horus) and often bear magical texts; examples are shown in the Fifth Egyptian Room. The Middle Kingdom ivory wand-amulets mentioned above also carry representations of Thoeris, a goddess shown as a pregnant female hippopotamus, standing on its hind legs. This deity was at all periods much revered at all levels of society as the protectress of women in child-birth. Objects often designated as 'toys' may well in many instances have been used for ritual rather than for purely recreational purposes: the so-called 'dolls', small figures in wood and clay, some merely flat ovoid boards with painted faces and rows of beads to indicate hair (e.g. 22613), others three-dimensional in representation (55595). Toys as such were of course made and used. Two fine examples, executed in wood, are on display in the Fourth Egyptian Room, one a cat with a moveable jaw (13671) the other a horse mounted on four wheels (26687).

The belief in the efficacy of magic to achieve desired ends was not limited to the more humble classes of Egyptians. The consulting of lists of lucky and unlucky days, the use of amuletic texts for the protection of the individual against dangers in particular circumstances and the existence of papyri bearing magical compositions for various purposes (p. 109), all testify to the devotion of all Egyptians to magical practices.

Between the simple religious beliefs of humble Egyptians and the elaborate theological formulations of the great state-cults lay a further stratum of religious thinking which may occasionally be distinguished through rare personal utterances found in tomb-inscriptions and through the literary compositions which are usually termed pessimistic and wisdom texts (pp. 97–103). In such compositions may be discerned the most profound religious thinking manifested in ancient Egypt. In the Old Kingdom a trace of such independent thinking appears in the texts in tombs of certain high officials of the Sixth Dynasty, particularly at Saqqara. Ideas of responsibility and retribution occur for the first time when the authority of the Egyptian king was experiencing its first serious challenge. In many Old Kingdom texts the Great God occurs as a divine being invoked for funerary benefits. Whether this Great God is to be identified with one particular member of the Egyptian pantheon has never been established— he may have been the deceased king; but the very existence of an unnamed deity reveals that the Egyptians could think about divinity perhaps without investing it with concrete form. During the First Intermediate Period this new attitude to religious matters developed in the painful circumstances that accompanied the dissolution of the central control. It was in this period that the first semi-philosophical texts were composed, and it is in these texts that moral and religious problems are first probed, even if only in a simple manner. God is here often considered as an abstract idea and not always in terms of named deities. The most unusual of these texts is the *Dialogue of a Pessimist with his Soul* (p. 101). During the New Kingdom the effect of this intellectual approach to religious and moral questions, which previously had been exercised largely in a personal manner, impinged to a small extent on religion within the framework of the great state-cults. In funerary religion it can be distinguished in the terms of the Negative Confession in Chapter cxxv of the *Book of the Dead* (p. 156). Organized state theology, however, gave few opportunities for the development of this type of religion, and the vehicle for its expression remained literary compositions. The *Teaching of Amenemope* (p. 98), for example, contains collections of didactic utterances after the manner of the biblical *Book of Proverbs*. Other Egyptian texts contain passages for which striking parallels can be found in the Bible, and outstanding among them is the hymn composed, perhaps by Akhenaten himself, in honour of the Aten, which in many particulars resembles Psalm 104 (p. 107). The acceptance of the cult of the Aten by Akhenaten during the Eighteenth Dynasty was in some respects a triumph for the strain of personal religion which subsisted behind the façade of the state religion. Most people who were sufficiently religious to seek spiritual satisfaction apart from the doctrinal and mythological complexities of the official system were in no position to do more than express their thoughts in semi-religious literary compositions or by introducing individual elements into conventional religious compositions. The inscription of Hor and Suty (p. 107), two architects at the court of Amenophis III, contains, besides a conventional prayer to the sun-god Re, a finely expressed prayer to the Aten (826, fig. 52). Such individual expressions are rare in Egyptian monumental texts, although some prayers to Amun reveal unusual personal piety; but this prayer of Hor and Suty shows that during the reign of Amenophis III even high officials were prepared to depart far from the conventional in their public religious pronouncements. Such behaviour on the part of private people probably incurred no disapproval, but the sponsoring of such ideas by the king himself was a different matter. The allegiance of Amenophis IV (who later changed his name to Akhenaten) to the cult of the Aten ran contrary to all that was expected of the king of Egypt. As a result the clash between himself and the entrenched priesthoods of the state-cults, particularly that of Amen-Re, was exceptionally bitter. The cult of the Aten could easily be tolerated as a subsidiary to the principal cults of the land, but as the chosen cult of the king himself it necessarily had to be resisted (p. 62). The nature of the cult was basically monotheistic; it was not anthropomorphic, its manifestation being the sun's disk, the giver of light, heat, life, and all that prospered the earth and its creatures. In sculptural representations the Aten is shown as the sun's disk with rays ending in hands holding the sign for 'life'. In the cult special emphasis was placed on Maat, the concept of 'truth and order', which always played an important role in Egyptian religion (see p. 140).

The new faith was free from involved theology and complicated mythology, but it lacked moral content and seems to have been considered a personal religion for Akhenaten and his family. Services to the Aten were conducted in open temples far different from the gloomy sanctuaries of the old state gods. In spite of the inherent potentiality of Atenism to become a universal creed, there is no evidence that it was ever held to be accessible to non-Egyptians.

52 Stela of the architects Hor and Suty

Official religion

Throughout the history of ancient Egypt divine cults were maintained in the principal towns of the land. Many of these cults were of great antiquity, but they remained local; others attained national importance for political reasons (p. 130). In every important sanctuary, however, a daily ritual was carried out which, already by the Old Kingdom, had achieved a remarkable standardization throughout the country. This ritual formed the basis of the official religion. In origin it was developed from the procedure of worship in the sanctuary of Re at Heliopolis; in its practice in provincial temples the local deities were identified with Re. The reason for this uniformity was not only the great influence of the Heliopolitan cult, but also the fact that the king, in all temples regarded as the high-priest, was the son of Re. Furthermore, the widespread adoption of the cult of Osiris towards the end of the Old Kingdom helped to standardize forms of worship. The relationship of the king with the god was equated with that of Horus with Osiris; in the practice of the cult the god therefore became Osiris, and the king, as principal officiant, was Horus. From the Middle Kingdom onwards the two strains of Heliopolitan sun-worship and Osirianism became inextricably woven together in the daily ritual, and the utterances used at every stage in the ceremonies reveal this theological tangle.

The organization of the temple ritual was designed to enhance the relationship between the king and the god, and was therefore an intensely personal form of worship at the highest level. Ordinary Egyptians may be said to have participated in it only in so far as their destiny was closely linked with that of the king and because his well-being was ultimately their own well-being. Ideally the king himself performed the daily ritual to the god, but for practical reasons he was rarely in a position to do so. His place therefore was regularly taken by a priestly deputy. In temple reliefs, however, it is always the king who is shown performing the services to the god. It is probable that the king himself endeavoured to fulfil his ritual duty in the greatest temples on the principal feast-days. The first act in the ceremonies was the procession at dawn to the temple and the ritual purification and dressing of the king in the House of the Morning. Every temple had such a building adjoining it and in it the king was sprinkled with water from the sacred pool by priests in the guise either of Horus and Thoth or of Horus and Seth; he was then purified with natron, dressed in the appropriate garments and handed the necessary ritual implements, after which he was ready to perform the service of the god. The form of this service was the same whether performed by the king or his deputy. The first act of the officiant within the temple was to kindle a fire and to charge a censer with charcoal and incense. The shrine containing the cult-statue of the god was then approached, the seals of the doors broken and the doors opened. After offering incense to the god the officiant made obeisance, recited a hymn, presented honey or a figure of the goddess Maat, and burnt more incense before the god. The offering of the figure of Maat was a highly significant part of the ritual, since Maat represented the divinely-appointed ordered state of the land, which had to be preserved for the well-being of the gods. Practically all the activities of the Egyptian state religion, including the building of the temples themselves, was devoted to the maintenance of Maat, so that the gods might be contented and Egypt would benefit as a consequence.

The next stage in the daily ritual consisted of the removal of the figure of the god from its shrine, stripping it of its garments and adornments of the preceding day, a general purification, and clothing it once more. The figure was then replaced in its shrine, ready to receive the ritual feast which followed. Before the shrine stood an offering-table on which the various courses of the feast were placed and consecrated. In turn each was offered to the deity symbolically, and at the end, after a final purification with incense, the doors of the shrine were closed and sealed. The final act of the officiant in the daily ritual service was the purification of the room containing the shrine and the careful sweeping away of all footprints. A shrine for a cult-image, exhibited in the Egyptian Sculpture Gallery (1134; fig. 53), comes from the island of Philae and may have contained a figure of the goddess Isis. In the Sixth Egyptian Room is a case containing bronze objects used in ritual ceremonies; among them are two censers (58543 and 41606), a sceptre of the type used in the presentation of the repast to the god (22842), libation vessels (e.g. 36318), and other vessels for sacred liquids; particularly fine are three great situlae of the Late Period (38212, 38213, 38214) used probably for offerings of milk. In the same case are shown bronze terminals of standards carried in religious processions (54010, 64545).

The daily service was the principal act of worship in the temple and in it the public had no part. Access to the inner parts of the temple was denied everyone except the priesthood attached to the temple and the king or his representative. Limited access to the front court seems to have been permitted and, from the Middle Kingdom, favoured persons were allowed to place votive statues there. Many of the private statues exhibited in the Fifth Egyptian Room belong to this category. Otherwise public participation in the rites of temple worship was limited to attendance at the great festivals, some of which have been

53 Monolithic shrine from Philae

already mentioned (p. 132). Every sanctuary had its calendar of festival days on which the important events of the myth of the local deity were commemorated publicly. In small religious centres these festivals were held as local celebrations, but the festivals of the national gods became great occasions for public demonstrations of enthusiasm. Many of the festivals coincided with important seasonal events and were closely associated with agriculture, such as the Festival of the Coming-forth of Min at harvest time and the Festival of Sokaris, celebrated at Memphis towards the end of the inundation season. Other festivals occurred when visits were made by one god to another in a neighbouring sanctuary; of these the greatest was the Festival of Opet, held in Thebes in the second month of the inundation season. At this time the god Amun journeyed from Karnak to Luxor to celebrate his union with the divine mother (Mut) in the Luxor temple. The procession by boat on the Nile with the bark of Amun accompanied by the barks of Mut and the divine child Khons was an occasion for great excitement. At such times Amun was accustomed to make oracular pronouncements, and, during the New Kingdom at least, the king always endeavoured to attend in person. Of less political importance, but of great popular appeal, was the Festival of the Valley in the second month of the summer season, when Amun left Karnak and crossed the Nile to visit the temples on the west bank. The necropolis workmen possessed special privileges to take part in the procession on this occasion.

From the point of view of the kingship the most important festival was the *Sed*, at which the union of Egypt under one crown was re-enacted and the authority of the king renewed. Normally the *Sed*-festival took place after the king had ruled thirty years, and thereafter it was repeated at three-yearly intervals. There are, however, instances of its being held earlier than the thirtieth year, perhaps on the thirtieth anniversary of the king's becoming crown prince. It was always held at Memphis and to it came all the gods of the land to pay homage to the king. A small ivory royal figure exhibited in the Sixth Egyptian Room (37996, fig. 54) is of early dynastic date and represents a king wearing the characteristic short cloak associated with the *Sed*-festival ceremonies. Among the various acts performed in the course of the festival were the double coronation of the king as ruler of Upper Egypt and of Lower Egypt, a ritual dance and the running of four courses by the king, and the conducting of the king in a litter to visit the chapels of Horus and Seth who presented him with four arrows to be discharged against his enemies at the four cardinal points of the compass.

54 Ivory figure of a king

The priesthoods in the temples throughout Egypt were organized in regular classes; each temple had its corporation of priests consisting of 'prophets' (ḥmw-nṯr, literally 'servants of the god') and 'ordinary' or 'weeb-priests' (wꜥbw, literally 'pure ones'). Theoretically the king was high-priest in every temple, but in fact the duties were carried out by the 'first prophet'. Until the New Kingdom in most temples, and for much longer in small temples, the senior priestly offices were occupied by high civil officials; in the Middle Kingdom, for example, the nomarch was regularly high-priest in the sanctuary of the principal nome-god. The weeb-priests were organized into four groups, often called phyles, and each group served in the temple for one month at a time. The phyle on duty was responsible for the day-to-day running of the temple; its members received payment in kind, partly from temple revenues and partly from the daily offerings to the gods. The daily ritual of the god was performed by the high-priest or his deputy. Priests were not exempt from state services, taxes, and other national obligations, but from time to time the priesthoods of specific temples were granted privileges of immunity for special reasons, as in the case of the priests and other staff of the great temple of Osiris at Abydos by Sethos I. By receiving special immunity and by the influx of vast wealth, certain priesthoods developed great power during the New Kingdom. The outstanding example of this development was the priesthood of Amun at Thebes. Its overt power in the Eighteenth and Nineteenth Dynasties was considerable, but this power became proportionately even greater during the Twenty-first Dynasty when it was able to establish a virtually independent priestly state within the kingdom of Egypt (p. 69).

The actual temple buildings at the various sanctuaries throughout Egypt were regarded as the dwellings of the gods and the places in which the king could communicate with the gods. It is probable that the foundation of all important new temples was carried out by the king in person. The foundation ceremonies began with the surveying of the site, and by fixing the four corners by means of astral observation directed on the circumpolar stars. The king himself made and laid the four corner-bricks and helped to prepare the first foundations. Sets of model tools, amulets, and other objects were deposited in pits at various points around the temple walls. Many of the model tools exhibited in the Fourth Egyptian Room came from such foundation-deposits. When the temple building was completed, purified and consecrated, the king handed it over to its god.

As a rule the Egyptian temple was set in a sacred enclosure surrounded by mud-brick walls. From the exterior, the walls of the temple proper have something of the appearance of a fortress, since that is exactly what the Egyptians considered the temple to be—a fortress defending Egypt against all forms of evil. Entrance to the temple itself was gained through two pylons, beyond which lay an open court. This court sometimes had colonnades along the sides and an altar in the middle (Plate 15). Next, along the temple-axis, came the hypostyle, a pillared hall often surrounded by small rooms devoted to the storage of temple equipment and to the performance of subsidiary rites. Finally, there was the sanctuary, a dark room containing the cult-figure of the god placed in a shrine. Outside the walls of the temple, but within the sacred compound, were the domestic buildings of the priestly staff, the workshops, storerooms, and other ancillary structures. Great temples, like the cathedrals of Europe, were not built quickly; the building was continued by successive kings and plans were frequently modified. The most remarkable example of this constant growth is the great temple of Amen-Re at Karnak which, with its subsidiary temples, buildings, and lakes, occupies an enclosure, each side of which is about one-third of a mile in length. Such buildings were far more than religious centres; the great mortuary temple of Ramesses III at Medinet Habu became in the Late New Kingdom the administrative centre of the whole Theban Necropolis (p. 67). The temples were also great landowners, and the administration of their estates and revenues demanded large non-priestly staffs. It is probable that a new temple at the time of its foundation was presented with an endowment of land with the income from which its upkeep could be financed. Originally, as all land in Egypt was strictly the property of the king, the possession of land-endowments depended on the favour of the king (p. 29). In time, however, property-holding, whether on the part of temples or private persons, came to be regarded more and more as a right and less as a privilege; in consequence large estates were built up, especially by temples. Records show that temples in Lower Egypt might hold land in Upper Egypt and vice versa. From time to time, as different cults achieved prominence, different temples were favoured with endowments; land thus endowed was no doubt frequently reclaimed by the crown if circumstances required it. Nevertheless, vast areas of Egypt were by the New Kingdom held as temple domains, and the evidence offered by the Great Harris Papyrus (9999, fig. 34) suggests that Ramesses III was in his life able to donate about one-tenth of the cultivable area of Egypt to temples. With land went people and small industries, and from the labour of the former and the products of the latter the temples derived their principal wealth. Large temples were sometimes also granted the revenues of mines and other undertakings normally regarded as royal monopolies. They received income in the form of personal tithes and voluntary donations by private persons.

Myths and legends

About every Egyptian god many stories were told, but the stories varied from period to period and from place to place. As a result, the mythology of Egyptian religion is very complicated. Nevertheless, certain traditions remained generally constant throughout history and may be considered the basic myths of the religious system. Such were the principal creation myths, the legend of the struggles of Horus and Seth, and the Osiris cycle.

The origin of the world and the nature of the gods who took part in its creation were subjects of constant interest to the Egyptians. Three distinct cosmogonies were formulated in the earliest times based on the traditions of Heliopolis, Hermopolis, and Memphis. In later periods the Heliopolitan system was generally accepted, elements of the other systems being incorporated. According to the Heliopolitan tradition the world began as a watery chaos called Nun, from which the sun-god Atum (later to be identified with Re) emerged on a mound. By his own power he engendered the twin deities Shu (air) and Tefnut (moisture), who in turn bore Geb (earth) and Nut (sky). Geb and Nut finally produced Osiris, Isis, Seth, and Nephthys. The nine gods so created formed the divine ennead (i.e. company of nine) which in later texts was often regarded as a single divine entity. From this system derived the commonly accepted conception of the universe represented as a figure of the air-god Shu standing and supporting with his hands the out-stretched body of the sky-goddess Nut, with Geb the earth-god lying at his feet. The second cosmogonical tradition was developed at Hermopolis, the capital of the fifteenth nome of Upper Egypt, apparently during a time of reaction against the religious hegemony of Heliopolis. According to this tradition, also, chaos existed at the beginning, before the world was created. This chaos possessed four characteristics identified with eight deities who were grouped in pairs: Nun and Naunet, god and goddess of primordial water, Heh and Hehet, god and goddess of infinite space, Kek and Keket, god and goddess of darkness, and Amun and Amunet, god and goddess of invisibility. These deities were not so much the gods of the earth at the time of creation as the personifications of the characteristic elements of chaos out of which earth emerged. They formed what is called the Hermopolitan ogdoad (company of eight). Out of chaos so conceived arose the primeval mound at Hermopolis and on the mound was deposited an egg from which emerged the sun-god. He then proceeded to organize the world. The Hermopolitan idea of chaos was of something more active than the chaos of the Heliopolitan system; but after the ultimate triumph of the latter system, a subtle modification (no doubt introduced largely for political reasons) made Nun the father and creator of Atum. The third cosmogonical system was developed at Memphis, when it became the capital city of the kings of Egypt. Ptah, the principal god of Memphis, had to be shown to be the great creator-god, and a new legend about creation was coined. Nevertheless, an attempt was made so to organize the new cosmogony that a direct breach with the priests of Heliopolis might be avoided. Ptah was the great creator-god, but eight other gods were held to be contained within him. Of these eight, some were members of the Heliopolitan ennead, and others of the Hermopolitan ogdoad; Atum, for example, held a special position; Nun and Naunet were included; also Tatjenen, a Memphite god personifying the earth emerging from chaos, and four other deities whose names are not certain, but who were probably Horus, Thoth, Nefertum, and a serpent-god. Atum was held to represent the active faculties of Ptah by which creation was achieved, these faculties being intelligence, which was identified with the heart and personified as Horus, and will, which was identified with the tongue and personified as Thoth. Ptah conceived the world intellectually before creating it 'by his own word'. The whole Memphite system was in fact intellectually based, and remained throughout Egyptian history a system particularly attractive to religious theorists. A treatise embodying the essence of the Memphite theology is preserved on a slab of basalt now exhibited in the Egyptian Sculpture Gallery (498). It was composed at an early date, and committed to stone during the Twenty-fifth Dynasty by the order of king Shabaka. Unfortunately this stone —the so-called 'Shabaka Stone'—was subsequently used as a nether mill-stone, and much of the text has been lost. The document known as the Bremner-Rhind Papyrus (10188) includes, among other religious texts, two monologues of the sun-god describing how he created all things.

Many distinct traditions contributed to make the legend of the struggle between Horus and Seth not only one of the most important but also one of the most confused episodes in Egyptian mythology. The original tale of the struggle between the two gods became unusually complicated when Osirianism was incorporated into the main stream of Heliopolitan theology. Horus then as the son of Osiris achieved a new significance. In origin, however, the tradition seems to be based on a simple story of antagonism between two divine persons. The Heliopolitan Horus, on the one hand, was the warrior-god, the king-god, and at the same time a god of heaven; his eyes were originally identified with the sun and the moon. A modification brought about undoubtedly by the Heliopolitan identification of Re as the sun-god led to the solar eye being attributed to Re, while Horus was assigned the lunar eye. Seth, on the other hand, was a god of the desert and of malevolent design; he snatched away the eye of Horus which was retrieved only after a violent struggle. This eye, known as *udjat*, according to some versions was cast away by Seth before it could be retrieved, and it was found by Thoth lying in pieces. Thoth restored it whole and from this act it perhaps received its name *udjat*, which can mean 'that which is sound'. An important act in the drama of this struggle is the trial that took place to decide between the rival claims of Horus and Seth. There seems little doubt that the basic issue to be decided was one of sovereignty, at first, who should receive the crowns of Upper and Lower Egypt, subsequently, who should succeed Osiris as king. The final justification of Horus in his claim is the classic prototype of the judgement of the deceased before Osiris in the after-life (p. 156). In a literary composition of the New Kingdom, the *Contendings of Horus and Seth*, the struggle is given as being over the solar eye of Re, and the trial, involving a series of contests between Horus and Seth, is carried out before the tribunal of the gods. Another version of the struggle is preserved in the inscriptions in the Ptolemaic temple of Horus at Edfu. Here Horus is represented as the warrior-protector of Re in a series of campaigns against Seth.

The cycle of legends concerning Osiris belonged originally to a very different tradition from that which gave rise to the creation myths already described. It is thought that the simple story of Osiris may have been based on actual historical events that took place at an early period in the Delta. Its appeal was more immediate than that of the cosmogonical theologies of Heliopolis and elsewhere, hence its remarkable success after its introduction into the corpus of royal religious traditions in the course of the Old Kingdom. The story never occurs in a consecutive form in Egyptian texts, but the host of references to component incidents in these texts confirms the general sequence of events given in the account related by the Greek author Plutarch. Osiris, according to the legend, was a just and beneficent king ruling over Egypt from the Delta. His reign was brought to an end by Seth, his brother, who, for reasons of jealousy, slew him. Plutarch relates that Seth prepared a fine chest and invited Osiris to a feast attended by a group of conspirators bent on killing him. The chest was offered to the guest who fitted it and the conspirators all tried it in turn, with no success. Osiris' turn came and as soon as he lay inside, the lid was fastened and the chest thrown into the Nile. Earlier allusions to this occasion suggest that Seth killed Osiris by drowning. The body of Osiris was then recovered by Isis, his wife, perhaps from Byblos, but Seth succeeded in stealing it and dividing it into fourteen (or sixteen, according to other versions) pieces which were scattered throughout Egypt. Isis with the help of her sister Nephthys sought the pieces and found them all with the exception (according to Plutarch, but not to most ancient sources) of his phallus. His body was reconstituted by the magic of Isis, who then succeeded in conceiving and bearing a child called Horus. She brought him up in secret in the Delta, and when he was old enough he took up the struggle with Seth, determined to avenge the death of his father. After many contests Horus prevailed and defeated Seth. In certain details the Osiris story owed much to other myths, especially that of the struggle between Horus and Seth. It exhibits that genius possessed by the Egyptians for adapting and harmonizing different traditions and systems without actually discarding anything. Texts of all periods contain references to Horus, Seth, and Osiris which show that the Egyptians were capable of regarding the various mythological threads either as individual stories or as parts of complicated traditions. The widespread success of the cult of Osiris was undoubtedly due to the realistic elements in the tale of his sufferings and to the hope offered by the belief in his resurrection after death. At first the king alone was identified with Osiris on his death, but from the Late Old Kingdom the possibility of enjoying a similar posthumous fate was extended to all classes of Egyptians. Osiris was further venerated as the personification of the Nile in inundation and as the god of vegetation, but it is unlikely that in his earliest form he was so regarded.

LIST OF PRINCIPAL GODS

AMEN: *see* Amun.

AMON: *see* Amun.

AMUN (AMEN, AMON), 𓇋𓏠𓈖: the great god of Thebes of uncertain origin; represented as a man, sometimes ithyphallic; identified with Re as Amen-Re; sacred animals, the ram and the goose.

ANAT, 𓈖𓏏𓏭: goddess of Syrian origin, with warlike character; represented as a woman holding a shield and an axe.

ANHUR: *see* Onuris.

ANPU: *see* Anubis.

ANQET: *see* Anukis.

ANUBIS (ANPU), 𓇋𓈖𓊪𓃥: the jackal-god, patron of embalmers; the great necropolis-god.

ANUKIS (ANQET), 𓈖𓏏𓈋: goddess of the cataract-region at Aswan; wife of Khnum; represented as a woman with a high feather head-dress.

ARSAPHES (HERISHEF), �face: ram-headed god from Heracleopolis.

ASAR: *see* Osiris.

ASTARTE, 𓈖𓏏𓏭𓁐: goddess of Syrian origin; introduced into Egypt during the Eighteenth Dynasty.

ATEN, 𓇋𓏏𓈖: god of the sun-disk, worshipped as the great creator-god by Akhenaten.

ATUM (TUM), 𓏏𓅓: the original sun-god of Heliopolis, later identified with Re; represented as a man.

BAST: *see* Bastet.

BASTET (BAST), 𓎼𓏏: cat-goddess whose cult-centre was at Bubastis in the Delta; in the Late Period regarded as a beneficent deity.

BES, 𓃀𓋴: dwarf-deity with leonine features; a domestic god, protector against snakes and various terrors; helper of women in child-birth.

BUTO: *see* Edjo.

EDJO (WADJET, BUTO), 𓇅𓏏: the cobra-goddess of Buto in the Delta; tutelary deity of Lower Egypt, appearing on the royal diadem, protecting the king.

ERNUTET: *see* Renenutet.

GEB, 𓆬𓏤: the earth-god; husband of Nut; member of the ennead of Heliopolis; represented as a man.

HAPY, 𓇤: god of the Nile in inundation; represented as a man with full, heavy breasts, a clump of papyrus on his head, and bearing heavily laden offering-tables.

HAROERIS, 𓅃𓅆: a form of Horus, the 'Elder Horus'; identified with the falcon-god and particularly the patron of the king.

HARPOCRATES (HOR-PA-KHRED), 𓅃𓀔: Horus-the-Child, a late form of Horus in his aspect of being son of Isis and Osiris; represented as a naked child wearing the lock of youth and holding one finger to his mouth.

HARSIESIS, 𓅃𓇤𓏏: a form of Horus, specifically designated 'son of Isis'.

HATHOR, 𓉡: goddess of many functions and attributes; represented often as a cow or a cow-headed woman, or as a woman with horned head-dress; the suckler of the king; the 'Golden One'; cult-centres at Memphis, Cusae, Gebelein, Dendera; the patron deity of the mining-region of Sinai; identified by the Greeks with Aphrodite.

HAT-MEHIT, 𓄙: fish-goddess of Mendes in the Delta; sometimes represented as a woman with a fish on her head.

HEQET, 𓆓: frog-goddess of Antinoopolis where she was associated with Khnum; a helper of women in child-birth.

HERISHEF: *see* Arsaphes.

HOR-PA-KHRED: *see* Harpocrates.

HORUS, 𓅃: the falcon-deity, originally the sky-god, identified with the king during his lifetime; also regarded as the son of Osiris and Isis, for the former of whom he became the avenger; cult-centres in many places, e.g. Behdet in the Delta, Hierakonpolis and Edfu in Upper Egypt. *See also*, Haroeris, Harpocrates, Harsiesis, Re-Harakhty.

IMHOTEP (IMOUTHES), 𓇓𓅃𓊪: the deified chief minister of Djoser and architect of the Step Pyramid; in the Late Period venerated as the god of learning and medicine; represented as a seated man holding an open papyrus; equated by the Greeks with Asklepios.

IMOUTHES: *see* Imhotep.

ISIS, 𓊨𓏏: the divine mother, wife of Osiris and mother of Horus; one of the four 'protector'-goddesses, guarding coffins and Canopic jars; sister of Nephthys with whom she acted as a divine mourner for the dead; in the Late Period Philae was her principal cult-centre.

KHEPRI, ⚱𓏤: the scarab-beetle god, identified with Re as a creator-god; often represented as a beetle within the sun-disk.

KHNUM, 𓎡𓃸: ram-headed god of Elephantine, god of the Cataract-region; thought to have moulded man on a potter's wheel.

KHONS, ⬭⌇𓀭: the moon-god, represented as a man; with Amun and Mut as father and mother, forming the Theban triad.

MAAT, 𓆄𓏤: goddess of truth, right, and orderly conduct; represented as a woman with an ostrich-feather on her head.

MIN, 𓀠: the primeval god of Coptos; later revered as a god of fertility, and closely associated with Amun; represented as an ithyphallic human statue, holding a flagellum.

MONTH (MUNT), 𓏠𓈖𓏏𓅆: originally the local deity of Hermonthis, just south of Thebes; later the war-god of the Egyptian king; represented as falcon-headed.

MUNT: see Month.

MUT, 𓆑𓄿: the divine wife of Amun; cult-centre at Asheru, south of the main temple of Amen-Re at Karnak; originally a vulture-goddess, later represented usually as a woman.

NEBET-HET: see Nephthys.

NEFERTUM, 𓄤𓏏𓅓: the god of the lotus, and hence of unguents; worshipped at Memphis as the son of Ptah and Sakhmet; represented as a man with a lotus-flower head-dress.

NEHEB-KAU, 𓆓𓂓𓂝: a serpent deity of the underworld, sometimes represented with a man's body and holding the eye of Horus.

NEITH (NET), 𓋍𓏏: goddess of Sais; represented as a woman wearing the red crown; her emblem, a shield with crossed arrows; one of the four 'protector'-goddesses who guarded coffins and Canopic jars; identified by the Greeks with Athena.

NEKHBET, 𓇓𓏏𓏏: vulture-goddess of Nekheb (modern El-Kab); tutelary deity of Upper Egypt, sometimes appearing on the royal diadem beside the cobra (Edjo).

NEPHTHYS (NEBET-HET), 𓎟𓏏: sister of Isis; one of the four 'protector'-goddesses, who guarded coffins and Canopic jars; with Isis acted as mourner for Osiris and hence for other dead people; represented as a woman.

NET: see Neith.

NU: see Nun.

NUN (NU), ⬚: god of the primeval chaos.

NUT, ⬚: the sky-goddess, wife of Geb, the earth-god; represented as a woman, her naked body curved to form the arch of heaven.

ONNOPHRIS: *see* Unnefer.

ONURIS (ANHUR), ⬚: god of This in Upper Egypt; the divine huntsman; represented as a man.

OSIRIS (ASAR), ⬚: the god of the underworld, identified as the dead king; also a god of the inundation and vegetation; represented as a mummified king; principal cult-centre, Abydos.

PTAH, ⬚: creator-god of Memphis, represented as a man, mummiform, possibly originally as a statue; the patron god of craftsmen; equated by the Greeks with Hephaestus.

PTAH-SEKER-OSIRIS, ⬚: a composite deity, incorporating the principal gods of creation, death, and after-life; represented like Osiris as a mummified king.

QADESH, ⬚: goddess of Syrian origin, often represented as a woman standing on a lion's back.

RA: *see* Re.

RE (RA), ⬚: the sun-god of Heliopolis; head of the great ennead, supreme judge; often linked with other gods aspiring to universality, e.g. Amen-Re, Sobk-Re; represented as falcon-headed; *see also* Re-Harakhty.

RE-HARAKHTY, ⬚: a god in the form of a falcon, embodying the characteristics of Re and Horus (here called 'Horus of the Horizon').

RENENUTET (ERNUTET, THERMUTHIS), ⬚: goddess of harvest and fertility; represented as a snake or a snake-headed woman.

RESHEF (RESHPU), ⬚: god of war and thunder, of Syrian origin.

RESHPU: *see* Reshef.

SAKHMET, ⬚: a lion-headed goddess worshipped in the area of Memphis; wife of Ptah; regarded as the bringer of destruction to the enemies of Re.

SARAPIS: a god introduced into Egypt in the Ptolemaic Period having the characteristics of Egyptian (Osiris) and Greek (Zeus) gods; represented as a bearded man wearing the modius head-dress; the Egyptian writing of the name (⬚, i.e. Osiris-Apis) may not signify the true origin of this god.

SATET: *see* Satis.

SATIS (SATET), 𓊨: goddess of the Island of Siheil in the Cataract-region; represented as a woman wearing the white crown with antelope horns; the daughter of Khnum and Anukis.

SEBEK: *see* Sobk.

SEKER: *see* Sokaris.

SELKIS (SELKIT, SERQET), 𓋴: a scorpion-goddess, identified with the scorching heat of the sun; one of the four 'protector'-goddesses, guarding coffins and Canopic jars; shown sometimes as a woman with a scorpion on her head.

SELKIT: *see* Selkis.

SEPDET: *see* Sothis.

SERQET: *see* Selkis.

SESHAT, 𓋇: the goddess of writing; the divine keeper of royal annals; represented as a woman.

SET: *see* Seth.

SETH (SET, SUTEKH), 𓈖: the god of storms and violence; identified with many animals, including the pig, ass, okapi, and hippopotamus; represented as an animal of unidentified type; brother of Osiris and his murderer; the rival of Horus; equated by the Greeks with Typhon.

SHU, 𓏃: the god of air; with Tefnut, forming the first pair of gods in the Heliopolitan ennead; shown often as a man separating Nut (sky) from Geb (earth).

SOBK (SEBEK, SUCHOS), 𓋴: the crocodile-god, worshipped throughout Egypt, but especially in the Faiyum, and at Gebelein and Kom Ombo in Upper Egypt.

SOKAR: *see* Sokaris.

SOKARIS (SOKAR, SEKER), 𓋴: a falcon-headed god of the necropolis; cult-centre in Memphis.

SOPDU, 𓇪: the ancient falcon-god of Saft el-Henna in the Delta; a warrior-god, protector of the eastern frontier; represented often as an Asiatic warrior.

SOTHIS (SEPDET), 𓇼: the dog-star Sirius, deified as a goddess; shown as a woman with a star on her head.

SUCHOS: *see* Sobk.

SUTEKH: *see* Seth.

TATJENEN, 𓇾: the primeval earth-god of Memphis; later identified with Ptah.

TAURT: *see* Thoeris.

TAWERET: *see* Thoeris.

TEFNUT, ⟨glyph⟩: the goddess of moisture; with Shu forming the first pair of the Heliopolitan ennead.

THERMUTHIS: *see* Renenutet.

THOERIS (TAURT, TAWERET), ⟨glyph⟩: the hippopotamus-goddess; a beneficent deity, the patron of woman in child-birth.

THOTH, ⟨glyph⟩: the ibis-headed god of Hermopolis; the scribe of the gods and the inventor of writing; the ape as well as the ibis being sacred to him.

TUM: *see* Atum.

UNNEFER (WENEN-NEFER, ONNOPHRIS), ⟨glyph⟩: a name meaning 'he who is continually happy', given to Osiris after his resurrection.

UPUAUT: *see* Wepwawet.

WADJET: *see* Edjo.

WENEN-NEFER: *see* Unnefer.

WEPWAWET (UPUAUT), ⟨glyph⟩: the jackal-god of Asyut in Middle Egypt; a god of the necropolis and an avenger of Osiris.

CHAPTER SIX

FUNERARY BELIEFS AND CUSTOMS

Most of the objects preserved from the ancient civilization of Egypt come from temples and tombs and this fact necessarily leads to the supposition that the Egyptians were a particularly religious people obsessed with death and burial. If more were generally known of the daily life of the Egyptians and of the purely secular side of their life, their interest in the gods and the after-life would seem less of an obsession. One fact that would emerge clearly is that the apparently overwhelming pre-occupation with death springs essentially from the Egyptian's devotion to life and the good things available to him in the beneficent land of Egypt. In general it was thought that the best existence a man could expect in the after-life was one that contained all that was most desired in the life on earth. The ideas of what a man might have to encounter in his progress to achieve this idyllic reconstruction of his life in Egypt varied from period to period according to the current dominant religious beliefs, but the end was apparently always the same, whether declared explicitly or hoped for implicitly. The hope was present undoubtedly in the earliest simple burials in which modest offerings and equipment were included; as time advanced this hope was established more firmly and the funerary arrangements were elaborated to provide fully for the expected state of bliss.

The tangle of confused and contradictory ideas which form the main body of Egyptian funerary beliefs was the result of thousands of years of development in which new conceptions were continually being incorporated without ousting those with which they were not in harmony. Consequently it is not possible to give accounts of most of the important elements in funerary thought which will apply to all places and all classes of society. In death, as in life, the Egyptian expected to belong to an hierarchic society in which the best was reserved for the king and the nobles and it is from their graves that most of the information about Egyptian burial customs comes. The resulting account is therefore necessarily one-sided; yet it may be said that at every level the Egyptian's aspiration for his existence after death was that it should consist of the best available to him in his life on earth. In order that he might fully participate in his appointed life hereafter it was necessary that his name should continue to exist, that his body should remain intact and that he should be regularly supplied with necessary food and drink. In the periods of high civilization these ends were achieved by the provision of a tomb containing the incorruptible mummy and inscribed with texts incorporating the owner's name and with scenes that would secure for him by magical means food and drink and other desirable things when the services of the appointed tomb-servants ceased to be carried out.

The early history of the ideas underlying these funerary beliefs is unknown; the first truly informative funerary texts occur in the Old Kingdom and it is clear that many centuries of slow development lie behind the formulations they embody. One concept which in origin applied only to the king but which later was extended to all classes was that of the possession of a spiritual entity called the *Ka*. It is not possible to give a wholly consistent account of the *Ka* because it was an elusive conception capable of various interpretations at different periods. To a certain extent it corresponds with the 'self' of a man. It was born with a man and formed an integral part of his being and was yet in some respects regarded as distinct from him, certainly from his bodily 'self'. It was for his *Ka* that a man provided all the paraphernalia of funerary equipment, food and drink in his tomb, and the tomb itself was known as the 'house of the *Ka*'. Another spiritual entity which can be identified approximately with what is now called the 'soul' was the *Ba* or *Bai*. The *Ba* was thought to leave the body at the moment of death and it was generally represented as a human-headed bird (Plate 14). It was more generally the concrete manifestation of the innate ability possessed by a man's soul to assume different forms both in life and in death; this ability was particularly important when the man was dead for it was necessary for the soul to leave the tomb during the daytime to revisit the outer world where it could transform itself into whatever form might be useful to accomplish its purpose. At night the *Ba* returned to the tomb and the body which was its proper home.

The beliefs of the Egyptians about the after-life were greatly developed when the solar religion of the Old Kingdom, which was principally royal in application, was superseded by the cult of Osiris, which envisaged a posthumous existence which could be enjoyed by men of all ranks. Osiris, the dead king and king of the dead, offered hope of survival in the after-life and the dead person was in fact identified with Osiris. In order to achieve this identification and to secure the Osirian resurrection the deceased needed to be tested and declared 'true of voice' a process carried out in the presence of forty-two assessor-gods. The judgement scene from the *Book of the Dead* prepared for the scribe Ani is a typical example (Plate 13). In the Hall of Judgement Ani, with his wife Tutu, stands by the scales on which his heart (for the Egyptians, the seat of intelligence) is being weighed against a feather representing Truth. The scales are watched by Anubis, the jackal-god of the necropolis, and a record is being kept by Thoth, the ibis-headed god. The deceased denies a specific sin to each assessor, the sins being related to behaviour in life and revealing the general moral attitude of the ancient Egyptians. This 'Negative Confession' completed, the deceased is declared 'true of voice' and led into the presence of Osiris.

Mummification

The preservation of the body, held to be so important for the well-being of a dead man in his after-life, became one of the principal aims of Egyptian funerary practices at a very early period. In the Predynastic Period bodies were buried for the most part in simple shallow graves and covered sometimes with a skin or a mat of woven work. The hot dry sand acted as a powerful desiccating agent and the body was naturally preserved as is shown by the example in the reconstructed predynastic burial in the Second Egyptian Room (32751). The appearance of the body after this drying process is that of a skeleton covered with skin; some hair remains on the head. Towards the end of the Predynastic Period burials became more elaborate and a kind of chamber was prepared for the body. No longer did the corpse come into contact with the hot desiccating sand and the natural process of putrefaction took place: a measure intended to afford greater protection had in fact the opposite effect. It seems possible that this change in the fate of the corpse was soon appreciated and attempts were made to secure artificially the effect formerly achieved naturally by the contact of the body with sand. Evidence is very scanty for the first three dynasties; but the discovery of bodies whose individual limbs were wrapped tightly with linen bandages suggests that at first it was thought that by keeping the body carefully covered decomposition could be prevented. The contrary, however, would have been the case and it is not until the Fourth Dynasty that good evidence exists to show that the Egyptians realized that one necessary step towards preventing decomposition was the removal of the internal organs. The tomb of Hetepheres, mother of the king Cheops, contained a partitioned calcite chest with bandaged packages of viscera still soaking in a dilute solution of natron. During the Old and Middle Kingdoms no fixed method of preparing the corpse was practised and very few bodies from these periods which can properly be called mummies have survived. In some cases the viscera have been removed, in others the brain; sometimes the body has been dehydrated; sometimes the appearance of a well-preserved corpse has been effected by the use of large quantities of linen wrappings and masks fashioned in the image of the deceased. By the New Kingdom, however, the basic requirements needed to obtain adequate preservation were fully understood. Even so, the results achieved fell far short of good preservation. The process was basically one of dehydration of the body after the removal of the brain and viscera. The name 'mummy' comes from an Arabic word (of Persian origin) meaning 'a body preserved by bitumen', the word for 'bitumen' in Arabic being *mumiya*; but bitumen was not in fact normally used in the embalming process. Late documents from Egypt (e.g. the demotic papyrus 10077, fig. 33) and the works of Greek writers, particularly Herodotus, provide most of the written evidence about mummification. The period spent on preparing the body for burial between death and interment was seventy days, about one-half of this time being devoted to the drying of the body. Immediately after death the corpse was handed over to the embalmers whose first task was to remove those parts which would putrefy most quickly, namely the viscera and the brain. The former were removed through an incision made in the left side of the abdomen and the latter through the nose by puncturing the ethmoid bone. The heart, however, as the seat of understanding, was regularly left in the body. It used to be thought that the principal stage in mummification was a long period of soaking in a bath containing a solution of natron, a naturally occurring compound of sodium carbonate and sodium bicarbonate. Recent investigations have shown, however, that it is far more probable that dry natron was used, the effect of which was to dehydrate the body efficiently, to dissolve body fats, and to leave the skin supple but not tender. The internal organs were treated with natron separately. All the materials used in this process were carefully preserved and buried in the vicinity of the tomb, if not in the tomb itself, for it was important that the essential juices extracted should not be divorced completely from the body. Finally the body-cavity was sometimes packed with linen and the abdominal incision sewn up and covered with a plate of leather or other material bearing a representation of the eye of Horus, a powerful protective amulet. The eye sockets likewise were plugged with wads of linen or inset with artificial eyes. After the body had been treated with ointments, spices, and resins it was wrapped in a series of bandages, part of the intention of which was to restore to the body some of the bulk and form which it had lost during the dehydrating process. The relative failure of mummification to retain the form and appearance of the body in life was evidently a matter of great concern to the Ancient Egyptians and many different methods were practised from time to time to improve the results obtained. Most elaborate measures were taken during the Twenty-first Dynasty when the skill of the embalmers reached its highest peak of achievement. The bodies of important people were subjected after dehydration to a packing of the limbs with materials such as linen, fats, and even mud so that the limbs might be restored to their forms before dehydration. In the same period the internal organs were replaced in the abdominal cavity (see below). Everything in fact was done to restore the body to its form during life. These elaborate measures were continued for only a short period and in subsequent times the treatment of the corpse became progressively more simple, the skill of the embalmers being exercised increasingly on bandaging. A good example of a well-bandaged mummy is that of Pasheryenhor (6666) exhibited in the First Egyptian Room (fig. 55); it dates to the period between the Twenty-second and Twenty-sixth Dynasties. In the Roman Period the outer wrappings were frequently arranged in intricate patterns of cross-strapping (13595).

In order to protect further the mummified, carefully wrapped body, amulets of various kinds were placed on the body and within the wrappings. Perhaps the most important was the heart scarab which was placed on the breast. It carried on its under-surface a short exhortation to the heart not to act as a hostile witness against the deceased when it was in the balance in the Judgement Hall of Osiris. A group of heart scarabs is exhibited together with other amulets in wall-cases 96 and 97 in the Third Egyptian Room; the most interesting and one of the earliest is that of King Sobkemsaf of the early Seventeenth Dynasty (7876). Ordinary small scarabs were also used for amuletic purposes on mummies of the New Kingdom and later. The legends engraved on such scarabs (many examples of which are shown in the Sixth Egyptian Room) consist mostly of divine symbols and short amuletic texts. Other amulets commonly found on mummies are the Eye of Horus, the *djed*-pillar, the girdle of Isis, and the *uadj*-sceptre; also small figures of deities were regularly used for amuletic purposes. Of special interest is the set of composition amulets from a mummy of the Twenty-sixth Dynasty, found at Nabesha in the Delta, which is exhibited, according to the arrangement on the body itself, in wall-case 96 (20577). Amulets of this type became common during the New Kingdom and even more numerous in the Late New Kingdom and Late Period. Two special categories of amuletic objects found with mummies are ivory wands and hypocephali. The former are found in graves of the Middle Kingdom and appear to have been used in life as well as in death (p. 135). They are regularly made of hippopotamus ivory and are engraved with the creatures

55 Mummy of
Pasheryenhor

they were intended to combat as well as those gods particularly associated with the home, Bes and Thoeris (fig. 51). Hypocephali are found in burials of the Saite Period and later; they are usually made of linen stiffened with plaster, although a few examples are made of other materials such as bronze (37330). They are found beneath the heads of mummies and are decorated with vignettes depicting various universal deities and with extracts from Chapter CLXII of the *Book of the Dead* designed to bring warmth to the body.

In the account of mummification given above it was stressed that one of the essential preliminaries to successful mummification was the removal of the internal organs. Equally important for the continued well-being of the deceased in his after-life was the careful preservation of these organs, and from the Old Kingdom onwards until the Ptolemaic Period it was customary to place the embalmed viscera in four jars which are now called Canopic jars. The name Canopic is strictly speaking incorrect; it was used by early scholars who saw in these jars with human-headed stoppers confirmation of the story related by classical writers of Canopus, the pilot of Menelaus, who was buried at Canopus in Egypt and was worshipped locally in the form of a jar with a human head and a swollen body. The earliest Canopic jar in the collection was made for a man called Wahka who lived in the late Eleventh Dynasty (58780) and the earliest complete set belonged to Gua, an official of the early Twelfth Dynasty (30838). Gua's jars are of alabaster with human-headed stoppers of painted wood, the set being contained in a wooden Canopic chest. The viscera placed in the four jars were protected by four minor deities, the sons of Horus, named Duamutef (the stomach), Qebhsenuef (the intestines), Hapy (the lungs), and Imsety (the liver), and the jars themselves were identified with the four protective female deities Neith, Selkis, Nephthys, and Isis. Until the end of the Eighteenth Dynasty the jar-stoppers were in the form of human heads; thereafter each jar had a stopper carved in the form of the head of its appropriate protective genius: for Duamutef a jackal head, for Qebhsenuef a falcon head, for Hapy an ape head, and for Imsety a human head. During the Twenty-first Dynasty, when it was usual to replace them inside the body-cavity, the viscera were made up into four packages, each one accompanied by a wax figure of the corresponding son of Horus. Yet the practice of including a set of Canopic jars in the full equipment of a tomb was so established that jars were supplied simply to fulfil the formal need. A fine set of this kind is shown in fig. 56; it was made for Neskhons, the wife of Pinudjem, High Priest of Amun at Thebes (59197–200). Dummy solid jars were also used during the Ptolemaic Period

6 Canopic jars of Neskhons

when the process of mummification was carried out in a very perfunctory manner, the viscera often being left in the body. A representative series of Canopic jars and chests is exhibited in the First Egyptian Room.

A development of the Egyptians' identification of certain of their gods with particular animals was the practice of animal mummification. In general the mass mummification and burial of sacred animals was a phenomenon of the Ptolemaic and Roman Periods. The animal-cemeteries were situated in the neighbourhood of the appropriate cult-centres. Thus Bubastis, the centre of worship of the cat-goddess Bastet, has large cat cemeteries, while Hermopolis in Middle Egypt has large ibis cemeteries, the local god being the ibis-headed Thoth. The actual mummification of animals and birds was very crude and the body was often skeletal before being bandaged; but the bandaging was carried out with great skill and every effort made to produce a wrapped mummy convincing in appearance. Although most animal mummies are late in date the practice of venerating particular animals in this manner existed in earlier periods, particularly the sacred bulls of Memphis, Heliopolis, and Hermonthis. The Apis bulls of Memphis were buried in a vast catacomb in the Saqqara necropolis known as the Serapeum. The mummification of these animals, only one of which existed at any one time, was performed thoroughly; a full embalming process was employed, and the large alabaster tables used for the preparation of the body have recently been found in the neighbourhood of the temple of Ptah at Memphis. The bull-mummies were finally buried in huge stone sarcophagi. Examples of animal mummies and coffins are exhibited in the First Egyptian Room.

Coffins

Coffins were in general not used in the burials of the Predynastic Period; in the earliest times the body was placed in
a shallow grave and covered sometimes with skins or matting to
protect it from the sand and other filling piled directly above it.
In later predynastic times wood-revetted or bricked chambers
with roofs were made to receive the body which was then placed
in the grave wrapped as formerly or in a wicker basket. A few
burials have been found in which primitive coffins of wood, clay
or pottery were used but they are exceptional and it was not until
the Early Dynastic Period that a coffin became a regular part of
the funerary equipment. No actual examples of coffins made for
kings or important nobles have survived from this period; men of
humbler position were buried in coffins constructed of reeds
(fig. 57), or were laid in simple trays or wooden chests, the last
occasionally with panelled sides reproducing the form of the early
great mastaba-tombs (p. 175). Typical coffins of wood and
reeds, dating from the First Dynasty, are exhibited in the Second
Egyptian Room.

During the Old Kingdom a type of coffin was developed which
was used until late in the Middle Kingdom. The form was a
simple rectangular chest made from large planks of imported
wood, mostly cedar. The coffin of Nebhotep (46629) of Sixth-
dynasty date, illustrates the form and also the way in which such
coffins were constructed out of unevenly shaped planks. It also
exhibits on one side the two eyes of Horus which were regularly

57 First Dynasty burial
in a reed coffin

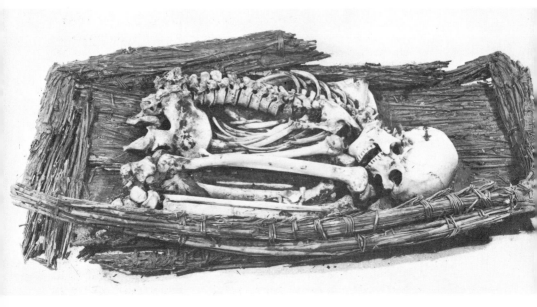

placed at one end both to act as amuletic protection of the body within and also possibly to enable the dead man to look out. This coffin has no decoration apart from simple bands of texts; in some other coffins the sides bear painted representations of doors beneath the double Horus-eyes and of palace-façade decoration. This latter type of decoration is found commonly on the great stone sarcophagi placed in the tombs of kings and high officials during the Old Kingdom to receive the inner wooden coffins. During the First Intermediate Period burials became less elaborate and tombs were rarely decorated; more attention was paid to the coffin, the ultimate receptacle of the corpse. Inner and outer wooden coffins of the chest type were frequently used, usually decorated on the insides with texts and representations which largely fulfilled the purpose of the mural scenes and inscriptions in Old Kingdom tombs. Coffins of this kind were most common during the Eleventh Dynasty and they were also used in the burials of provincial nobles and high officials during the Twelfth Dynasty. The most important part of the decoration consisted of excerpts from the *Coffin Texts*, a body of funerary texts, which derived from the old royal *Pyramid Texts* (p. 171) of the Fifth and Sixth Dynasties. The adaptation of the *Pyramid Texts* for use by non-royal persons was one result of the democratization of Egyptian life which followed the breakdown of the exclusive royal power at the end of the Old Kingdom. The purpose of these texts was to ensure the well-being of the deceased by magical means. Figure 58 shows the inside end of the inner coffin of Gua (30840), a high official whose tomb was found at El-Bersha in Middle Egypt; it bears a substantial extract from the *Coffin Texts* and part of the so-called 'frieze of objects' commonly included in the decoration of these great wooden coffins. This frieze usually contains representations of objects some of which were amuletic and some useful in a more practical way. The floors of this inner coffin and of the outer coffin of the same man (30839) are inscribed with texts from the *Book of the Two Ways* accompanied by a plan by which the deceased could find his way in the underworld. These coffins of Gua, and others of similar type, are exhibited in the Second Egyptian Room.

Stone coffins were rarely used except in royal burials during the Middle Kingdom when they were usually simple coffers with flat lids. Occasionally, as in the case of those made for the princesses buried at Deir el-Bahri, the sides were decorated with scenes of daily life and offering-texts.

A change in the manner of preparing the mummified body for burial during the Twelfth Dynasty prompted a modification in coffin design. It became customary to cover the head of the corpse

with a mask made usually of layers of linen and gesso, moulded to the form of the face, the latter being sometimes gilded. A good example of a Middle Kingdom mask of this kind on exhibition belonged to an unidentified lady of high rank, probably a princess (29770). The characteristic mummy of the period with heavy bandaging and mask became the basic form on which coffins were modelled thereafter. In so preparing the body and burying it in a coffin shaped like a mummy, the Egyptians reinforced the identification of the deceased with the god Osiris who was

58 Texts and painted decoration on the inner coffin of Gua

regularly shown as a mummified king. The decoration of the earliest anthropoid mummiform coffins, which were heavily built of wood, was designed to achieve the same effect; the surfaces were commonly painted with a feather design, thought to represent the wings of the goddess Isis, protecting the body of Osiris. Feather decoration of this kind is usually called *rishi*— the Arabic word for 'feather'. One of the Museum's coffins of this type has the decoration gilded, the colour of the gold being an unusually light lime-colour (6652). This coffin was made for a king Inyotef (possibly Nubkheperre) of the Seventeenth Dynasty.

In the New Kingdom coffins were normally made of wood or cartonnage (moulded linen and plaster) and were mummiform. Stone sarcophagi on the other hand were not common except in royal burials. During the Eighteenth Dynasty the kings were buried in simple but finely inscribed stone sarcophagi which contained inner and outer mummiform coffins of gold and gilded wood. In the Nineteenth Dynasty the royal stone sarcophagus was no longer rectangular, but mummiform and inscribed with funerary texts and representations. Parts of the lid of the great alabaster sarcophagus of Sethos I are in the Museum, though not exhibited; the fine coffer of this sarcophagus is preserved in the Sir John Soane Museum in Lincoln's Inn Fields. Of rare stone sarcophagi made for non-royal persons, a good example is that of the Viceroy of Kush, Merymose, who served under Amenophis III, which is exhibited in the Central Saloon of the Egyptian Sculpture Gallery (1001). It is mummiform and made of black granite finely carved with texts and divine representations. Fragments of an outer mummiform sarcophagus for the same man are also preserved in the Museum. The decoration of non-royal wooden and cartonnage coffins was mostly simple in the Eighteenth Dynasty, texts being inscribed in yellow paint on a ground of black paint. Towards the end of the dynasty and during the Nineteenth Dynasty coffin-equipment was often more elaborate, like that of the lady Henutmehit. Three separate units are preserved, each heavily decorated and gilded; first a cartonnage mummy-cover with figures of gods in open-work, backed by purple linen; next an inner coffin with finely modelled face and heavy wig; finally, an outer coffin, similarly decorated (48001, 48001A; Plate 12).

In the later New Kingdom inner and outer anthropoid mummiform coffins were heavily decorated within and without with religious scenes and amuletic symbols. A series of these coffins is shown in the Second Egyptian Room. The base colour regularly used is yellow and the decorations are painted in bright colours, some of the individual elements being first modelled in relief in gesso. Among the common scenes and symbols found on the outside are the winged sun-disk, the winged scarab-beetle, representations of the deceased adoring various gods, figures of gods and goddesses, often winged and shown in protective attitudes, the sun-god passing through the divisions of the underworld in his bark, the funeral procession, the judgement-scene in the underworld, the resurrection of Osiris, and various demons of the underworld. On the insides, the regular scenes include the goddess Nut, the *djed*-pillar, the deified Amenophis I, the human-headed *Ba*-bird, the adoration of the sun-god and other deities, underworld demons, and sacred symbols. In the period following the Twenty-first Dynasty the decline in the craft of mummification was accompanied by a deterioration in the design and decoration of coffins. One development, which can be traced to the practice of placing moulded mummy covers over the corpse as early as the Eighteenth Dynasty, was the close-fitting cartonnage case shaped to the form of the mummified body. These cases were decorated with scenes similar to those found in the inner coffins of the preceding period, but they did not in general take the place of the inner coffin. Burials of rich and influential people were still provided with at least two wooden coffins, sometimes with three; the outer coffins were increasingly ponderous and crude in design and were decorated with scenes and texts executed in indifferent style. Stone mummiform coffins also became fashionable again, sometimes being used instead of the outer wooden coffin. Wooden coffins of the Late Period are exhibited in the First Egyptian Room and stone coffins in the Egyptian Sculpture Gallery. Also in the Sculpture Gallery can be seen examples of the great stone sarcophagi which contained the nests of coffins in the burials of kings and very important nobles in the Late Period. Of special interest are those of the princess Ankhnesneferibre of the Twenty-sixth Dynasty and the king Nectanebo of the Thirtieth Dynasty. The former (32) is a rectangular chest finely inscribed with texts from the *Book of the Dead* and with low-relief representations of Ankhnesneferibre (on the lid), the goddess Nut (on the reverse side of the lid, fig. 59; not now visible), and the goddess Hathor (on the bottom of the coffer). The coffin of Nectanebo (10) is rounded at one end and is inscribed with scenes and texts from the *Book of what is in the Underworld*.

In the Ptolemaic Period the tradition of the Late Period was continued. Outermost coffins were frequently made in the form of a chest with vaulted lid and four corner posts in a type developed towards the end of the Late Period. The mummy itself was often covered with an openwork cartonnage case and all

59 The goddess Nut carved on the schist sarcophagus of Princess Ankhnesneferibre (see also fig. 25)

elements of the equipment were inscribed with religious texts. The First Egyptian Room contains many examples of coffins of the Ptolemaic Period and also of the subsequent Roman Period (p. 243).

Shabtis and other funerary equipment

From the earliest times the tombs of the Egyptians were provided with an equipment designed to satisfy the needs of the deceased in his after-life. At first this equipment consisted principally of objects that might be used by the deceased in the way in which they were used in the daily life of the time. In simple graves there were pottery vessels and baskets containing food and drink, simple tools, and other utensils. In the tombs of kings and nobles from the time of the early dynasties there were placed, in addition, articles of furniture, chests of clothing, jewellery, and other objects of value. Many of the objects exhibited in the various rooms of the Egyptian Department in the British Museum came from tombs and formed originally parts of individual tomb-equipments. Most of the vessels of pottery, composition, stone, and metal may so be classified and also most of the 'objects of daily life' exhibited in the Fourth Egyptian Room. These objects, however, were actually used in the daily life of the times when they were placed in tombs and are not to be regarded solely as funerary equipment. This term is applied here to those objects the purpose of which was more closely connected with the fate of the deceased in the after-life, and which had no part in daily life. Some of the objects of this kind found in close association with the mummy, such as amulets, have already been mentioned (p. 159); others are *shabti*-figures, Ptah-Seker-Osiris figures, papyri with religious texts, and magical bricks. Model utensils and tools and the wooden models of scenes were made specially for burials, but represent actual objects used in daily life, or activities carried on in daily life.

Shabti-figures are exhibited in the Third Egyptian Room. The name *shabti* is of uncertain meaning. The same figures were called *shawabtis* in the New Kingdom and *ushabtis* in the Late Period; hence it would appear that the Egyptians themselves were in doubt about the original meaning. The Ancient Egyptians believed that in the underworld, as in Egypt itself, there would be a regular need for work on the land such as was required after the annual inundation of Egypt by the Nile (pp. 24 f.). Each year the rehabilitation of the land, involving the re-establishment of property boundaries, the rebuilding of dykes and cutting of canals, followed the subsiding of the flood waters, and these tasks were accomplished by the conscription of

Plate 12
Inner coffin of Henutmehit (*opposite*)

Plate 13
Weighing the heart from the Book of the Dead of the scribe Ani (*overleaf*)

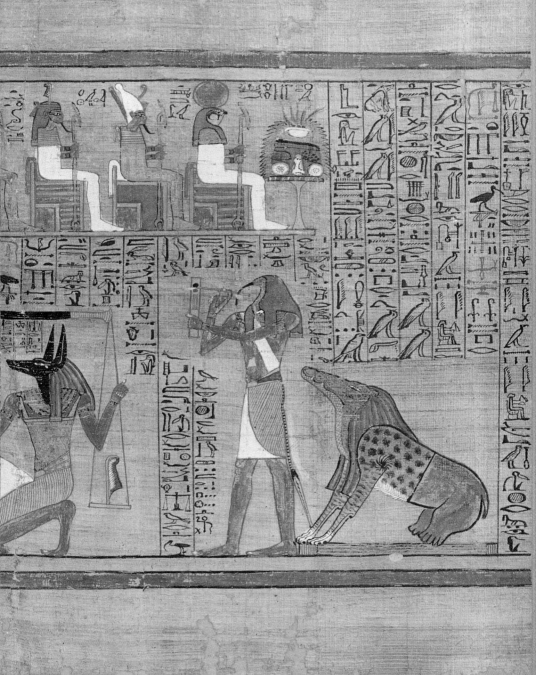

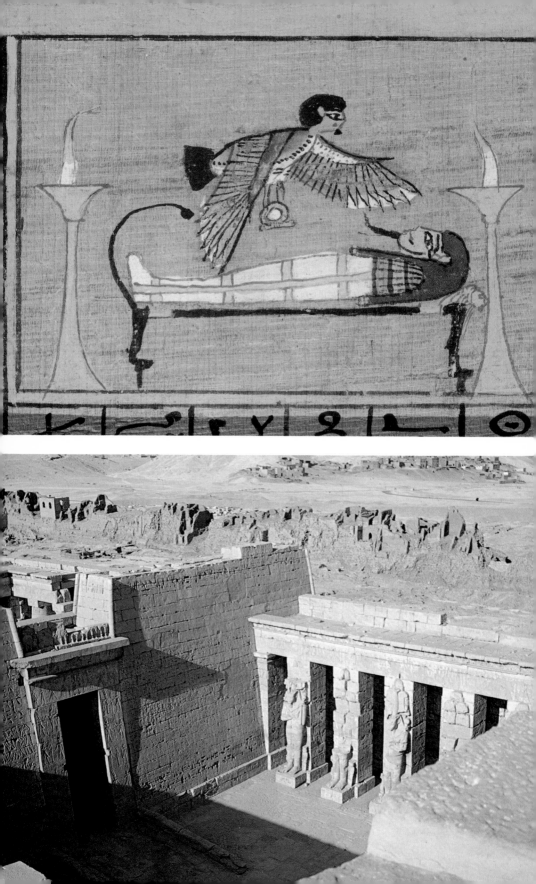

Plate 14

Vignette from the
Book of the Dead of
the scribe Ani
showing the *Ba* (soul)
hovering over the
mummy

labour. It was possible, however, for a man of means to avoid this *corvée* by supplying a deputy, and the intention of the *shabti*-figure was to act as the deceased's deputy for such tasks in the underworld. The coffin of Gua mentioned above (p. 163) carries an early version of the magical text used to secure this substitution; in the New Kingdom the text (incorporated as Chapter VI of the *Book of the Dead*) usually ran as follows: 'N. says "O shabti! If N. is detailed for any tasks to be done there (in the underworld), as a man is bound, namely to cultivate the fields, to flood the banks (of the fields—i.e. to water them) and to carry away sand to the east and to the west, then say thou, 'Here am I'."' The earliest *shabti*-figures were made of wood or wax in the form of a mummy and simply inscribed with the name of the deceased owner; they were sometimes placed in small coffins. In the New Kingdom more care was used in making the figures, which were usually carved in stone and inscribed with the *shabti*-text. The form remained that of a mummy, for it represented the deceased as Osiris. At this time *shabtis* were first made with tools in their hands—baskets, mattocks, hoes. Some *shabtis* are finely carved, especially those made for kings, such as that of Amenophis II (35365; fig. 60). In the Eighteenth Dynasty glazed composition was first used in their manufacture and thereafter it was the material most commonly employed, almost to the exclusion of other materials. The design of *shabtis* deteriorated throughout the Late New Kingdom and Late Period until the Twenty-sixth Dynasty when very finely modelled pieces were again made. The practice of providing *shabtis* in burials seems to have died out at the end of the Dynastic Period. A rare, apparent *shabti*-figure of the Roman Period, in polychrome glazed composition, is that of a sailor named Soter (30769). The *shabti*-figures of members of the Napatan royal family of Twenty-fifth Dynasty date and later represent an interesting development of Egyptian culture in Nubia where, in the Late Period, the ruling family was devoted to the worship of Amun and followed Egyptian funerary practice (p. 73). In the Middle Kingdom *shabtis* were provided singly in burials, sometimes in small coffins, and were thus true deputies. In later times, however, large numbers were buried, especially in royal tombs. Some New Kingdom *shabtis*, buried singly in coffins (e.g. 53892), may have had some other function. In the Late New Kingdom it became customary to provide one *shabti* for each day of the year with 'overseer' figures added to control the gangs into which the 'worker'-*shabtis* were organized. These overseers are represented usually not as mummies; they wear skirts and carry whips of office. The large numbers of *shabtis* were accommodated in special *shabti*-boxes, examples of which are exhibited with

Plate 15

Part of the temple
built by
Ramesses III at
Medinet Habu

the *shabtis* in the Third Egyptian Room. The burial of the lady Neskhons contained two boards bearing decrees concerning her *shabti*-figures. One of these boards is in the Museum (16672); the text shows that Neskhons paid for the *shabtis*, but it is not clear whether she bought them as slaves or made the payment to reimburse them for their work.

An object characteristic of burials of the Late Period is the Ptah-Seker-Osiris figure representing a triune deity embodying some of the characteristics of Ptah, the god of creation, Seker (or Sokaris) the god of the necropolis, and Osiris, the god of the underworld. The earliest figures belonging to this category, coming from Nineteenth Dynasty burials, represent Osiris alone, shown as a mummiform king standing on a pedestal. In some cases the figure is hollow and was intended to hold a copy of the *Book of the Dead* inscribed for the deceased owner. Such a figure was that made for the priestess of Amen-Re, Anhai, who lived in the Twentieth Dynasty (20868); the fine papyrus contained in the figure is now exhibited in the Third Egyptian Room (10472). The papyrus of Hunefer (9901) was also found in a Ptah-Seker-Osiris figure (9861). In the Late Period the figures have the triple divine association with Ptah, Sokaris, and Osiris, and it often happens that the bases of the figures contain small papyrus rolls in substitution for the larger rolls and also small portions of the bodies of the deceased. The figure made for Nesuy (9737) exhibited with that of Anhai in the Third Egyptian Room has a small figure of the god Sokaris, represented as a mummified falcon, placed on the pedestal which is made in the form of a coffin. This base no doubt represented the coffin in miniature and the fragment of body placed within represented the whole body of the deceased.

The placing with a burial of papyri inscribed with specialized funerary texts was a custom which developed in the Eighteenth Dynasty and became common thereafter. The idea of furnishing a burial with funerary texts was, however, very much older. In the Old Kingdom the tombs of private persons contained many texts, mostly consisting of short, set formulae, designed to ensure the continuation of offerings for the deceased in the future. Royal pyramids of the same period (p. 178) contained large extracts from the body of texts known as the *Pyramid Texts*. In the Middle Kingdom the great wooden coffins of private persons were inscribed with *Coffin Texts* (p. 163), which were the literary and religious descendants of the *Pyramid Texts*. A papyrus preserved in the British Museum (10676) written in a Middle Kingdom hieratic, close in character to the script used on the coffins, contains many sections of the *Coffin Texts* and it is possible that it was originally used in a Middle Kingdom burial

60 *Shabti*-figure of Amenophis II

in the way in which the later copies of the *Book of the Dead* were used. Part of this papyrus is exhibited with examples of the *Book of the Dead* in the north-eastern division of the Third Egyptian Room. The *Book of the Dead* is the name now given to a collection of religious and magical texts known to the Egyptians as the *Chapters of Coming-forth by Day*. This extended composition was the descendant of the *Pyramid Texts* and *Coffin Texts* and its principal aims were to secure for the deceased a satisfactory after-life and to give him the power to leave his tomb when necessary. No copy contains the text of the whole work, each owner clearly having obtained for himself those sections which he particularly needed or as much as he could afford. In many cases the copies were prepared especially for individual customers; other copies were written as 'stock' examples with blank spaces in which the names of the purchasers could be inserted. The finest copies are beautifully illustrated with coloured vignettes, examples in the collection being those made for Ani (10470), Hunefer (9901), and Anhai (10472; Plate 2). In the Late New Kingdom and Late Period, the vignettes were commonly done as brush and black-ink drawings. The best examples of this type are contained in the Papyrus of Nesitanebtashru (10554), a daughter of Pinudjem I, High-priest of Amun, and Neskhons. Good illustration is not, however, always accompanied by good text; the text of the Papyrus of Ani is full of errors; on the other hand the Papyrus of Nu (10477) has an excellent text accompanied by relatively simple vignettes. Of the many sections making up the whole work the one that is found in most copies is Chapter cxxv, which deals with the judgement of the deceased before Osiris; this chapter is often accompanied by a vignette showing the weighing of the heart before the 42 assessor-gods (pp. 156 f. and Plate 13). In the Saite Period the text of the *Book of the Dead* underwent a considerable revision, new sections being added, old sections discarded, and others reworded. The new version, used thereafter, is now called the Saite recension; a good example is the Papyrus of Ankhwahibre (10558) of the Ptolemaic Period. From the Late New Kingdom other religious works were sometimes placed with burials. Of these the most common was the *Book of what is in the Underworld*, a composition which in the early dynasties of the New Kingdom was inscribed on the walls of the royal tombs. It deals primarily with the progress of the sun-god in his bark through the underworld by night—a progress with which the fate of the deceased could be identified, a journey from death to resurrection through the divisions of the underworld in the course of which the deceased experienced regeneration. The Papyri of Henttowy (10018) and

Ankhefenkhons (9980) contain versions of this work. Among other compositions found in funerary papyri of the Late Period and concerned with the fate of the deceased person are the *Book of Traversing Eternity* (see, e.g. Papyrus 10091) and the *Book of Breathings*, a copy of which is contained in the Papyrus of Kerasher (9995) which is illustrated with vignettes appropriate to the *Book of the Dead*. Some late funerary papyri contain very little text, but a wealth of illustrations, the vignettes being taken from the repertoire of all the contemporary funerary texts. Examples of such papyri, which are purely magical in intention, are those of Pashebutenmut (10007) and of Pedikhons (10004) exhibited with the other funerary texts in the Third Egyptian Room.

The vignettes of the funerary texts of the New Kingdom and later are filled with strange deities, the significance of many of whom remains unestablished. In the tombs of kings of the Eighteenth and Nineteenth Dynasties wooden figures resembling some of these deities have been found. A collection of such figures is exhibited in the north-west section of the Third Egyptian Room. They are all bird- or animal-headed and come from royal tombs in the Valley of the Kings at Thebes.

In the same section of the Third Egyptian Room is a group of objects found in the burial of a lector-priest named Idy who lived during the Sixth Dynasty. It consists of stone vessels and a large number of copper model tools and utensils including a small altar fully equipped with miniature vessels (fig. 61). The practice of

1 Model copper objects and altar from the tomb of a priest, Idy

placing model or miniature objects in tombs was prompted by a magical intention similar to that underlying the representation of objects on the walls of tombs. The models and the representations served in place of actual, usable objects. The original reason for employing models was economy, but it seems that in later periods models were sometimes used in preference to actual objects because they could be made specifically for funerary purposes and be more elaborate than the real objects. The gilded wooden ointment and incense model containers inscribed with the name of Ramesses II, exhibited in the Fourth Egyptian Room, seem to be models of this kind. The wooden false vessels for ointments painted to simulate different hard stones and glass, which are shown in the Third Egyptian Room, may also have been used in preference to actual glass and stone vessels and not because they were cheaper to produce. Many of the model tools in the Fourth Egyptian Room were likewise made as parts of funerary equipment. Specially interesting are the miniature hoes and baskets which were intended for the use of the deceased or his *shabti* in carrying out work on the land in the after-life (e.g. those of Heqreshu, 32693).

In tombs of the late Old Kingdom to Middle Kingdom were placed wooden models representing many kinds of domestic, agricultural, and other activities. They were substitutes for the scenes, painted or carved on the walls of earlier tombs, showing similar activities, and, like these scenes, they were intended to serve as magical substitutes for the existence the deceased hoped to enjoy in the after-life. Among the examples exhibited in the Fourth Egyptian Room are models of butchery (41576, 58083), brewing (55728, 36423, fig. 5), baking (45197, 40915), ploughing (51090, 52947), and brick-making (63837, fig. 80); also miniature granaries (2463, 21804) and boats. Of the last the majority are model cargo-boats or travel-boats; but two (9524, 9525, Plate 17) are funerary boats with mummies on deck intended probably to represent the journey of pilgrimage to Abydos, which was commonly regarded as desirable from the Middle Kingdom onwards. The burials of humble people in the Middle Kingdom were not equipped with sets of models, but frequently they contained pottery model houses, in the forecourts of which were representative offerings, the whole being intended to provide sustenance and homes for the *Kas* of the deceased owners. These pottery houses are usually called soul-houses, and examples are exhibited with the wooden models.

A further form of amuletic protection provided for burials of the New Kingdom comprised a set of four magical bricks placed in niches in the four walls of the burial chamber. These bricks were by prescription made of unbaked mud and each carried an amulet, the northern a mummiform figure of wood, the southern a reed fitted with a wick, representing a torch, the eastern a figure of a jackal made of unbaked clay, and the western a *djed*-pillar of blue composition. The bricks were inscribed with short individual texts which formed part of Chapter CLI of the *Book of the Dead*, and their intention was to prevent the approach of the enemies of the deceased from the four cardinal points.

Tombs and tomb-stelae

The graves of the Predynastic Period have already been mentioned (p. 157). In general they were simple oval or rectangular pits, mostly shallow, sometimes brick-lined or revetted with wood, but commonly without structural features of individual distinction. The more elaborate, carefully constructed graves had wooden roofs, above which were piled rough mounds of sand and rubble. Burials at that time, and throughout Egyptian history, were made on the desert-edge, beyond the cultivation, where they in no way diminished the area of cultivable land available and were above the level of the flood-waters of the Nile. The simple burial in the desert-sand consisting of a shallow pit and mound continued to be the normal type of grave for people of humble situation during the Early Dynastic Period. Tombs of kings and important officials and nobles, on the other hand, were from the beginning of the First Dynasty elaborate structures.

In the First and Second Dynasties the great tombs of nobles consisted of subterranean burial chambers with large mud-brick superstructures. At first the superstructures were surrounded on all sides with deep recesses in imitation probably of the façades of palaces and other great secular buildings of the period. Later the recesses were reduced in number to two, placed at the north and south ends of the eastern side. These recesses served as false doors, the larger southern one as a chapel for the practice of the funerary cult. The subterranean parts of these tombs contained many store-chambers for the less-important funerary goods. The superstructure was rectangular, low in proportion to its length and with a convex roof; the sides were painted with coloured patterns which represented, probably, the woven mat-hangings of secular buildings. In many cases subsidiary burials were placed around the principal tomb which suggests that, at the beginning of the Early Dynastic Period, the primitive custom of burying the great man's relatives with him at the time of his death was retained. The subsidiary burials were similarly provided with small superstructures with two false door recesses. Tombs with low rectangular superstructures are usually called mastabas, this name having been used by the native workmen of early excavators, who saw a similarity between the superstructures and the benches (mastabas) found outside native houses. The stelae with which some of the earliest tombs were supplied were simple stone memorials bearing, in the case of a royal burial, the name of the king (e.g. 35597 that of Peribsen of the Second Dynasty, fig. 62), and, in the case of a private person, his name and title. Not until the end of the First Dynasty were the first truly funerary stelae produced, that is stelae carved with scenes and texts directly connected with the securing of posthumous benefits for the deceased. From the first, the scene on funerary stelae took the form which persisted throughout the Old Kingdom on the panel incorporated in the large false door stelae. It consisted of a representation of the deceased seated at an offering table piled with sliced loaves of bread and of simple texts enumerating various food and drink offerings and the titles and name of the deceased. The early funerary stela was placed apparently in the southern niche on the eastern side of the mastaba.

In these early mastabas stone was used only to a limited extent for lining burial chambers, for the lintels and jambs of doorways and for the portcullises which sealed the entrance passages. In general stone was introduced to give greater security to the most important part of the tomb, the burial chamber. Most of the changes in design and technique in the development of tomb-architecture in the early period were the result of attempts to make the burial more secure from tomb robbers. The most remarkable development, however, was the construction of the Step Pyramid at Saqqara for Djoser, the first king of the Third Dynasty. The whole complex of funerary buildings connected with this pyramid was within a great enclosure wall and was built of stone. The pyramid itself has six steps and rises to a height of about 60 metres; it is not square in plan, being approximately 125 metres from east to west and 110 metres from north to south. Beneath the pyramid are the burial chamber and a network of passages and small chambers used for storing the funerary equipment and for the burials of members of the royal family. At the south end of the enclosure is a great mastaba beneath which is a duplicate set of chambers reproducing those immediately connected with the burial chamber beneath the pyramid. The walls of some of the rooms under the mastaba and pyramid are decorated with blue glazed composition tiles, arranged to represent primitive hangings of matting, and fine low reliefs showing Djoser performing various religious ceremonies. On the north side of the Step Pyramid is a mortuary temple and a small chamber containing the statue of the dead king. The former was intended for the practice of the funerary

62 Stela of Peribsen

cult of the king and the latter as a substitute for the body of the king for the reception of offerings. The chamber containing a statue of the deceased became a regular feature of Old Kingdom burials and it is now usually called the *serdab* (the Arabic word for 'cellar'). The Step Pyramid enclosure contained also a number of buildings planned for the celebration of the dead king's jubilee ceremonies in his after-life; the purpose of other buildings in the enclosure is unknown. The whole complex was intended to provide for the dead king a setting in which he could fulfil his function as a monarch after death and it is probable that it contained in its plan most of the features characteristic of the royal palace at Memphis.

The step pyramid form was used by the later kings of the Third Dynasty, but it was then superseded by the true pyramid which was thereafter used by kings throughout the Old Kingdom and during the Middle Kingdom. The change in design was probably due to a change in religious beliefs. The Great Pyramid at Giza, built for Cheops, the second king of the Fourth Dynasty, may be taken as characteristic of the type. It is built mostly of local limestone and was originally faced with fine limestone from the quarries of Tura on the east bank of the Nile. Its four sides were almost identical in length, having been originally about 230 metres long: its height when complete was about 146 metres. From fig. 63 it can be seen that two changes of plan

63 Section of the Great Pyramid at Giza

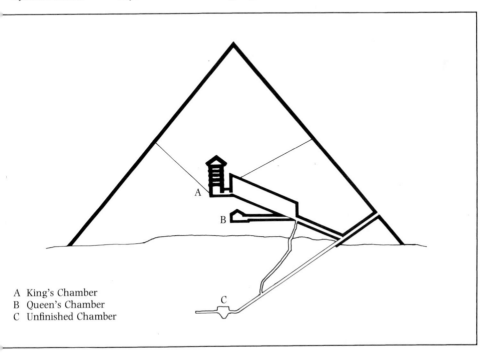

A King's Chamber
B Queen's Chamber
C Unfinished Chamber

were made in deciding the position of the burial chamber. At first a subterranean chamber was excavated at the end of a long descending corridor. Before it was completed it was abandoned and a second chamber prepared within the masonry of the pyramid; this chamber has erroneously been called the Queen's Chamber. For some reason it was later decided to prepare another room for the royal burial and the so-called King's Chamber was constructed above the Queen's Chamber. It was approached by a lofty gallery of majestic proportions. The King's Chamber is built of granite and its roof is relieved of the weight of the pyramid-mass above by five cell-like relieving chambers. A large granite sarcophagus for the royal body (contained, no doubt, in a wooden inner coffin) is still in the chamber. No royal mummies of the Old Kingdom have been found intact; it used to be thought that the wooden coffin and human remains found in the pyramid of Mycerinus, also at Giza, belonged to the original burial. The coffin, preserved in the reserve collections in the British Museum (6647), is now recognized as a replacement coffin provided probably in the Saite Period when the interest in their past led the Egyptians to investigate the monuments of their ancestors. Moreover, scientific tests have shown that the human remains are of relatively modern date, being probably those of an Arab intruder during the Middle Ages.

On the east side of the Great Pyramid is the mortuary temple, in which the funerary cult of the dead king was practised, and from it a stone causeway leads to the edge of the desert to the so-called Valley Temple in which the final rites were performed on the body of the king before it was taken to the pyramid. The Valley Temple of the Great Pyramid is unexcavated as it lies beneath a modern village. The walls of the two temples and the causeway were probably decorated with painted reliefs; the pyramid itself was uninscribed within and without.

During the Fourth Dynasty very large pyramids were built for three kings, Sneferu, Cheops, and Chephren. Thereafter far smaller pyramids were constructed, no doubt because the effort and resources needed for them constituted less of a drain on the economy of the country. Basically, however, the plan of a royal pyramid-complex remained the same, consisting of the pyramid, mortuary temple, causeway, and valley temple. The pyramids of Unas, the last king of the Fifth Dynasty, and of the kings and the last queens of the Sixth Dynasty were distinguished by having the burial chambers and ancillary rooms decorated with funerary texts, known as *Pyramid Texts* (p. 171).

Private burials during the Old Kingdom continued to be made in mastaba-type tombs wherever the nature of the site available permitted; elsewhere rock-cut tombs were prepared. The plan of

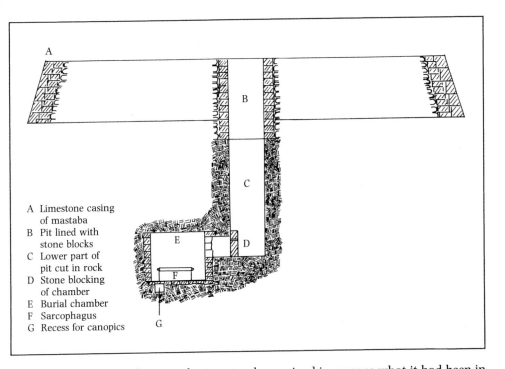

A Limestone casing
of mastaba
B Pit lined with
stone blocks
C Lower part of
pit cut in rock
D Stone blocking
of chamber
E Burial chamber
F Sarcophagus
G Recess for canopics

64 Section of a
mastaba

the mastaba-type tomb remained in essence what it had been in the Early Dynastic Period, consisting of a subterranean burial-chamber and a rectangular superstructure with a chapel for the performing of the funerary cult (fig. 64). Many changes and developments, however, took place during the course of the Old Kingdom, the principal being the use of stone in the construction of the superstructure, the increase in size of the chapel, and the placing of the burial-chamber at the bottom of a deep shaft. In the early Old Kingdom the superstructures were commonly built of solid masonry and rubble with the chapel added either as a separate small structure or as a chamber partly built outside the main mass of the superstructure and partly penetrating it. At Giza the mastabas of the nobles, who served under Cheops, were grouped in regular lines around his pyramid. At Saqqara and elsewhere this regularity was not so strictly observed although it remained customary for great officials to have their tombs in the neighbourhood of the pyramid of the king whom they had served. This change in custom resulted partly, no doubt, from the weakening of the great authority of the kings. A further indication of the diminution of dependence on the part of the nobles can be seen in the mastabas of the Fifth and Sixth Dynasties when compared with those of the Fourth Dynasty. As mentioned above, the chapels of the early Old Kingdom mastabas were small chambers; they were equipped

with a funerary tablet and offering table. Figure 65 shows 65 Stela of Rahotep
a typical Fourth Dynasty funerary stela (1242) which comes
from the mastaba of Rahotep at Maidum. The mastaba-chapels
of the early Old Kingdom at Maidum sometimes are decorated
with a few scenes of daily life. Later in the Old Kingdom the
chapel developed into a series of rooms which eventually filled
the whole of the superstructure of the mastaba. One room was
reserved for use as the mortuary chapel and it held the offering
table and texts intimately connected with the cult of the deceased.
These texts usually included an offering list containing sometimes as many as a hundred items, which was intended to act
as a magical substitute for the proper provision of actual offerings; it was accompanied by scenes of the deceased receiving
offerings and of the preparation and bringing of offerings. Most
important, however, was the false door or stela through which
the dead man was believed to gain access to the earthly world
from the tomb; it incorporated the old funerary tablet and texts
consisting of the titles and dignities of the deceased and prayers

to the funerary deities for the continuation of offerings. Adjacent
to the mortuary chapel was the *serdab*, the room containing the
statue of the deceased. It was generally a sealed room with a
squint through which the statue could see and also receive
(if only symbolically) the offerings placed in the chapel or
represented on its walls. The other rooms in the superstructure
of a large mastaba were used partly as stores for funerary equipment, but principally for the representation of scenes showing
the deceased owner watching and participating in activities
common in his life on earth which he hoped to continue enjoying in the after-life. In the Egyptian Sculpture Gallery, at the
south end, are many good examples of Old Kingdom false doors
and most of the scenes of one small mastaba chapel (718).
The last was made for a high official, called Urirenptah, at
Saqqara. It consisted of one room only which held false doors
for the deceased and his wife and scenes of daily life. The false
door devoted to Urirenptah incorporates a long offering-list; the
scenes include sowing and reaping, representations of ships,
offering bearers, butchers, musicians at the funerary feast, and
the preparation of the deceased's bed.

During the Late Old Kingdom it became customary for high
local officials, the nomarchs, to be buried in their provincial
localities and not in the neighbourhood of the royal pyramid. In
many places the land on the west bank of the Nile was not suitable for cemeteries of the kind found in the Memphite area and
a new type of tomb was evolved which made use of the cliffs
which were near the Nile in Upper Egypt. In such rock-cut
tombs no superstructure was built, but the chapel and other
rooms which in mastabas were included in the superstructure
were excavated in the cliff-face. A shaft or descending passage
led from one of these rooms to the burial chamber. In the case of
very important people the tombs were often provided with
terrace platforms, sometimes incorporating elaborate architectural features, and formal façades. The approach to a tomb
of this kind might be by a causeway from the cultivated land
or by a flight of steps. The types of scene and inscription found
in these tombs are similar to those in contemporary mastaba-
tombs in the Memphite necropolis. Frequently, however, inasmuch as the provincial noble felt himself more independent
than the noble at court, he showed this independence by including in his tomb a fulsome account of his career and personal
achievements.

During the First Intermediate Period and Middle Kingdom the
rock-cut tomb remained the common type in Upper Egypt. In
some cases, as at Beni Hasan and Qaw, very elaborate tombs
were cut deep into the cliffs and, at Qaw, they were provided with

unusually grand ancillary buildings, including valley temples after the manner of pyramid-complexes. In the neighbourhood of the royal pyramids at El-Lisht, Illahun, and Dahshur, court officials were buried in mastabas, continuing the burial traditions of the Old Kingdom in the Memphite necropolis. The decoration of these tombs was in general similar to that found in tombs of the Late Old Kingdom. Many rock-cut tombs have no wall decorations, sometimes because the condition of the rock was too poor to receive them, sometimes possibly for reasons of economy. In such cases it was common for the burial to be provided with models representing some of the activities usually shown in the painted or relief-decorations (p. 174). The use of models subsequently was extended even to burials provided with good mural decorations. Poor rock which was not suitable for carving was often plastered and painted; where the rock was very bad the chambers of a tomb were sometimes lined with fine limestone slabs which could be carved. After the end of the Old Kingdom the false-door stela became less common and new smaller types of stela were evolved, the texts and representations of which incorporated the essential elements of the Old Kingdom stelae in the offering scene, the dignities and titles of the deceased, and formulae for securing offerings for the deceased. In addition it was not uncommon for the stela to include an account of the deceased's career. A fine example is the stela of Tjetji (614, fig. 12), a high official who served under the kings of the Early Eleventh Dynasty, exhibited in the Sculpture Gallery. Many smaller funerary stelae of Middle Kingdom nobles and officials are also exhibited in the same gallery; among them are some from Abydos where, at this period, it was common for a man of position to set up a cenotaph, associating himself in death thereby with Osiris, the god of the underworld, whose chief cult-centre was Abydos.

A dramatic change in the form of the royal tomb came with the construction at Deir el-Bahri on the west bank of the Nile at Thebes of the mortuary-complex of Nebhepetre Mentuhotpe II, the great king of the Eleventh Dynasty who reunited Upper and Lower Egypt after the divisions of the First Intermediate Period (p. 50). In plan this structure was original: the mortuary temple was built on a raised terrace and embodied a podium bearing a small pyramid or, possibly, a square mastaba, and surrounded by colonnades. At the end of a long corridor lay the tomb proper beneath the cliffs; under the pyramid was a cenotaph approached by a long tunnel from the forecourt. The temple was connected with the valley temple by a very long open causeway. This type of structure was never repeated although a similar complex was probably planned for Mentuhotpe III. During the Twelfth

Dynasty the kings established their capital in the north and returned to the pyramid type of burial characteristic of the Memphite necropolis. The pyramids of this time were, however, far inferior in size and construction to those of the great period of the Fourth Dynasty. In some cases the cores were brick-built. The associated temples and other buildings were likewise less grand. Great care was taken, however, over the construction of the internal chambers in these pyramids, the work being executed with extreme accuracy in the hardest materials. In certain cases the arrangement of the passages was deliberately complicated, with corridors on different levels, accessible only through concealed entrances. The purpose of these measures was to protect the burial from plunderers, but in no case were they wholly successful.

Royal burials during the Second Intermediate Period continued to be made in pyramids; the few surviving examples in the Memphite region show a continuation of the style of construction of the Twelfth Dynasty. In Thebes no actual royal pyramids have survived, but traces found by excavation reveal that they were very modest structures of mud-brick. The prominence which a pyramid gave to a burial no doubt greatly attracted the attentions of tomb robbers and it is surprising that the form remained in fashion for so long. It was ultimately abandoned in Egypt for royal burials early in the Eighteenth Dynasty. From the reign of Tuthmosis I, throughout the New Kingdom, kings were buried in rock-cut tombs in the so-called Valley of the Kings, a remote valley lying in the hills on the west bank of the Nile at Thebes. These tombs consisted of a series of corridors and rooms, extending many hundreds of feet into the rock (fig. 66). The farthest room was usually the burial chamber,

66 Plan of the tomb of Seti I

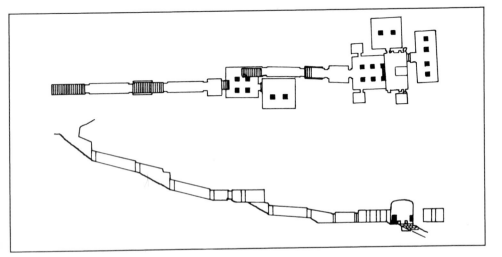

the others being reserved for the storage of equipment and for the performance of funerary ceremonies. The walls were covered with mythological texts and representations designed to facilitate the progress of the deceased king to his ultimate goal in the after-life (p. 172). Royal mortuary temples and valley temples were now no longer built in close connexion with the tombs; each king constructed a single mortuary temple on the edge of the cultivation on the west bank of the Nile, some distance from the Valley of the Kings. A different plan was adopted for the tomb and temples constructed for Queen Hatshepsut. For her, a valley temple was constructed on the edge of the cultivation and connected by a long causeway with a mortuary temple of very unusual design constructed in a bay in the cliffs at Deir el-Bahri, close to the mortuary temple built for Mentuhotpe II. This temple consisted of a series of open terraces with colonnades and the royal tomb was situated in the cliff behind (p. 59).

New Kingdom private tombs of officials and nobles, of which the best examples are in the Theban necropolis, are, for the most part, more simple than the tombs of people of similar station of the Old and Middle Kingdoms. The basic plan consisted of a transverse entrance chamber and a short corridor which led to the chapel (fig. 67). The burial-chamber was reached by a shaft

67 Plan of a New Kingdom private tomb

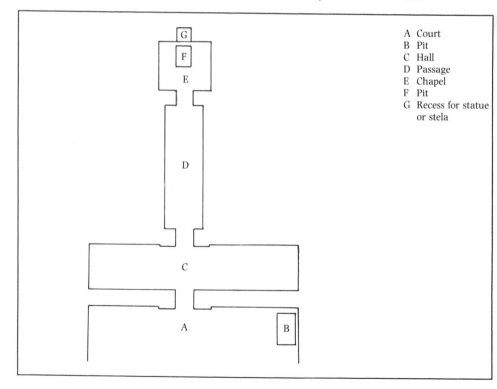

A Court
B Pit
C Hall
D Passage
E Chapel
F Pit
G Recess for statue or stela

or a descending passage from inside or outside the upper rooms. Most Theban tombs are rock-cut, but some have constructed façades and exterior courts. The special interest of these tombs lies in the painted and relief decoration found on the walls of the chapels and transverse chambers. These decorations contain some of the most lively representations of Egyptian daily activities. Parts of painted scenes from Theban tombs are exhibited in the Third Egyptian Room (p. 205 and Plates 3–5, 9). The principal stela in a typical Theban tomb was found at the end of the chapel (occasionally at one end of the transverse chamber) with an offering table in front. No longer was the stela used to present the biography of the deceased; information on his life and career were now incorporated in the texts included on the walls of the tomb. Lesser officials and members of the families of great men associated themselves with the principal burials by placing stelae in the forecourts of the great tombs, or by carving them on any available space in the neighbourhood. Such stelae bear texts devoted to securing funerary benefits for their owners, with appropriate prayers to the funerary deities. Similar small stelae are found with burials of men of modest station elsewhere in Egypt and many examples can be seen in the Egyptian Sculpture Gallery. This custom persisted until the Roman Period.

Few royal burials of the Late New Kingdom and Late Period have been discovered and the royal necropolises of the various dynasties in most cases remain to be identified. At Tanis in the Delta some tombs of kings of the Twenty-first and Twenty-second Dynasties have been found, consisting of stone chambers built just below ground level, with modest superstructures above. They were sited within the temple enclosure in the city. The Ethiopian kings of the Twenty-fifth Dynasty were buried in their southern capital, Napata, where they constructed at El-Kurru and Nuri small pyramids of which the angles of the faces were far less acute than those of the traditional Egyptian pyramid. One or more subterranean chambers were provided for the burial and in some cases the walls of one of these chambers were inscribed with the Negative Confession from Chapter cxxv of the *Book of the Dead* (p. 157).

The most remarkable private tombs of the Late Period are those constructed in the Theban necropolis for people like Mentuemhat, a fourth prophet of Amun (1643), and Pedamenope, also a high priestly official. These tombs are vast subterranean complexes of rooms, the walls of which are covered with religious texts derived from the sacred books formerly reserved for royalty. The tomb of Mentuemhat also has finely carved and painted reliefs inspired by Old and Middle Kingdom prototypes. Elaborate mud-brick chapels with pylons were constructed for these burials. In the Memphite necropolis the important tombs of the Late Period consisted of chambers inscribed with versions of the *Pyramid Texts*, placed at the bottom of exceptionally deep shafts.

It would appear that after the end of the New Kingdom, the varied fortunes suffered by Egypt affected not only the political stability of the country but also the regular evolution of funerary architecture. In consequence large cemeteries of great tombs were not developed and uniformity in tomb-design, so characteristic of the great necropolises of earlier periods, was not maintained. The exhaustion of land suitable for burials in the neighbourhood of the principal cities contributed to this development and late tombs are often found fitted among earlier tombs wherever space was available. By the Ptolemaic Period the custom of having elaborate tombs had largely been abandoned, except no doubt in the case of royal persons and the very highest officials; but of such tombs few are known. Burials of this period, both of simple people and of minor officials, were often made within the superstructures of earlier tombs especially in places where old cemeteries were silted up with sand and with the decayed brickwork of ancient superstructures. Coffins were placed simply in brick compartments or straight into shallow graves; funerary equipment was scanty and unelaborate. The depressed status of the Egyptian in this late period is suitably reflected in the humble nature of his burial.

CHAPTER SEVEN

ARTS AND CRAFTS

The burial customs of the Egyptians described in the previous chapter and the climatic and topographical features described in the first chapter account for the vast number of objects of funerary purpose or daily use which have survived from Egypt. Most of this material comes from Middle and Upper Egypt. The Delta, with a higher water-table and more Mediterranean-like climate, its settlements lying in less close proximity to the desert edge, has proved hitherto less rewarding in finds of material remains. Only a few town sites have been scientifically excavated and these too have as a rule yielded little reward.

The exploitation of the full richness of the country's natural resources is reflected in the wide range of techniques and manufactures practised by the Egyptian craftsman. Illustrative material will be found in the Upper Egyptian Rooms. In the Fourth Egyptian Room are examples of stone vases, wooden models, furniture and receptacles, metal tools and weapons, weights and measures, toys, musical instruments, toilet objects, household utensils in faience and metal, and woven fabrics and basketry. The Fifth Egyptian Room contains small sculpture in stone, wood and metal, terracotta and ivory; it includes some of the finest achievements of the Egyptians in this field of art. Jewellery, bronze, faience, and glass objects, and pottery are displayed in the Sixth Egyptian Room. Taken in conjunction with the scenes of craftsmen at work in the tombs, these remains provide a body of evidence for the arts and crafts, skills and manufactures, unrivalled in the ancient world from the point of view of quantity, state of preservation, diversity of material, and quality of production.

Most of the techniques employed by the Egyptian craftsman are already in evidence in the earliest settlements which can be traced back to predynastic times. It is not possible to do more than guess at the process of accident or experiment which resulted in the discovery of the means of exploiting the various resources of Egypt. With the unification of Egypt greater skills were developed in the use of materials long familiar, owing to the increased availability of metal for tools. By the Old Kingdom Egypt had already reached a standard of material culture which was not fundamentally altered until the Roman Period.

Stoneworking
Of all the crafts in which Egyptians showed early mastery, stoneworking is perhaps the most characteristic of the ancient

civilization, and certainly it was the craft in which it achieved some of its finest and most memorable work. The great natural wealth of Egypt in diverse ornamental stone, which lay close at hand on the desert edge or in the great ranges of the eastern hills, was exploited in the Predynastic Period for the making of stone vessels (fig. 68). The earliest of them are usually of basalt, of simple design with broad flat rims and flat spreading bases of the type illustrated by 64354. Vessels of this kind were found in a disturbed context at the site of El-Badari and may be contemporaneous with the earliest of the predynastic cultures. Certainly by the time of the Naqada I Period stone vessels were made in great quantity, the usual forms being slightly curved in a barrel- or heart-shape with two lug handles for suspension. Egyptian alabaster (calcite), basalt, breccia, granite, and porphyritic rock were all worked in the earlier Predynastic Period as well as the softer limestone. In the later Predynastic Period, in addition to these stones, schist, serpentine, and steatite were also used.

Great numbers of stone vessels have been recovered from royal and private tombs of the Early Dynastic Period and of the Third and Fourth Dynasties. The hoard of vessels from the subterranean galleries of the Step Pyramid of Djoser is numbered, for instance, in thousands. This was the period of highest artistic achieve-

68 Stone vessels dating from the Pre-dynastic period to the Eighteenth Dynasty

ment, a variety of stones being chosen and a wide range of shapes fashioned. The complete mastery of the material is well demonstrated by the manner in which the craftsmen could shape and fashion hard stone as if it were clay. A fine example of this plastic quality is a red breccia vase (35306) in the form of a sitting dove or pigeon, measuring from beak to tail 19 cm. The body has been hollowed out to form an effective receptable, the opening being a hole with narrow rim placed on the top of the back of the bird, the diameter of which is just over 2·5 cm. On the side of the bird, where the wings would come, are two pierced lug handles for suspension by cords. The head and neck are finely modelled, with eyes made by smooth bored holes, one of which still retains its original inlay of blue.

Representations in tomb scenes of the vessels being made as well as examination of finished and unfinished examples show that the hollowing out was done, once the outside had been roughly fashioned, by drilling the stone. The drill, rotated by a bow, was fitted with a tubular bit made probably of copper, its action assisted by the use of an abrasive powder, perhaps finely ground quartz. The cylindrical core left by the drill was broken away by driving wedges into the drill-cut. The central hole was then enlarged by means of a drill, rotated by a wooden crank handle weighted on each side, fitted with crescent-shaped bits of flint or other hard stone, of varying sizes and shapes. The process was continued until the required size of hole was achieved; the manner in which the drill was used for the under-cutting of the shoulders is not known. The final stage of the work was the careful shaping of the inside of the vessel and the polishing of the surface with stone burnishers.

Stone vessels continued to be made throughout the Dynastic Period, but from the Old Kingdom onwards there was consider-ably less use of the harder stones, alabaster being by far the most common material. Vessels are often inscribed with short vertical columns of hieroglyphs enclosed within a rectangular frame, giving the names of kings with conventional epithets; of more interest than usual is the text on the alabaster vase 57322 which is inscribed on one side with the name of Djedkare-Isesi (c. 2390 BC) and on the other with the information that the vase contained ointment for one of the king's ladies.

In the Middle Kingdom the majority of vessels were small and were used for containing cosmetic preparations. Particularly attractive are small vases of pale blue anhydrite, a stone which was used only in the Twelfth Dynasty. With the New Kingdom several new shapes were introduced, the more common being provided with one or two loop handles, often in the form of the head and neck of an animal or a bird. Another popular form was an amphora with ribbed handles, the base of which fitted into a stone stand. Examples of finely polished hard stones have survived; 24432 is a ribbed loop-handled vase with a diorite lid, 4734 is a diorite amphora with ribbed handles, one of which is partly restored. Stone anthropoid vessels, probably intended for magical purposes, are also found (30459, 29907). Fine vessels continued to be made in the Late Dynastic and Ptolemaic Periods, in the latter usually imitating classical forms. An interesting example from the point of view of technique is an alabaster hydria, of the Ptolemaic Period, which was made in four separate parts originally cemented together (35295).

With the exception of the small cosmetic jars, the majority of surviving stone vases were doubtlessly intended for funerary use only, providing a more durable and permanent receptacle for food and drink among the tomb equipment than the everyday clay pots. A wide variety of special types of stone vessel, however, was used for measuring liquids. Each variety had its special name, and in addition to being containers for beer, wine, milk, oil, and honey, some types were also used to measure solids like grain and incense. 4659 is an alabaster jar with lid of New Kingdom date, of the type called by the Egyptians *hin*; the inscription states that its capacity is $8\frac{1}{6}$ *hin*. Actual measuring gives as its equivalent about $8\frac{1}{2}$ pints, the *hin* corresponding approximately to a fraction over a pint. From the New Kingdom large high-sided bowls of stone filled with water were also used to measure time: two fragments of such clepsydrae or water-clocks in the collection date from the end of the Dynastic Period. No. 933 is a basalt fragment inscribed on the outside with texts relating to Alexander the Great; on the inside of the vessel the twelve hours of the night are marked by vertical lines of small holes, a different line being used for each month. The vessel was filled with water which drained away through a small hole in the base (fig. 45). No. 938 is another basalt fragment inscribed on the outside with a scene of Philip Arrhidaeus before the god Min.

The skill in stoneworking acquired from the manufacture of stone vessels was first applied to architecture at the beginning of the First Dynasty. The more plentiful supply of copper and the making of copper tools (see below pp. 222 f.) enabled the stone to be quarried from the rock bed and huge slabs to be dressed. This new development was first employed for monuments of a funerary nature, both royal and private, to make pavements, stairways, doorways, and portcullises and to line a room with a course of masonry (p. 176). The first building completely of stone was the funerary complex of Djoser at Saqqara (the Step Pyramid) which was constructed throughout of small blocks of fine limestone (p. 44); the style of architecture clearly imitates the early reed and wood constructions of the preceding ages, a feature which remains a dominant motif for the columns and capitals in Egypt throughout its ancient history and provides one of the most pleasing aspects of its architecture.

From the time of the Step Pyramid, increasing use was made of stone to build the superstructures of the funerary monuments of both royal and private persons, the primary reason for its adoption as a building material being its durability and its protective possibilities for monuments which in Egyptian belief were to last for ever. Ordinary houses, palaces, and until the New Kingdom probably also the great majority of local cult temples, were still constructed of sun-dried mud-brick, except for those parts which practical experience had shown required some stronger, more durable, and more impervious material like thresholds, lintels, door-posts, bases for columns of wood, and slabs for the wash-room (p. 32). For these local limestone was easily available.

The three main building stones were limestone, sandstone, and granite. Core masonry of Old Kingdom constructions at Giza and Saqqara was of the local surface rock taken from the vicinity of the building site. For the outer casing, great quantities of a good quality limestone free of nummulites were transported across the river from the vast quarries in the Moqqatam hills to the south-east of Cairo, in the region of Tura and Masara. The stone was soft, easily quarried with the copper tools available, but hardened on exposure to the air. It was capable of receiving and retaining the most sensitive and delicate work of the sculptor's chisel. It was removed economically, a block being isolated on four sides by means of trenches cut into the rock and detached from its bed by the making of slot holes at the base into which were inserted wooden wedges. These were wetted; as they swelled, so the block split away horizontally. The good strata of the rock were followed by tunnelling, a hollow space being first driven along the whole length of the layer to be worked between the roof of the tunnel and the top of the first blocks to be detached, to enable a mason's gang simultaneously to cut vertically downwards behind and around the block, and so gradually lower the floor of the quarry. The quarrymen used chisels of stone and metal, which were struck with wooden mallets (fig. 69), and stone hammers or pointed stone mauls, apparently not fitted with hafts. This fine limestone from Tura was highly prized throughout the Dynastic Period and the great man-made caves, with pillars of the living rock left to prevent a collapse of the roof, were already a familiar tourist sight in Greek and Roman times (Herodotus ii. 124; Strabo 17, i. 34).

69 Stonemason's mallet

Though there is little good quality limestone in the Theban area, the remains of Middle Kingdom constructions there show that limestone continued to be the chief building stone. Sandstone was also used to a limited extent. The capillary attraction of water up through the lower courses of limestone masonry and the subsequent crystallization of salt on the surface, as well as ancient and modern re-use of the blocks and the burning of the stone to make lime for fertilizer, account for the almost total disappearance of Middle Kingdom temples.

Limestone continued to be chiefly employed in the early part of the Eighteenth Dynasty, but in the reign of Tuthmosis III increasing use was made of sandstone which became henceforth the building stone of the great temples of Upper Egypt (p. 32). The change was due to the closeness of good quality sandstone to the river on both sides at Gebel es-Silsila, which could easily be transported to Thebes, to satisfy the great demand for stone which the lavish building programmes of the New Kingdom pharaohs required. The method of quarrying was the same as that for limestone, the blocks being extracted by both open and underground quarrying. Its use enabled a greater span of architrave to be achieved. The surface, however, rarely allowed the same fineness of relief as limestone to which there was a partial return in the reign of Sethos I (p. 65).

Granite, both the pink and the black varieties, was regularly used throughout the Dynastic Period for greater strength and greater effect, a preference being shown for the coarser-grained stone. The manner in which limestone was painted to imitate granite is itself proof of its desirability in Egyptian eyes. Doorways, columns, whole shrines, and burial chambers were constructed of the stone. It came from the region of the First Cataract by Aswan. In the first instance use was probably made of detached boulders, but as early as the Old Kingdom the stone was already being quarried from the rock-bed for columns and casing stones. To reach a block of the suitable strength and quality, the top stratum of rock was broken away by first heating and then rapidly cooling it with water. A block of the required size was then detached by pounding a trench with balls of dolerite and splitting it from the rock bed by means of wedges, the slots being made by a stone or metal tool worked in conjunction with an abrasive powder.

Other stones used to a limited extent in building were alabaster, quartzite, and basalt, usually in connexion with the most important rooms. The resources lay for the most part close to water transport, though the most highly prized alabaster came from Hatnub, some 15 miles into the desert south-east of El-Amarna. When the stone had been extracted, it was lashed to sledges which were dragged, usually by teams of men but also by oxen. Water or other liquid was poured on the ground to ease the passage of the sledge. Wheeled transport does not seem to have been used to shift loads in the Dynastic Period, though a wheel used to push forward a scaling ladder is shown in a relief in the Fifth Dynasty tomb of Kaemheset at Saqqara. The difficulties of overland transport of the stone explain the large numbers of men recorded on the rocks in the Wadi Hammamat by the quarrying expeditions; these expeditions to the desert quarries were major operations conducted at irregular intervals according to the need of the moment and the taste of the individual pharaoh. They were maintained by the king and in the New Kingdom comprised prisoners of war as well as levies of Egyptians. They normally took place during the period from December to April when men could best be spared from the land and be put to hauling the quarried blocks (p. 45).

The blocks were taken by the most practical route to the nearest point on the river; from there they were transported by water on barges as close as possible to the building site. Sites were levelled, the floor beaten down and the lines of the walls and doorways marked out by use of a surveyor's cord. Rough architectural plans of buildings on both papyrus and ostraca have survived; one ostracon in the collection (41228) from Deir el-Bahri, of New Kingdom date, gives the plan of a small peripteral chapel, 27 cubits square (i.e. a little over 14 metres square). No true foundations were laid, the lines of the walls being marked at the most by shallow trenches. Much of Egyptian masonry is no more than a core of rubble enclosed by ashlars of dressed stone. To raise the blocks in the course of construction, no pulley seems to have been used before the Roman Period; the blocks were manhandled into position by means of wooden baulks, rockers, and ramps of earth and brick. To assist in the final placement, a thin layer of gypsum plaster was spread over the joints to act as a lubricant rather than as a binding material.

The method of decorating the stonework with carvings in relief is shown by the large number of models and trial pieces and also by the unfinished state of surviving monuments. After the final dressing of the blocks (or in the case of rock-cut tombs the preparation of the rock face) the surface was divided up into squares by a series of horizontal and vertical lines which might be incised on the stone or made by stretching at regular intervals across the walls a string dipped in red ochre. Over this grid the design was roughly sketched out, usually in red but sometimes in black paint, the draughtsman working from a drawing on a small scale similarly divided.

In some cases the image was merely engraved on the stone with incised lines. In the other cases the outline was first isolated by a furrow cut around it, the background was lowered to the required depth and the details of the figures modelled. The delicate shallow raised relief, for which the Tura limestone provided an ideal vehicle, shows Egyptian art at its best. This type of work had, however, the disadvantage that it could be easily damaged or usurped and doubtlessly this consideration, as well as the saving in time and labour, gave rise to the less decorative deep-sunk relief, in which the design and modelling were cut below the level of the surface.

The representation of the human figure in the reliefs followed strict conventions. The figures are invariably shown with the head in profile but the eye as if from the front; the shoulders are represented frontally, chest in three-quarter view and legs in profile. Feet and hands may be represented without distinction between left and right. The oddity of the anatomy is lessened by the fluency and firmness of the Egyptian line and by the strict canon of proportion maintained, admirably illustrated by a drawing-board with a seated figure of Tuthmosis III over a grid (New Kingdom from Thebes, 5601).

At the same time as the Egyptians were applying the newly gained skill in quarrying and dressing stone blocks to masonry and relief, they began also to fashion stone sculpture in the round, not only in soft stone but also in the hard or ornamental stones highly prized for their ability to receive and retain a high polish. Only a little, and that usually on a small scale, has survived from before the Third Dynasty; from then onwards the increasing adoption of stone for the construction of royal and private tombs, of mortuary and later cult temples, is reflected in the number of surviving stone statues which formed part of their embellishment. In the Old Kingdom the mortuary and valley temples attached to the pyramids were adorned with numerous statues of gods and of the king for whom each complex was intended. These representations of the kings, which by the Fifth Dynasty had already reached the proportions of the monumental and colossal, are generally held to be among the finest achievements of Egyptian art.

In Old Kingdom statuary the king was invariably represented standing with the left foot advanced or seated on a cubic block representing throne or chair. The statues were frontally posed and there is no suggestion of movement or action. Statues were provided with a back pillar reaching from the base up to the level of the shoulder, neck or head. It is uncertain whether this pillar, which is a constant element in Egyptian statues, was deliberately incorporated into work for technical reasons—as 70 Sesostris III

a safeguard against the splintering of the stone—or whether it had some symbolic purpose. The body of the figure was summarily executed, according to a fixed canon of proportion similar to that used in relief and in painting. The effect was to emphasize the head and it was to the modelling of this part of the statue that the greatest skill and art were devoted. The features were idealized to convey the essential god-head of the king. Not until the Middle Kingdom, with the statues of Sesostris III (684–686; fig. 70), was there a suggestion in the lines of the features and in the heavy frowning expression of the human qualities of the king.

Royal statuary of the New Kingdom, usually of monumental proportions in hard stone from the time of Amenophis III, displays a conventional idealized look without conveying the same sense of divinity as the best of the Old Kingdom royal sculpture. The style is well represented in the collection with the statues and heads of Amenophis III which have come from his mortuary temple, now destroyed, behind the Colossi of Memnon in Western Thebes. The two seated statues in black granite at the southern end of the Egyptian Sculpture Gallery (4; fig. 71, and 5) are typical of figures found in New Kingdom temples. The large limestone head (3) is noteworthy for the scale and care of its construction. The dramatic change which marks Amarna sculpture is foreshadowed by the unusual treatment of the same king in the nearby statues (6; fig. 72, and 7). The Nineteenth Dynasty is represented by a number of statues of Ramesses II, the largest of which (19; Plate 7), so typical of the monumental scale of the work of the reign, has been made from a piece of granite containing a geological flaw; the present sharp contrast between the upper and lower part of the head may originally have been concealed by painting. On a different scale is the attractive figure of the king as a young man (67).

In the fashioning of a statue, the design was first marked out in red ochre on a block roughly of the size and shape required. The next stage of the work was the rough blocking out of the stone without distinguishing face, arms, or legs. This process and the modelling of the features were carried out with the use of guide lines in subsequent stages. The working of soft stone was comparatively easy with the available copper (and later bronze) chisels; in the case of hard stone the modelling was done by pounding away with a ball of dolerite, and by rubbing with stones of various sizes held in the hand with the aid of an abrasive powder (probably quartz sand). Sawing, using at first only copper blades fixed in a wooden handle, made use of an abrasive. The stone was drilled and bored in the method long employed in the working of stone vessels (p. 189).

71 Amenophis III

72 Amenophis III (*inset*)

The final stages of the work, done by eye alone, consisted of modelling the features with patient light bruising and burnishing. In the completed statue all traces of the working were removed by the final polishing. The inscription would be added, and even in the case of statues with a high and pleasing polish, paint would be applied in flat washes of colour in order to make the statue as lifelike a replica of the owner as possible.

The earliest private sculpture in this Museum goes back to the Third Dynasty, the style and skill of which are illustrated by the red granite seated figure of the ship-builder Bedjmes, depicted

73 Bedjmes, a ship-builder

74 Katep and
Hetepheres

holding an adze over his shoulder (171; fig. 73). Private statuary
was intended for the tomb and its main development follows
closely the conventions set by royal sculpture. It was static,
frontally posed, the features idealized without, however, carrying
the authority of the divine kingship. Its quality depends largely
upon the care with which the details have been indicated and
the time which has been spent in the process of rubbing.

Common in the mastabas of the Fourth Dynasty is the painted
limestone statue of a man and his wife, represented in the
collection by the statue of Katep and Hetepheres (1181; fig. 74).

76 Meri, a steward

75 Nenkheftka
(*opposite*)

The large painted limestone statue of Nenkheftka (1239; fig. 75) is typical of the succeeding dynasty. The two seated statues of the steward Meri of the Eleventh Dynasty (37895 and 37896; fig. 76) indicate by the quality of their work the return to the strong centralized government and politically stable conditions after the First Intermediate Period. In the Twelfth Dynasty it was possible apparently for private persons to place statues of themselves in temples; new forms were introduced which reduced the time spent over the modelling of the body, like the standing or seated figures wearing long tight-fitting cloaks reaching from the neck to the ankles; block statues were also introduced in which the person is represented squatting, only the head, feet and arms protruding from the entire block. One of the earliest of this style is the statue of Sihathor, treasurer of the king in the reign of Ammenemes II, which still rests in its original niche

(569, 570; fig. 77). The type continued to the end of the Ptolemaic Period.

77 Stela and block statue of Sihathor

The seated limestone statuette of Tetisheri, grandmother of Amosis the founder of the Eighteenth Dynasty, one of a pair dedicated by a member of her household at Thebes, marks the return of good workmanship after the Second Intermediate Period (22558). The complete mastery of technique in the working of hard stones is exemplified in the statues of high officials of the Eighteenth Dynasty. Many of these statues are con-

78 Statue of a nobleman and his wife

ventional in form, but some, like the striking figure of Senenmut, holding the princess Neferure (174; fig. 15), are very imaginative in conception. During the New Kingdom, beginning just before the Amarna Period, great attention was paid to the elaborate representation of daily costume and wigs. This development is well exemplified in the collection by a statue of an unknown man and his wife (36; fig. 78). Considerable art was required to render these repetitive details without giving the impression of complete lifelessness.

The last period of great sculpture begins with the Twenty-fifth Dynasty, when in addition to close copying of Old and Middle Kingdom examples, a class of more realistic, more mature likenesses is met with, of which the crystalline limestone head of an old man (37883; fig. 79) is an outstanding example. In this period there is a noticeable increase in the use of the harder stones, particularly schist and basalt, and until the end of the Ptolemaic Period they continue to be carved by the Egyptian sculptors with their traditional skill.

79 Head of an old man

Painting

The earliest form of painting in Egypt is the decoration on pottery from the periods Naqada I and Naqada II (pp. 208 ff.; fig. 81). In the Dynastic Period paint was freely used on papyrus, plaster, pottery, stone, and wood. It is perhaps surprising that little use was made of linen as a painting ground; it is not until the Roman Period that linen shrouds were painted with representations of the deceased and with scenes and objects of significance in the funerary ritual. Among the rare exceptions are the small cloths of linen, dating from the New Kingdom, painted with scenes of funerary significance, originally placed over the breasts of wooden anthropomorphic coffins at Thebes (43215–16).

The pigments used in the preparation of paint were either naturally occurring minerals or artificially prepared mineral substances; carbon in the form of soot, lamp-black, or powdered charcoal was used for black; azurite and, from the Middle Kingdom, a frit (a crystalline compound of silica, copper, and calcium) for blue; powdered malachite (a copper ore) for green; oxide of iron for pink; red ochre, and, from the Roman Period, red lead for red, and yellow ochre for yellow. The pigment was finely ground on stone palettes and mixed with water. Glue, gum, or egg was added as an adhesive.

The paint was applied by means of brushes of many different kinds. The largest were generally made of sticks of fibrous wood, one end of which had been soaked in water and frayed out, and were used when large surfaces were to be covered. Details, out-lines, and work of a delicate kind were executed with finer brushes made of a single stem of rush with a frayed end, and identical with the type of brush used by the scribe (pp. 94 f.).

Painted scenes are found in tombs in place of carved relief, at first probably for reasons of economy. At Thebes the quality of the limestone of the necropolis area is poor and for that reason, with some notable exceptions, the majority of the tombs contain painted scenes of the type illustrated by the fragments in the Third Egyptian Room. A smooth ground for painting was prepared by covering the rough-dressed walls of the corridors and chambers of the tombs with a layer of mud plaster to fill up the irregularities of the surface. Over this a coat of lime plaster was superimposed. The surface was then divided into squares by means of strings dipped in red ochre paint, as in the case of the preparation of a wall for relief (p. 193). The design was roughly sketched out over this grid. The same conventions in delineating the human figure were observed; in the repre-sentation of a banquet scene from a Theban tomb (37984, Plate 9) the drawing of two of the woman-musicians full-faced and the bodies of the dancers in profile is exceptional. The method of rendering landscape, without perspective, giving as it were a bird's eye-view, is admirably illustrated by the repre-sentation of an ornamental fish-pond in the garden of the scribe Nebamun, around which a variety of trees has been planted (37983). Colour was applied flatly but some attempt was made from the Eighteenth Dynasty to render shading. It appears on the soles of the feet and on the toes of the women musicians in 37984. The long flowing garments are shown as transparent, the limbs first being painted in red or yellow and a thin streaky wash of white applied over them. Considerable skill with the brush is shown in the rendering of detail, particularly in the case of birds and animals, as in the body of the hare (37980), the fur of a cat, and details of butterflies and birds (37977), or in the markings of the geese (37978). By artistic convention the skin of men is represented as red-brown, while that of women is generally yellow. For the most part colour is rendered naturalistically, particularly in the cases of animals, birds, fish, and plants.

When the painting was completed, the paint was usually protected by a thin layer of varnish, originally colourless, the exact composition of which is uncertain.

Brickmaking

Though stone was employed from the Early Dynastic Period for funerary monuments of both royal and private persons and later also for the cult-temples or 'houses of the gods', the palaces of kings and houses of ordinary people were built of sun-dried Nile mud-brick. Brickmaking required less skilled craftsmen than the quarrying of stone: the bricks were easier to transport and handle in bulk than stone and the raw material lay plentifully at hand. Practical experience no doubt proved the suitability of such buildings as living quarters. Brick provided houses of sufficient durability, dramatic and sudden storms, which might leave a trail of damage, being very infrequent. Such buildings could also be easily adapted, enlarged or divided up to suit the changing needs of families.

The method of brick-making is illustrated by a wooden tomb model of Middle Kingdom date from Beni Hasan (63837; fig. 80). The mud used was the alluvial deposits of the Nile after the inundation. When a deposit of the right consistency had been selected near the building site, the mud would be carried in buckets or jars to the brickyard. Here it would be mixed with water, drawn from a convenient pool, the work being done with the foot or with the hoe. It was the usual practice to knead in at the same time some chopped straw or other vegetable matter. This improved the binding quality of the mud and also at the same time by chemical action increased the strength and plasticity of the mud.

The mud was then ready for shaping into bricks: it was carried in baskets or jars to the brickmaker who—as the Egyptians termed it—struck the bricks. He used a hollow wooden rectangular mould, the exact size of the intended brick, and held it by its handle flat on the level area of ground chosen to mould the bricks. After sprinkling the bottom and sides with a little chopped straw, he filled the mould with handfuls of the treated mud, pressing it down firmly. When the mould was full, it was

80 Wooden model of
brickmakers

removed, leaving behind the moist brick; another would be struck by its side until the whole area was covered with a regular series of bricks. Here they would be left for two or three days until the fierce heat of the sun had thoroughly dried them out. They would then be carried in slings from a yoke (5413, from Thebes, New Kingdom, 35928–29) which was normally balanced on one shoulder only. Bricks might be stamped while still moist with a wooden die inscribed usually with the name of a king (6012, Tuthmosis III; 6016, Amenophis III) but also with the name of the building for which they were to be used. Bricks stamped with the names of private persons (13176, of the Steward of Amun, Djehutymes) fall into a different category, since they were used for decorative purposes in private tombs.

Although the technique of preparing baked bricks was known from early times, the Egyptians only employed such bricks in places where they had a particular advantage, such as in floors or underground structures exposed to damp. The earliest known use of baked brick in this way dates to the Middle Kingdom (*c*. 1900 BC) and further instances occur in later periods. Baked bricks were more generally used in the Roman Period.

The actual size of bricks varies according to their use and their date. The bricks of the Early Dynastic Period are all small; then comes an increase in size until the Middle Kingdom, followed by a fluctuation until the Twenty-sixth Dynasty, after which there is a decrease until modern times. From the Old Kingdom to the Ptolemaic Period, two distinct groups of bricks were in use: a small type suitable for house building or for private tombs, commonly measuring 30 × 15 × 8 cm, and a larger type used for official buildings, such as temples and palaces, measuring from 35 to 45 cm in length.

Ceramic

The river clay was also the material for the manufacture of a wide range of domestic implements, the most common of which were household pots. The earliest pots date back to the Badarian Period (p. 39): they are of simple shape, mostly in the form of open bowls without true brims or handles. The walls of the pots are thin; the regularity and evenness of the shape are noteworthy, the more so since they were built up by hand without the use of a wheel. Before firing the pots were polished with a quartz pebble to give the characteristic burnished red look. For variety, pots were blackened around the rim—or completely —probably simply by placing them in the smoke of a charcoal fire. Also characteristic of the period is a ripple-line decoration produced by the running of a comb-like instrument over the wet clay (59667, from El-Badari).

The pottery of the succeeding predynastic cultures is essentially the same ware, though in both shape and size there is considerable development. Brims are found and two, sometimes three, lug-handles for suspending the vessel. The most noticeable innovation is the introduction of incised, painted, and occasionally modelled decoration. In the Amratian Period (Naqada I) incised representations of animals are found, like the hippopotamus (30965), the lion (49019), and the snake (30970). Five clay hippopotami decorate the rim of a shallow bowl from Matmar (63408). A lizard crawling upwards is modelled on the outside of another black and red pot of unknown provenance (53885).

The earliest painted designs are geometric patterns in white or cream coloured paint on the polished red clay. Pictorial scenes with animals, plants, or figure subjects are less common. The outline is usually filled in with cross-hatching. The ability of the Egyptian draughtsman to capture with an economy of line the

1 Painted pottery vessel

essential outline of an animal is well shown in the figure of a hippopotamus drawn in white on a red pot (53882).

In the Gerzean Period (Naqada II) the typical decoration is dark red or purple on buff-colour or pinkish-red, the colour of the pot being due to the use of clay deposits in the wadis of the eastern desert around Qena, still the centre of a thriving pottery industry. Geometrical designs continue to predominate but they are more varied and the outline patterns are blocked in. Particularly characteristic are bulbous pots, often standing over 60 cms high, with pictorial representations in a haphazard arrangement, the interpretation of which is, and is likely to remain, a matter of some uncertainty (fig. 81). They commonly show a semicircular design with a fringe usually thought to be ships with a bank of oars: at the prow there is often a plant design variously identified as the *aloe* or the Abyssinian banana tree. The boat is provided with a central cabin or shrine equipped with a standard bearing a design which sometimes, but not invariably, can be identified with the later nome-standards. By the side of the cabin there is often a female figure in a characteristic pose with both arms above her head. Wavy lines represent water and long-legged birds appear, of the type called *niw* in later Egyptian

texts and usually identified with the flamingo or ostrich. Other
pots of this period show spiral decoration perhaps in imitation
of stoneware (30908). A more unusual scene is shown on a
terracotta rectangular open box from El-Amra (32639; fig. 82).
On the long sides are representations of long-horned deer,
horizontal lines, and S-shaped patterns. On the short sides there
are, at one end, the usual type of boat, at the other, four fish
nibbling at a ball of food.

82 Painted pottery box

With the end of the Predynastic Period, the native decorated
ware of Egypt disappears: even the black-on-red pots which had
persisted throughout the predynastic cultures seem no longer to
have been made in Egypt proper, though their use continued in
Nubia and their type reappears in the burials of Nubians in
Egypt in the Second Intermediate Period (pan-graves). Large
numbers of foreign painted pots have been found in Egypt,
reflecting the busy flow of trade in the third and second millennia
BC. They are found from the end of the Predynastic Period,
throughout the Old and Middle Kingdoms with the apparent
exception of the Second and Third Dynasties. Foreign models also
supplied the prototypes for the more elaborate forms, like the
spouted ewer from El-Badari (58032, Fourth Dynasty). During
the Twelfth Dynasty and Second Intermediate Period are found
pots and sherds of Minoan, Cypriot, and Syrian origin; among
the pots more widely distributed in Egypt and Nubia are the
small jugs, ordinarily black, with incised designs filled in with
white pigment ('Tell el-Yahudiya' ware).

The native pottery of the dynastic period is utilitarian. The more common shapes are bulbous; true brims, handles, and spouts are lacking (except in imported ware) until the end of the Eighteenth Dynasty. The base of the pot might be flat, or pointed to stand upright in the ground, or rounded to be placed on a light wooden stand (2470, 2471, New Kingdom, c. 1400 BC) or round clay pottery rings. Occasionally ink hieratic inscriptions on the pots give an indication of the use to which they were put. The larger storage jars with pointed bases were for wine or beer; the small bulbous types were used for grain, fruits of various kinds, for meat, oil, honey, and cooking fat. Open-bowl types were probably mainly cooking vessels or crucibles: flat saucer-like types were used for serving food.

It is not until the middle of the Eighteenth Dynasty that the native ware of Egypt is again painted. The most striking examples come from El-Amarna. The jars are painted in light blue on a buff-coloured background with details picked out in red and black. The designs are most commonly floral patterns of petals and leaves in horizontal bands imitating the garlands shown in the painted tomb scenes to have decorated vessels at banquets (37984, 37985, New Kingdom from Thebes, c. 1400 BC). Two large vases with splayed bases and pottery caps of this type (59774–5) have hieratic inscriptions in ink describing the contents as wine from a Delta vineyard. Relief also reappears, like Hathor-heads (58460).

With the end of the Eighteenth Dynasty the native pottery types of Egypt revert to the drab and utilitarian. Not until Roman times did decorated pottery reappear; particularly noteworthy are the thin open beakers from Meroitic cemeteries, with painted designs of birds, animals, flowers, etc. (fig. 99), derived from pharaonic and Hellenistic art. The type is well represented in the collection from finds made at Faras in Lower Nubia. The tradition of painted ware continues into the confused period following the collapse of the Meroitic Kingdom, among the people known as the X-group, either the Blemmyes or the Nobatai of classical texts; typical examples of this last manifestation of the dynastic art may be seen in the material from Qasr Ibrim.

Terracotta

Although clay was widely employed for bricks, pottery and household utensils, there was relatively little use of the material for figurines. From the Predynastic Period come a number of crude steatopygous female figurines, with beak-like faces, prominent breasts, and thick legs usually in a kneeling position with arms raised. A more unusual figure is that of a woman from El-Badari (59679; fig. 8), more naturally modelled, in a standing pose with arms crossed: and at El-Amra there was found among the grave equipment an unusual model of four oxen (35506). After the Predynastic Period it is probably true to say that the Egyptians showed little predilection for the use of clay for plastic forms; the most common types, apart from figures of animals in the Old and Middle Kingdoms, are crude female figures of bound figures of captives (56912–13), the most likely purpose of which was for use in magical practices designed to secure fertility, safe child delivery, and power over personal enemies or malignant forces. An exception to the general rule is the series of anthropomorphic pots in burnished red clay, often in the form of a woman with a child on her back (24652, 54694). They date from the second half of the Eighteenth Dynasty.

It is not until the Late Period that terracotta becomes typical, as a result of the increasing influence of the Greek and later Hellenistic world upon the daily life of Egypt. A large number of terracotta heads of persons of many different races, dating perhaps from the seventh century BC, has been recovered from Memphis, and in the Ptolemaic and Roman Periods the use of terracotta becomes widespread.

The majority of figurines, which served as votive offerings or household images, are representations of healing and saviour gods. From the Roman Period also dates the widespread use of clay lamps. Some, like a lamp with two wickholders on a stand in the form of the god Bes from the Faiyum (15485), have some pretence to individuality, but the majority belong to the familiar types current throughout the Mediterranean world. The usual shape of the lamp is lentoid made in two pieces from moulds and frequently stamped on the base with the potter's mark, a letter, or simple geometric design. They are provided with a central opening for filling with oil and a nozzle with a hole for a wick of twisted flax or papyrus. A common type has modelled on its upper surface a representation of a frog, the body sometimes pricked with a stylus (38453). They belong perhaps for the most part to the third and fourth centuries AD. More uncommon are lamps in the form of a human face with oil-hole at the top of the forehead and burner at the base of the neck (15478), or a lamp with loop handle decorated with a frog and mythological animals (20785). Use of clay lamps continued late into the Coptic Period.

Faience and glazed stones

Faience, or more properly glazed composition, is more typical of dynastic Egypt for plastic art than terracotta. It appears as early as the Predynastic Period. Glazed objects from this early time are mostly beads; as well as the composition material, solid quartz or steatite is used as a core. Glazed solid quartz was in use until the end of the Middle Kingdom, mostly for beads, small amulets, and pendants, only a few larger objects being known. The hardness of quartz and the difficulty of shaping it probably prevented its greater employment; steatite, being a soft stone, was particularly suitable for carving into small objects like amulets and small figures of gods, and it proved an ideal base for glazing. It does not disintegrate under heat. Glazed steatite objects are found throughout the Dynastic Period and it is by far the most common material for scarabs.

Faience consists of a core made of small grains of quartz sand or quartz pebbles or rock crystal ground into a fine powder. In this dry form the body material was light and friable but had no coherence and it is uncertain by what means it was bound together for shaping. Of the suggestions which have been made, the most likely is the small addition of a weak solution of natron or salt which when heated would combine chemically with the quartz to produce a coherent but friable mass, which could be worked with the fingers. For small objects the material was shaped in open red pottery moulds, large numbers of which have been discovered from the New Kingdom. The popularity of this composition material for small objects of personal ornament (beads, pendants, rings), for funerary equipment (amulets, *shabti*-figures, pectorals), or house decoration (tiles, inlays of floral patterns) was due to the ability to mass-produce them in moulds from cheap materials.

The normal glaze used by the Ancient Egyptians is similar in composition to ancient glass and was made by heating together sand (silica with lime impurities) and natron or plant ash; it is therefore an alkali glaze and would not adhere to ordinary pottery. The introduction of a lead compound into glaze seems to occur first in the Late Dynastic Period. It did not replace the alkali glazes and was applied to the normal composition core. The glazing of pottery, made possible by the lead glazes, is not found before Roman times.

The precise method of glazing is uncertain, but the probability is that the glaze was applied as a viscous fluid coating the object. Glaze and body material were then fused together by heating, giving the manufactured object its strength and coherence.

The most common colour of the glaze is blue, green, or greenish-blue. The colour is due to the addition of a copper compound. A particularly vivid blue is characteristic of the New Kingdom, typical examples of which are a plaque with a figure of the royal scribe and treasurer, Amenemope, before Osiris (6133) and a bowl with a design of lotus and papyrus (4790; fig. 83); it is the common colour of the *shabti*-figures of

the Twentieth and Twenty-first Dynasties (p. 169). From about
the middle of the Eighteenth Dynasty white, yellow, and red
become common; polychrome faience work seems to have
reached its highest stage of development and is well exemplified
in objects from El-Amarna. A fine example of the variety of
colours of faience at this time is the floral collar with inlaid
lotus-flower terminals (59334). The component elements are
yellow mandrake fruits, green palm leaves, and lotus petals,
white with purple tips, separated by small coloured disks.
Among the more attractive combinations of colours is purple
on a white background found on a type of *shabti*-figure (8964,
34013) and on a kohl-pot inscribed with the cartouche of
Tutankhamun and his queen Ankhesenamun (2573). An

83 Blue faience bowl

example of faience work, unusual for its design, execution, and colouring, which shows the art of the New Kingdom at its best, is a small vessel for perfume found at Sesebi, in Upper Nubia, glazed white with an applied decoration in blue and black (64041; fig. 84); around the shoulder runs a frieze of lotus petals alternately indicated in blue and black. Below each of the two handles hangs a blue lotus flower flanked by two buds. Around the base is a design of an open lotus flower, its petals blue and black. Fine work in faience continues in the Ramesside Period, as is shown by the faience bowl (4796) inscribed with the name and titles of Ramesses II.

Characteristic of the Thirtieth Dynasty is the combination of dark blue on light blue; it is found on *shabti*-figures (35225) and on small objects of daily use like the dish with three compartments for ointment, with its lid, in the shape of a lotus capital (63980).

These small objects of daily use in faience demonstrate more clearly than any other class of antiquities from Egypt the taste and artistic genius of its ancient people. Inspired largely in their choice of decoration by the natural flora and fauna of the Nile Valley, and brilliantly coloured in monochrome or polychrome as a result of the alkaline glaze, they make an immediate appeal to the modern eye.

The achievements of the faience workers are best exemplified in the glazed composition tiles and inlays which decorated houses or palaces and in the drinking cups modelled in low relief, in imitation of engraved metal work. The earliest examples of tiles date back to the Early Dynastic Period; large numbers of them, measuring about 6×4 cms, and blue or green in colour, were used in the underground passages of the Step Pyramid of Djoser (Third Dynasty) to form a panelling imitating hangings of reed mat (2438–40). From houses and palaces of El-Amarna come numerous polychrome tiles with floral patterns, the more common being small plaques of white chrysanthemums with yellow centres. Similar tiles are found in Ramesside palaces at Qantir and Tell el-Yahudiya in the Delta and at Medinet Habu at Thebes. Particularly remarkable for the skill with which the different coloured glazes were fused to the composition core are tiles used to decorate the throne-dais from these palaces bearing representations of foreigners with the detail of their gaily patterned dress carefully executed. The larger tiles seem to have been modelled by hand, the composition material being made into a coarse paste, moulded, and dried by exposure to heat before the glazes were applied.

Faience cups become common from the Eighteenth Dynasty. The usual form which the cup takes is a lotus flower on a thin

84 Faience vessel

stem (24680, 26226, 26227) or a pomegranate fruit (21918, 59398). From the later Dynastic Period comes a series of vessels elaborately modelled in low relief: 65553 is a fragment from the base of a dish with a head of Bes on one side, and on the other a frieze of desert animals, a gazelle, an antelope, a lioness, an ostrich, an ibex, a camel, and another antelope. Animals, birds, and fishes occur on the interior of another dish (57385). The tradition continued into the Roman Period though the fine thin walls of the dynastic work and thin evenly applied glaze are replaced by a coarser ware and glassier glaze. No. 62639, with its figures of birds, animals, baskets of fruit, and petals, probably carved, is an example of Roman work at its best. Other techniques of decoration popular in the Roman Period are incised patterns on the core material before glazing (29352) or the application of strips of the body material of lighter colour to the vase to suggest a pattern of laurel leaves (58430).

Glass

Though the ancient glaze is itself glass, and glass may be said therefore to have been known to the Egyptians at an early date, it was not until the Eighteenth Dynasty that the material was used independently, with the sporadic exception of some small beads and amulets. The technique which was applied to the making of glass vessels was a natural development of the technique of glazing, the composition core being replaced by one of sandy clay which was removed on the completion of the manufacture. In view, however, of the date of its first appearance in Egypt, some hundreds of years after the production of faience vessels and figures, it is possible that the introduction of the manufacture of glass vessels in Egypt was a consequence of the contact with Syrian cities following the military conquests of the early Eighteenth Dynasty.

The ancient glass was formed by strongly heating quartz sand and natron in clay crucibles with a small admixture of colouring material, normally a copper compound, perhaps malachite to produce both green and blue glass, though an analysis shows also the use of cobalt which would have been imported. Heating would be continued until the ingredients fused into a molten mass. The exact point at which to stop the heating was probably known by experience, but tongs may have been used to remove small quantities for testing. As the mass cooled, it might be poured into moulds, rolled out into thin rods or canes about 3 mm in diameter, or the crucible broken away and the mass left to be used as required. Examples of the raw glass, recovered from glass factories, may be seen exhibited in the Sixth Egyptian Room.

In the manufacture of a glass vessel, the first stage was to fashion on the end of a metal rod a core of sandy clay to the shape of the interior of the intended vessel. The core was then dipped in a crucible of molten glass and perhaps spun a few times, acquiring thereby a coat of irregular thickness with spherical air bubbles. While the glass was still hot, the glass-maker might add with a pair of tongs a mass of molten glass and shape it into a splayed foot, pinch out the lip, and add a bent glass rod for a handle. When the vessel had cooled, the outer surface might be polished. The core was then scraped out.

The earliest dated glass vessels of this type bear the cartouche of Tuthmosis III; they are represented in the collection by a small vessel, blue in imitation of turquoise, on which the pre-nomen and floral pattern have been painted (47620, Plate 16). A dark blue, imitating lapis lazuli, is common, and yellow imitating gold, white imitating silver. Transparent glass is not found.

Glass of different colours was also partially fused together to produce a conglomerate, as in the dish 27727, but the most striking decoration is found in vases of polychrome ware. The sandy core was first dipped in a molten glass of dark colour, then, while the mass was still hot and the coating semi-viscous, thin rods of manufactured glass of different colours were wound around the object. The cold rods softened on contact with the still hot mass of the base and fused into the surface in horizontal bands of colour. By drawing a sharp metal instrument upwards and downwards over the surface, the glass-worker was able to tease the bands into a series of loops or chevrons. The remarkable skill with which this technique could be applied is illustrated by the reassembled polychrome vessel in the shape of a fish, from El-Amarna (55193).

The limitations of the technique, a certain intractability in the material, and the brittleness of the finished product prevented the same general range of employment of glass as of faience. For the most part objects made of glass are seldom more than 10 or 15 cms in height. It was used chiefly for the manufacture of eye-paint pots in the shape of a palm-column (2589, 64334, 64335) or perfume jars with lids (24391). An unusual example of a cosmetic container in glass is the dish in the form of a shell (65774). Glass was often used for inlay, like the profile faces of royal persons (16375, 54264, 64121). Glass figurines are rare; the damaged, but finely modelled, head of a king from a sphinx (16374) was first modelled and cast solid; the details of the head-dress and face were incised after moulding.

Glass, for reasons perhaps not merely connected with taste, does not seem to have been made in Egypt in the Late Dynastic Period. No glass, for instance, was found in the royal tombs of the

Twenty-first and Twenty-second Dynasties at Tanis. It does not reappear until the Ptolemaic Period. A firmly dated Ptolemaic example is a plaque of opaque glass, originally red in colour, but now mostly green, which formed part of a foundation deposit, inscribed in black on one side with the names of Ptolemy IV Philopator (221–205 BC) and his queen in Greek; on the other side the same text is repeated in the hieroglyphic script (65844).

Towards the end of the Ptolemaic Period, sometime in the first century BC, the technique of blowing glass was developed, and during the Roman Period Egypt was, with Syria, one of the main centres of glass-working. By the end of the third century AD, to judge from the number of fragments of glass vessels found at town sites, glass was generally used to provide rich and poor alike with vessels for the table or containers for a woman's toilet preparations. Opaque glass was still common in the Roman Period, like the cobalt blue cup 64188, but the majority of vessels were of clear glass, the shapes for the most part following the models of the potters. The ribbed examples 59835 and 64189 may have been the result of blowing glass into moulds. The clear glass of the ancient period has acquired in the course of time an iridescent colour, due to the flaking of the glass into layers which refract the light like a prism (59833, 59838).

Metal-working

Associated with the ancient fundamental rocks of the Eastern Desert are deposits of gold, silver, copper, lead, iron, and zinc. Of these neither zinc nor iron was mined in pharaonic Egypt. Zinc and brass (an alloy of copper and zinc) were unknown in the ancient world before the classical period. Iron objects found in archaeological excavations are few in number from dynastic Egypt, and analysis has shown that the earliest examples are of meteoric origin. In this connexion it should be noted that the piece of iron found by J. R. Hill (2433) in the course of excavations conducted by Colonel Vyse at the Great Pyramid in 1837 is almost certainly intrusive, in spite of the precise statement of the finder regarding the circumstances of the discovery. The scarcity of iron may be judged from the paucity and size of the iron objects found in the tomb of Tutankhamun in comparison with the number and weight of gold objects. Though there is an increase in the use of iron in Egypt from the Twenty-sixth Dynasty onwards, it is not until the Ptolemaic Period that iron tools are at all usual; in the Roman Period household implements of iron, like knives and flesh hooks, become common.

Lead, gold, silver, and copper were all known to the Egyptians from predynastic times. The process of extracting lead by roasting the ores was a simple one and was early mastered. Ores are reported from a number of areas, mostly near the Red Sea coast. The chief ore found in Egypt is galena, the sulphide of lead, which was used in the manufacture of *kohl*, the ancient eye-paint, from predynastic times. The raw material was finely ground on palettes which were among the most common items of grave equipment in the predynastic tombs. The palettes of the Badarian Period were flat and rectangular in shape with a notch in the side; in the subsequent predynastic cultures they were frequently made of green schist and shaped in the likeness of birds, animals, and fish. They reached the height of their development with the series of large ceremonial palettes from royal tombs finely carved on both sides with scenes commemorating political or religious events.

We hear almost nothing in Egyptian records of mining activities for lead. It was used in the main for small objects of daily use, or ornaments like sinkers for fishing nets, rings, etc. A siphon, strainer, and small cup, found together at El-Amarna, are of lead (55147-9). Like all metal in Egypt it could be used as a medium of exchange and valuation; from a problem in the Rhind Mathematical Papyrus (*c.* 1650 BC, p. 122) we learn that it had half the value of silver and a quarter that of gold.

The galena deposits of Egypt, unlike those at Laurion worked by the ancient Athenians, are not rich in silver content. Until the Middle Kingdom silver was of more value than gold, and analysis of objects of the Old and New Kingdoms shows that the ancient silver of Egypt is a natural alloy of gold with silver in a sufficiently high percentage to impart a white colour. The depreciation in the value of silver in relation to gold was no doubt due to its importation during the Middle and New Kingdoms from Asiatic sources by way of both trade and tribute. Imports must have been on a considerable scale, for in spite of the quantity of gold which came to Egypt from Nubia in the New Kingdom the ratio of gold to silver was constant at 2:1.

The gold-bearing region of the Eastern Desert extends, broadly speaking, from a short distance to the north of the modern road from Qena to Quseir, southwards into the modern Sudan. The main areas of exploitation are to be found in three concentrations which have their natural outlet on to the Nile Valley at Qena or Qift, and at El-Kab or Edfu, and at the mouth of the Wadi Allaqi, where in the Middle Kingdom the Egyptians built the forts of Kuban and Ikkur.

Gold occurs both in the alluvium of the wadi-beds and in the veins or dikes of white quartz which are present in the igneous rocks of the great central range of hills between the Nile and the Red Sea, running parallel to the river. Recovery of the gold from the alluvium was a simple matter, given a body of unskilled labour and water with which to wash the auriferous gravel. By running water down a sloping surface over the gravel, the lighter material was carried off and the heavier gold was left behind as fine particles or occasionally as small nuggets. In the case of the quartz veins, exploitation necessitated considerable organization, involving the use of skilled miners or quarrymen, to extract the rock and a large body of labour to crush the matrix with heavy stone mortars (rotary grinders were not known in ancient Egypt). The gold was then extracted by washing the finely ground quartz in the same way as the alluvial deposits.

The thoroughness with which the ancients prospected for gold, removing the alluvial gravel and following the gold-bearing quartz veins, has often been remarked upon. There are no centres of modern exploitation which do not have some indication of ancient working: deep galleries, open cuts, numerous stone ore-crushers, troughs, washing tables, and stone huts. It is, however, not always possible to say whether these workings are of pharaonic, Ptolemaic, Roman, or Moslem date.

The Egyptians themselves left few written records which bear directly upon the nature of their expeditions or upon the organization of the mines. There is nothing at the ancient sites in the nature of the official commemorative stelae and rock tablets which are found at the quarries of ornamental stone. The absence of official inscriptions may in part be explained by the nature of the rock—usually granite—in which the quartz veins occur; it does not lend itself to carving. The passage of workmen to and fro from the sites is attested by occasional *graffiti* in the sandstone area. Certainly at some periods there seem to have been permanent settlements in the desert, banishment to which was one of the punishments inflicted upon criminals by the courts, as we learn from the accounts of the investigations into the activities of the tomb robbers in the Twenty-first Dynasty (pp. 120 f.). The gold itself reached Egypt either in the form of dust tied in linen bags, or small fragments of metal fused into small ingots or rings (see the painted scene of Nubians bringing gold tribute from a Theban tomb, about 1400 BC, no. 921).

Copper does not occur in its metallic state in Egypt; it was extracted from ores as early as the Badarian Period, being used for small implements like needles and borers. A number of areas show traces of ancient mining and smelting both in the Eastern Desert and also in Sinai, at the Wadi Maghara and Serabit el-Khadim. The ore was smelted close to the site at which it was mined or it was dragged on sledges to the nearest point at which sufficient supplies of fuel could be obtained. The crushed ore was mixed with charcoal on the ground or in a hollow pit; practical experience no doubt taught the value of siting the fire in the best position to take full advantage of air currents. Representations of metal-working in scenes from the tombs show the metal being placed in an open clay crucible on a charcoal fire the temperature of which was raised by using blow-pipes. Some time, early in the New Kingdom, a form of bellows was introduced; a pair of inflated skins was worked by foot and a current of air directed on the embers by means of clay nozzles. Primitive though the method was, it was sufficient to obtain the required temperatures for casting metal, but the amount of ore normally worked upon at any one time must have been small and the metal produced contained considerable impurities, the heating and reheating of it being the only method of refining.

The addition of a small proportion of tin to copper produces bronze, and results in a lower melting-point, an increased hardness, and a greater ease in casting. The date of the introduction of bronze into Egypt is uncertain. The alloy does not seem, on present evidence, to have been known in Egypt before the Middle Kingdom, but from that time onwards it was regularly used for tools and weapons until it was replaced by iron. Tin does not occur in Egypt and it is not known whether the bronze used was originally all imported in a manufactured state or whether the alloying was done in Egyptian workshops. It may perhaps be significant that among the many names known in the hieroglyphic texts for minerals, there is none which can be certainly identified as the word for tin. Before the introduction of tin, Egyptian copper was hardened by the addition of arsenic. It is not yet known how or whence the arsenic was obtained, though a foreign source seems likely. Arsenical copper was employed from the Early Dynastic Period right up to and including the Middle Kingdom, after which it was largely supplanted by bronze.

In the workshop the crude metal was weighed before issue to the metal-worker. Scenes of metal-working regularly include a representation of the weighing of metal in a balance, which is otherwise depicted only in vignettes of the weighing of the heart in the judgement scene from the *Book of the Dead* (Plate 13). The Egyptian balance in its simplest form consisted of a wooden beam suspended from its centre point by a cord held in the hand and drilled at the ends to take a single cord and hook for pans, in one of which the weights were placed and in the other the metal. From at least the Fifth Dynasty the beam was supported by an upright standard. A plummet line was hung parallel to the upright so that the weigher could check the accuracy of the balance by comparing the plummet with a rectangular board attached at right angles to the balance arm. In the course of time improvements in design were made ensuring greater precision, though the basic principle of weighing remained unaltered throughout the Dynastic Period. From the Middle Kingdom the pans were suspended by four cords (38241, bronze pan, Ptolemaic Period; 57369, pair of silver pans, Ptolemaic Period, with a hieroglyphic inscription referring to the goddess Hathor, from a balance used perhaps in the rites of her temple at Dendera). By the New Kingdom two further refinements increased the accuracy of the balance. The rectangular board was replaced by a pointed metal tongue. Tubular beams, terminated with flanges in lotus or papyrus form, were introduced so that the strings of the pans came out together from inside the beam and diverged from the lowest point of the edge of the flange. This is the design of the elaborate standard balances illustrated in vignettes in the *Book of the Dead* of the New Kingdom. Representations of the Roman Period (e.g. 9995, sheet 4, Papyrus of Kerasher) suggest that the balance had disappeared from daily use and that the draughtsman was reproducing a thing of which he had no direct knowledge.

Large numbers of weights have survived from Egypt. They are, for the most part, made from the harder stones and are simple in shape, the duck, lentoid, and animal forms familiar in Western Asia being rare. The great majority of weights are unmarked. Actual weighing shows that there were a number of different standards in use. Weights marked with the unit and standard to which they belonged (or with their equivalent value in another standard) are uncommon. No. 38546, a felspar weight of 1,021 grammes from Gebelein, inscribed with the figure 5 and the name of Amenophis I, belongs to the ancient gold standard, indicated by the writing of the hieroglyphic ideogram for 'gold' (*nub*). It is the most commonly named of all the standards. In texts of the New Kingdom the weight of metal is usually expressed in a number of *deben* which consisted of 10 *kite*, approximately 140 grains or 91 grammes.

The dynamic development of the material culture of Egypt, which coincided with the unification of the country, must be largely attributed to the more plentiful supply of copper and to its use in making tools. Flat objects, like chisels, knives, axeheads, and adzes, were cast in open pottery moulds, the final shaping of the tool and the hardening of its cutting edge being done by hammering. Since, in the early period, the Egyptians did not possess tongs suitable for holding hot metal, this hammering was done cold.

Metal tools or models of tools are not uncommon from funerary equipment or foundation deposits (p. 143). Because of the value of all metal, care was taken to weigh tools before they

85 Copper tools

were issued to workmen and again when they were returned to store, to ensure that there had been no pilfering of the metal. Theft of metal tools figures large in the surviving records of trials. Of particular interest, both for their rarity and for their firm dates, are the tools marked with royal names, two chisels (66208–9) and an adze-head (66207) with the name of Userkaf (fig. 85), an adze-blade of the Hyksos king, Auserre Apophis (66206), an axe-head tied with its original leather thongs to a wooden handle inscribed with the name of Tuthmosis III (36770), an axe-head of Amenophis II (37447), and another inscribed 'King of Upper and Lower Egypt, Usermare-setepenre, beloved of Horus Lord of Tanis' (66211), probably Sheshonq III.

The personal weapons of the Egyptian soldiers comprised daggers, swords, spears, and axes. Daggers were short with rounded cheek pieces of bone or ivory. The sword was little more than a long dagger for thrusting and slashing in close-in fighting; the short, straight, two-edged blade had grooves, which might take the form of lotus stems and birds (27382, 32211, Eighteenth Dynasty). A curved scimitar-like sword with handle fashioned in one piece (called in Egyptian texts *khepesh*) was introduced on the pattern of Western Asiatic models during the

Second Intermediate Period (27490, from Tell el-Rataba, Eighteenth Dynasty). The spear had a pointed metal blade and metal butt riveted to a wooden shaft. The main weapon of the Egyptian infantryman was the battle-axe. In the Old and Middle Kingdoms rounded and semicircular forms, designed for slashing and cutting, predominated, the most popular of these being the type with three rear tangs forming open scallops in the blade. A particularly fine scalloped axe in the collection consists of a bronze blade riveted to a hollow silver tube which was originally fitted on a wooden haft (36776, Middle Kingdom, fig. 86). An identical battle-axe hafted in precisely this manner is shown in the hand of one of the body-guards of a Twelfth Dynasty nomarch (1147, fig. 87). In the Second Intermediate Period, a new form of battle-axe was evolved, suited for piercing rather than slashing, with a narrow, elongated blade and concave sides. The elaborate axe-heads with open fretted designs which appear from the beginning of the Middle Kingdom were more often ceremonial rather than functional. The designs most favoured were details of the hunt, or fighting animals, like the two bulls with their horns engaged (36764). No. 36766, from the early Eighteenth Dynasty, gives one of the earliest representations on Egyptian objects of a man riding bareback on a horse. These axe-heads were fitted to wooden hafts and secured by leather thongs in the manner well illustrated by 65663. Until the New Kingdom, the Egyptian soldier seems to have had no defensive armour except for his shield of tough leather stretched over a wooden brace (49245, Middle Kingdom) to which it was attached without an additional frame. Defensive mail coats made by riveting small bronze plates to leather jerkins were also adopted during this period; helmets first appear on battle scenes with representations of foreign mercenary elements in the Ramesside Period. From the Roman Period comes a suit of armour in crocodile skin in three pieces, one for the breast, one for the shoulder, and one for neck and head (5473, from Manfalut).

86 Bronze axe with silver handle

Copper, and later bronze, provided material for a wide range of domestic utensils in addition to tools and weapons. Household vessels, cauldrons, ewers, basins, ladles of metal formed, with textiles, part of a householder's negotiable property which could be used for barter. Among articles of the toilet, circular flat disks were used for mirrors from the beginning of the Dynastic Period, the polished metal giving a good reflecting surface (22830). The surface of the mirrors was not decorated before the Twenty-first Dynasty, when scenes of ritual significance were sometimes incised upon them. The mirrors were fitted to metal, wooden, faience, or ivory handles, mostly shaped like a papyrus column,

a club, or a Hathor head. Two protecting falcons also appeared on the cross-pieces. Glass mirrors did not occur before the Roman Period.

Pins, tweezers (for the extraction of thorns as well as the removal of hair), and razors are also common. The last in the New Kingdom consisted of a small flat piece of metal, shaped not unlike a miniature axe with sharp edge, which was fixed in a curved wooden handle and rotated by the fingers. These objects of daily use are for the most part simple in design; among the more unusual examples is the handle of a toilet implement in the form of a man on horseback (36314).

The use of metal for figure subjects is comparatively rare before the Late Dynastic Period. The Palermo Stone records the making of a copper statue of Khasekhemwy of the Second Dynasty; a remarkable copper statue of Pepi I in Cairo of the Sixth Dynasty is, however, the earliest surviving example of metal sculpture. The precious nature of all metal in Egypt no doubt accounts for the rarity of early pieces, since much of the metal would eventually have been melted down and re-used. On the other hand, the wealth of Egypt from the New Kingdom onwards, when the empire was at its height, may explain the apparent increase in the number of metal statues of kings and gods from the Eighteenth Dynasty. The kneeling figure of a king making an offering (64564), inscribed on the girdle with the prenomen of Tuthmosis IV without cartouche, is the earliest in the series of the inscribed statues of kings. The outline of the eyes and eyebrows is inlaid with silver: small pieces of alabaster painted black to indicate the iris and eyeball are inserted in the eye sockets.

Of statues of private individuals, the standing figure of a priestly official under Psammetichus I, Khonsirdais (14466; fig. 88), 34 cms high, is exceptionally fine in its detail. Khonsirdais is shown standing with left foot forward clad in a long pleated garment over which is the priestly 'leopard skin' passing over the left and under the right shoulder. Originally he held in his hands a figure of a god which was cast separately and secured to the group by a metal tenon. On the right shoulder is incised a figure of Osiris; the front of the skirt has an incised scene of the dead man before Osiris.

The majority of bronzes reproduce figures of gods, sacred animals, and emblems, and date for the most part from the Saite and Ptolemaic Periods. The method of casting was that of the lost-wax technique (cire-perdue). Small objects were normally cast solid; a model of the object was first fashioned in beeswax and coated with clay. When this was heated the clay hardened and the wax melted and ran out through holes left in the clay. When the clay mould had hardened, the metal was introduced through the holes. After the metal had cooled, the mould was broken away.

In the interests of economy, larger statues were shaped in quartz sand which was then thinly coated with beeswax. A clay mould was made in the same manner as if the object were to be solid cast. On heating, the core hardened and the metal was introduced to replace the thin coating of beeswax—now melted—which lay between the mould and the inner core of sand. It is not known how this inner core was held rigid during the process. When the metal had cooled the clay was broken away and the object was given final touches with the chisel.

Gold and silver were also cast to make small statues in the same manner as copper and bronze. The two metals are first found early in the Gerzean Period (Naqada II), mostly in the form of solid beads. The ability to work large masses of the material is shown by the gold coffin of Tutankhamun in Cairo which weighs more than 300 lb. Gold was the first objective of the ancient and modern tomb plunderer; bowls, figure sculpture, and solid gold funerary masks are uncommon and most surviving examples of the goldsmith's craft are items of personal jewellery which was worn by both sexes. Notable examples of this work in the collection are the pair of gold bracelets with inlay of semi-precious stones made for Nemareth, son of Sheshonq I (14594–5), an open-work plaque with a representation of Ammenemes IV offering unguent to the god Atum (59194; fig. 13) and two gold spacer beads with three recumbent cats inscribed on the back with the name Nubkheperre Inyotef and his queen Sobkemsaf (57699–700). Three strands of a necklace passed through it,

88 Khonsirdais, a priestly official

probably of gold beads and semi-precious stones; the most
important of the stones used in jewellery are agate, amethyst
(particularly in vogue in the Middle Kingdom), beryl, carnelian,
crystal, felspar, garnet, haematite, jasper (green, red, and yellow),
lapis lazuli, and turquoise. Drilling the beads by means of a
multiple bow-drill is shown in the fragment of tomb painting
in the Third Egyptian Room (920, Eighteenth Dynasty). Other
items of gold jewellery were diadems for the hair or wig, finger
rings, girdles, and anklets. Ear-rings were introduced from
Western Asia during the New Kingdom.

When the gold was not cast solid, it was beaten on a flat stone
with another stone in the craftsman's hand into a sheet of even
thickness. The design was executed with a hand punch on the
back (repoussé work) and with a chasing tool on the front. Gold
wire was made from the sheet by cutting narrow strips off the
edge or, for a more continuous thread, by cutting the sheet in
the form of a spiral. By the Middle Kingdom the art of attaching
grains of the metal to a gold surface for decoration was mastered
(granulation). A type of jewellery particularly characteristic of
Egypt is an open-work pectoral, in which the design was
executed on the back frame in fine chased repoussé work: on
the front were a series of gold cells (cloisons) which were filled
with coloured inlay of semi-precious stones or glass held in
position generally by a bed of cement but in the best work also
by the walls of the cells. Heat was not used in the case of glass
inlay as is the practice in true cloisonné enamel work.

Gold in sheet form was used to decorate wooden furniture:
thick sheet gold (i.e. foil) was hammered directly on to the wood
and fixed by small gold rivets. Thinner sheets were attached by
an adhesive, probably glue, on a prepared base of plaster. The
finest sheet (gold leaf) was freely used to gild statues, mummy
masks, coffins, and other items of funerary equipment. It was
applied over a layer of plaster, but the nature of the adhesive
used by the Egyptian craftsman has not been identified by
analysis.

Woodworking

Wooden objects are found from the Predynastic Period but fine
woodwork was not possible before the Early Dynastic Period
when copper tools became available. Examples of the carpenter's
tools (fig. 89), mostly found together in a woven basket in a
Theban tomb of New Kingdom date, are exhibited in the Fourth
Egyptian Room. For the preliminary shaping of a length of wood
or log, use was made of axes, to trim and split the timber, and of
saws, which occur from the Early Dynastic Period. The saw used
by the Egyptians was of the pull variety, that is to say the cutting

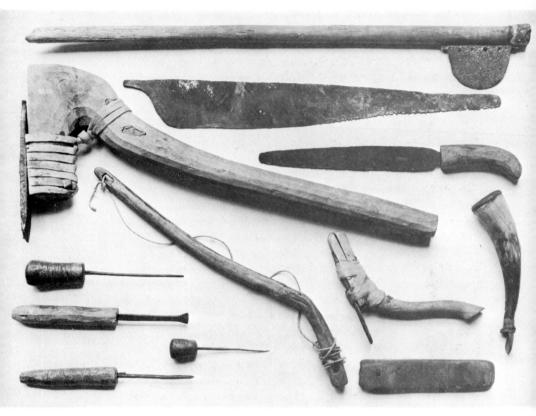

39 Carpenter's tools

edge of the teeth was set towards the handle and the saw-cut made on the pull of the saw, and not on the push. The most efficient method of using this type of saw was to cut vertically down from the top with the tip of the saw pointing upwards. Small pieces of wood, easy to work, were held upright by hand, but heavier timber was tied to a pole fixed firmly to the ground. The lashing was kept tight by a stick weighted with a heavy stone acting as a tourniquet. The saw could then be operated with two hands from a standing position. A small wedge was inserted in the saw-cut to prevent binding; as the carpenter cut down the piece it was necessary for him from time to time to relash it higher up the vertical post. For shaping, planing, and smoothing the wood, adzes of different sizes were used. Joints were cut by chisels, with different sizes and shapes to the cutting edge. They were struck by wooden mallets. Hammers of modern form, with metal heads, were not used. Holes were bored by bradawls of metal with wooden handles or drilled by means of a bow-drill. The metal bit of the drill was held upright, its top turning in half a dom-palm nut held in the hollow of the hand. Rapid sawing with the bow rotated the bit. An important item in the equipment was an oil flask and honing-stone. The plane was unknown in ancient Egypt, the work of smoothing being done by adzes and by rubbing the object with sandstone rubbers. There is no firm evidence for the use of the lathe for turning before the Roman Period. The rounded terminals and legs of furniture, for instance, were fashioned by hand and eye: square, level, and plumb-rule could be used to check.

With the help of these tools, the woodworker was capable of extremely fine joinery which made possible the construction of strong wooden boxes, coffins, and furniture. Wood was carefully cut into lengths and firmly joined by dovetailing and cramps; corners were fitted by different kinds of mitre joints and separate pieces by mortice and tenon joints and sometimes lashed together with leather thongs. Dowels of wood were used in the construction of coffins; small wood or ivory dowels or pins of copper or gold fixed inlay work of faience and ivory. Glue was probably used to secure inlay as early as the Early Dynastic Period but it was not widely used otherwise before the New Kingdom. A piece of six-ply wood from a coffin discovered in the Step Pyramid of Djoser, the separate layers of different woods secured by pins, shows the rapid development of the craft of woodworking. Veneer is found in furniture of the Eighteenth Dynasty.

The general nature of the Egyptian box or chest did not greatly vary over the centuries. Typical examples from the New Kingdom are an ebony box inlaid with tinted and untinted ivory and plaques of faience (5897), a shallow painted wooden casket from Akhmim (21818), and a chest of sycomore wood (5907) which belonged to the ship's captain, Denegro. The designs on boxes are usually drawn from hieroglyphic signs of amuletic significance or from conventional floral motifs and block patterns. The covers of these examples are detachable. Hinged lids also occur in the Eighteenth Dynasty. Metal locks and keys were unknown before the Roman Period. Examples are found of coffin lids being permanently sealed by an elaborate device of tumblers. Boxes were sometimes constructed to enable the cover to be secured, thus preventing the contents from spilling out if they were knocked or dropped, but the only means of safeguard against pilfering was to secure the lid to the box by lashing around the projecting knobs on the lid and the side of the box which could then be sealed with a lump of mud bearing a seal impression.

Though wooden furniture is represented in tomb scenes from the Old Kingdom, actual surviving examples before the New Kingdom are not very common. Egyptian houses were probably always sparsely furnished, use being made of low divans of mudbrick covered by cushions. The normal items of furniture were chairs, stools, tables, and jar-stands. Some of the light open wicker-work examples of stools (2476) and of jar stands (2470, 2471) clearly derive in design from reed and rush constructions of the Predynastic Period. Other stools are three-legged (2481, a type used by craftsmen at their work) or four-legged (2472). Particularly popular in the New Kingdom was a type of folding stool (29284), consisting of two pairs of crossed uprights pivoted about half-way down, with carved duck-head terminals inlaid with ivory and ebony. The seat was of leather, stretched across two curved wooden cross-pieces. Chairs are usually low, with seats of plaited cord mesh, generally no more than 20–25 cms from the ground. The legs are carved usually in the form of a lion's paw or, less commonly after the New Kingdom, a bull's hoof; backs are high and straight, often decorated with open-work designs of amuletic signs and figures of Bes; in 2480 the back panel has small insets of ivory in the design of four lotus stems and flowers. No. 2479 is a higher chair, with straight, uncarved legs, and sloping back. No. 2469 is a low table supported on three splayed legs. On the flat surface is painted a representation of the goddess Renenutet in snake form before an offering table; an inscription contains the conventional formula of the funerary offering for a certain Paperpa, from whose tomb the table doubtlessly comes.

An Egyptian would also possess a wooden bed-frame provided with a footboard. The finely carved fragments from a bed (21574) overlaid with decoration in silver and gold come perhaps from a royal tomb at Thebes. In place of pillows, which would have been too uncomfortable for the hot nights of Egypt, the bed would be provided with a head-rest, the greater number of which are of wood. The rest consisted of a carefully carved, fitted, crescent-shaped piece for the back of the head, supported on a wooden pedestal; more elaborate forms are also found, like that shaped in the likeness of a crouching hare (20753). Head-rests may be carved with the name and title of the owner, perhaps also with a prayer for a good night's rest, and in examples made for funerary rather than everyday use, with Chapters from the *Book of the Dead* on the base of the pedestal (35804).

The technical skill of the Egyptian woodworker is best seen in boat-building and chariot-making; in both cases the ability of these objects, built up of small pieces, to withstand the stresses and strains in their use depended upon knowledge of the natural quality of different woods, and the strength and accuracy of the joinery which gave them their strength and rigidity. The earliest boats were made of papyrus or reed, and the characteristic high prow of the typical Egyptian boat is a legacy of this early material. Already by the Early Dynastic Period local wood was used for constructing river craft. The smallness of the planks which could be obtained from timber from local sources resulted in the development of a technique described by Herodotus ii. 96 and depicted in a number of tomb scenes. The shell of the boat was built up by joining small pieces of wood; there was no keel and no ribs. Sea-going vessels were constructed of larger imported planks along the same lines as river craft, with the exception that greater rigidity and strength was given to the frame by trussing the boat at the prow and the stem and running between them a hogging truss which passed over wooden crutches.

The chariot is believed to have been introduced by the Hyksos invaders; it was used in the struggle between them and the Theban kings of the Seventeenth Dynasty. It was employed in the New Kingdom in warfare, in hunting, inspection of estates, and for official appearances. It consisted of a light wooden frame with open back, set forward of a short axle fitted to two wheels of four or six spokes. A pole projected from the centre of the axle beneath the carriage, terminating in a yoke to which a pair of small-framed horses were harnessed by leather accoutrements. Particularly remarkable is the skill with which the wheels were joined together from separate segments and bound with leather tires. To bend the wood, a piece was tied to a forked post stuck in the ground, welted, and bent with the help of a lever.

The carving of solid woods into statues, models, and household equipment was also practised with high skill throughout the ancient period. It is clear that in many cases the provision of statues of offering bearers and of models in the period from the end of the Old Kingdom to the Middle Kingdom was a substitute for carved stone relief and stone statues. If such figures charm, it is rather in the state of their preservation, particularly of their colour, and the interest of the subject-matter rather than in their skill of carving. The statues of the tomb owner were, however, also often of wood—such indeed form a large proportion of surviving wooden statues—and the choice of material was not necessarily dictated by reasons of economy. Wood statues were provided, for instance, for royalty from the First Dynasty and persisted to the New Kingdom. Three of these large over-life-size figures, all of New Kingdom date, from the royal tombs of the Valley of the Kings at Thebes (854, 882–3) are in the collection.

The statues of private persons, broadly speaking, follow in their pose and style the conventions of stone sculpture. They are usually carved in one piece, except for the arms which are fitted on by mortice and tenon joints. Some of the best examples of this class of work are: the statue of Meryrehashtef as a young man

90 Figure of
Meryrehashtef

(55722, fig. 90), one of a group of statues from his tomb at Sedment of Sixth-dynasty date, in which the arms are carved in one piece with the body; the small but attractive standing figure of Netjernakhte from his tomb at Beni Hasan, Twelfth Dynasty (65440); and the standing figure of an official elaborately draped from the time immediately following the Amarna Period (2320). No. 47568 is a finely carved bust of what must have been a large statue, from a tomb at Akhmim of the Sixth Dynasty.

In these statue-figures the woodworker was limited by the religious conventions of the patron; greater freedom of style is to be found in the small objects of wood. Particularly attractive is the series of cosmetic jars and containers from the New Kingdom carved in various forms, a running jackal with a shell in his mouth (38187), a negro girl carrying a small chest on her head (32767), a swimming girl (38186), a cucumber (5980), or a bouquet of lotus flowers and buds, some of the latter in tinted ivory (5965, from Memphis). The figure of a young girl playing a harp (48658) is also a good example of the less formal style of Egyptian art.

Ivory-work

Ivory from the tusks both of the hippopotamus and of the elephant was used, like wood, for a variety of small objects as well as for inlay, either in its natural state or stained pink. The use of ivory had a certain magical significance; it was employed, for instance, for the making of flat curved wands (often referred to as knives) on which were incised with a fine line the figures of various demons and deities (p. 135; fig. 51). Finely carved objects include handles for knives and wands, toilet spoons, button seals, and gaming pieces. The ivory pieces are mostly small, but larger objects were also built up, for instance the head-rest of Gua (30727, Twelfth Dynasty) with the support in the form of the girdle of Isis.

Fine carving goes back to the Badarian Period; a particularly skilful example from that time is an unguent pot (63057) from Mostagedda in the form of a hippopotamus.

Figurines in ivory date back to the Predynastic Period; they are mostly in the form of naked women (p. 128; fig. 47). An exceptionally fine early ivory is that of a standing figure of a king (37996; fig. 54), found in a temple at Abydos, probably of the First Dynasty, clothed in a garment usually associated with the sed-festival, the detail of the quilted pattern of the cloak being carefully done (p. 142).

Weaving

Weaving was one of the earliest crafts to be developed; fragments of woven textiles date back to the earliest of the predynastic cultures and already show advanced skill. The small fragment of woven linen from the Faiyum (58761) is of two-ply thread, lightly spun, with 8–10 warp threads and 10–12 weft threads per centimetre. It dates from before 3100 BC, perhaps even 4000 BC. Textiles of the Early Dynastic Period were woven with 64 threads to a centimetre in the warp and 48 in the weft (modern cambric of a fine quality contains about 56 threads to the centimetre). Throughout their history the Egyptians had a high reputation as skilled weavers; a particularly fine cloth is frequently mentioned in the Old Testament as byssus.

The woven cloth of Egypt was almost invariably of linen. Until the Middle Kingdom there was no breed of sheep which produced wool; a small piece of woven woollen material (55137) was found at El-Amarna, but the scarcity of wool from the Dynastic Period suggests that there may have been a certain religious taboo against its use for garments. Silk was not introduced until the Ptolemaic Period: cotton fragments from Nubian sites have been found dating to the Roman Period, but in Egypt itself woven cotton does not occur before Coptic times.

Flax, the source of linen thread, is frequently shown in agricultural scenes in tomb reliefs and paintings. It was pulled up by the roots (not cut with the sickle like cereal crops), and taken to a man who removed the boles by pulling the flax through a wooden combing implement. The stalks were then trussed together for transporting.

The preparation of the thread was begun by soaking the stalks for a number of days in water to soften them (retting) and to begin the separation of the fibrous matter (i.e. the tow) from the woody tissues. The operation was completed by beating the soaked matter on a block of stone with a wooden mallet, after which the fibres were removed with a sharp-toothed comb (hackling).

When the fibres were dry, they were drawn out length-wise and loosely twisted into roves following the natural direction of the twist of the drying fibres to the left. The work was done by women who rolled the fibres on the upper part of their thigh, squatting on the ground with their right knee tucked under the body. It was at this stage of the work that the thread began to be formed and to acquire the strength and elasticity needed for woven fabrics, the individual fibres being pressed together and adhering by virtue of the irregularities on the surface. When sufficient quantity had been obtained, the roves were loosely wound on scraps of pottery or on pottery reels into balls. They were placed in pots to prevent them rolling away and spun by hand on a spindle, a slender stick tapering at one end and weighted towards the top with a whorl, generally of wood or stone but sometimes of pottery. The typical Middle Kingdom whorl was flat and cylindrical (35928), that of the New Kingdom was domed (6477). The shaft of the spindle did not greatly vary. It had a spiral groove at the top to receive the thread. Later this was replaced by a metal hook (38147).

Until the New Kingdom spinning seems to have been the work of women. Thenceforth it was done by both men and women. The simplest method of spinning was for the woman to stand and guide the single roves from the pot through her fingers on to the spindle which she rotated by raising one knee and rolling it on her thigh. The distaff, a stick to hold the prepared fibres from which the thread was spun, did not come into general use in Egypt until the Roman Period. A quicker method of spinning was to draw the rove out of the pot, pass it over a forked stick, and attach it to the spindle which was rotated between the palms of the two hands. The finest quality thread was produced by a third method, in which the action of the spindle helped in drawing and attenuating the thread. The rove was drawn through the fingers of the left hand, attached to the spindle which was rotated by a flick of the fingers, and allowed to drop and swing, the weight of the whorl helping to maintain the spin.

The earliest looms in Egypt were horizontal. The warp was stretched between two wooden beams attached at the corners to four short pegs which were driven into the ground. The warp might be set up directly on the beams of the loom or might be wound over three pegs set in a wall and transferred to the loom. The threads of the warp were then divided into two; the odd-number threads were lashed to a wooden stick (heddle rod) and raised to make a space through which the weft thread passed, either as a ball or wound on a stick spool. The space for the return of the weft thread was made by turning on edge a flat piece of wood passing through the weft (sled-rod).

By the New Kingdom, probably as one of the innovations of technique introduced during the Hyksos Period, the horizontal loom was replaced by a vertical loom in which the warp was stretched between two beams fastened to an upright wooden frame. In contrast with work on the horizontal loom, representations show that the loom was operated by men, sitting or squatting at the base of the frame. The method of making the passage for the weft threads was unaltered.

Most woven material from the Dynastic Period consists of linen wrappings and bandages from mummies; lengths of cloth were also commonly included in the burial equipment, usually inscribed in ink in hieratic with the name of the owner, the date at which it was taken into use, or the quality of the cloth. The size of these sheets may be considerable; no. 37105 measures

4·57 × 1·83 ms. and is marked 'Cloth of the singer of the god's wife, king's wife and king's mother, Aahmes Nefertari (may she live) Sitdjehuty'. The cloth was intended to serve the dead person for everyday purposes.

Actual garments from the Dynastic Period are rare. Until the New Kingdom the regular dress was white and the garments were draped and pleated, not tailored. Representations of coloured or patterned textiles are rare, and usually they are worn by foreigners. Fragments of patterned textiles do not survive from before the New Kingdom; their introduction at this time may be due to the vertical loom. Most of the patterned textiles which have survived date from the fourth century AD and in style and choice of pattern and decoration owe little to pharaonic Egypt (see pp. 255 ff.). The main fabric is usually plain linen cloth; where the decoration was to be applied, warp and weft were not inter-woven but placed side by side; the pattern was then woven on one, two, three, or more threads which formed the warp, while the weft consisted of the coloured and more bulky material, usually wool. This was afterwards beaten down with large wooden weaver's combs to hide the warps (20747, 35926).

Mat-making and basketry, crafts closely allied to textile weaving, were also fully developed in the Predynastic Period. The fragment of woven reed matting (59700) comes from Badari; boat-shaped baskets of grass stems, possibly for sowing grain, like no. 58696, are characteristic of the predynastic Faiyum.

Mats were woven on horizontal looms of rush, reed, and the coarse grasses of Egypt. The patterns of the mat weaves are reproduced in early architecture (see p. 191) and remain one of the dominant artistic motifs of the Dynastic Period.

Baskets were made by coiling a fibrous core spirally into the shape required; the principal material employed was palm leaf with the split rib of the branches for foundation. Baskets were the most common form of household container after clay pots and might serve a number of purposes analogous to wooden boxes. No. 2566, of palm leaf, originally contained a linen tunic, no. 6026 a set of carpenter's tools, and no. 6027 model bronze tools with the name of Tuthmosis III. Receptacles were also made of cane and papyrus (but not plaited); 2561 contained a wig (2560). An unusual example of cane and reed construction is the model table with offerings (5340, Eighteenth Dynasty).

Reed, flax, and halfa-grass were also employed for ropes from predynastic times. In the Dynastic Period palm fibre was generally employed, but the large thick cables required in the hauling of stone were of papyrus. The process of making these papyrus ropes is illustrated in the copy (lower register, right) of a painted scene from the tomb of Khaemwese at Thebes of New Kingdom date. Three men are at work; two stand twisting together two separate strands. The third is seated holding a spike between the strands. There are four finished ropes coiled above the figures, a bundle of papyrus stems, and a group of six tools: two spikes, two twisting tools, a mallet, and a knife.

CHAPTER EIGHT

ROMAN AND CHRISTIAN EGYPT AND THE KINGDOM OF MEROE

The defeat of the Egyptian navy at the battle of Actium in 30 BC, the ensuing death of Antony and suicide of Cleopatra VII, mark the beginning of a new and distinct period in the history of Egypt. The country and the people were drawn more firmly than ever into the world of the eastern Mediterranean. The effect of the Roman occupation is readily apparent in the material remains of Egypt reflecting the daily life of the inhabitants. Certain aspects of the change have already been noted in the previous pages: the widespread use of terracotta for clay lamps (p. 212), of glass for household purposes (p. 216), and of iron for domestic implements (p. 218); the adoption of the reed pen (p. 94), of metal keys and locks (p. 230), and of the lathe in carpentry (p. 230). Even in matters of dress and jewellery the fashions in Egypt differ little from the general pattern of the eastern Mediterranean.

In theory the Roman emperors were the legitimate heirs of the pharaohs, possessed of full traditional titles and absolute powers; on the carved reliefs of the Upper Egyptian temples most of the emperors until the middle of the third century are found depicted in accordance with the ancient iconography, their names written within cartouches in the hieroglyphic signs. In practice the country was incorporated as a province of the empire and was administered by a prefect formally appointed by the emperor from the equestrian order. It remained part of the Roman, and later Byzantine, Empire until the Moslem invasion of AD 641.

Towards Egypt the early emperors maintained an attitude of suspicion which explains the unique character of the province in the Roman world. Behind this attitude lay the memory of the havoc caused by the intervention of Cleopatra upon the lives of Julius Caesar and Antony. Moreover the agricultural wealth of Egypt and the strength of its natural frontiers were factors very much present in the minds of the early emperors, who, in their determination that the country should not become a base for treason, forbade access to it by high officials without permission.

The last two centuries of Ptolemaic rule had been marked by dynastic feuds and a general weakening of authority. Considerable disorders had occurred, particularly in Upper Egypt. Something of the general condition of Egypt may be gathered from Strabo's account of his journey through the country soon after the Roman occupation (*Geographica*, Book 17). Heliopolis is described as entirely deserted, Abydos as only a small settlement, and Thebes as a collection of villages: the last was destroyed by Ptolemy IX Soter II after an abortive revolt in 88 BC. The Romans had little difficulty in quickly bringing order to the whole of Egypt as far as Aswan, the traditional southern frontier.

There can be no doubt that the general security, peace, and ordered government which the Roman administration established brought prosperity, at least for the first two centuries. Improvements were effected in agriculture, and it was probably during the Roman Period that the *saqia*, or waterwheel driven by an ox, and the *norag*, a wheeled sledge drawn over the threshing-floor to extract the grain from the ears, were introduced.

The bulk of the population consisted of the Egyptian-speaking element whose way of life can have been hardly affected by the change of rule, except in so far as the Roman administration was more efficient in the collection of taxes. Receipts for these taxes written in the demotic script on limestone flakes or pottery sherds form the greater proportion of the large numbers of ostraca in the native language found from the Roman Period. The ancient religion still enjoyed a measure of official patronage, particularly in Upper Egypt where the great series of temples, at Dendera, Esna, Kom Ombo, and Philae were completed or further embellished during the first two centuries AD. Like the work of the Ptolemaic Period, the construction during the Roman Period scarcely differs in its architecture from the tradition of the Upper Egyptian temples of the New Kingdom, except for the introduction of new types of capitals, the inclusion of underground chambers, and the erection of *mammisi* ('birthplace'), small temples in the style of the old peripteral shrines in which the ritual of the birth of the infant god was performed. In these temples the daily ceremonies were still performed and the great feasts celebrated. The continued vigour of the native culture is shown by the fact that the majority of our existing copies of demotic literary works were made in the first two centuries AD; most categories of the ancient literature are represented, and some of the wisdom literature and stories, in particular, compare favourably with any earlier compositions of their kind.

A smaller proportion but still numerous element of the population were the descendants of the Greek, Macedonian, and other racially mixed but hellenized immigrants who had been attracted to Egypt, mainly as soldiers, administrators, traders, and bankers, following the invasion of Alexander the Great and the founding of the Macedonian dynasty of the Ptolemies. Some had been established in Egypt for nearly three hundred years

Plate 16
Vase decorated with the prenomen of Tuthmosis III

Plate 17
Wooden model funerary boat

and they thought of Egypt as their homeland. They had settled not only in the Greek foundations of the Ptolemies but also throughout the Nile Valley in the old nome-capitals. Their numbers received a fresh influx of strength from the settlement, particularly in the Faiyum, of disbanded veterans of the legions. This cosmopolitan group was distinguishable from the old indigenous population by their mode of speech and education. They spoke and wrote in Greek and were educated in the normal Hellenistic pattern on the classical authors, particularly Homer, and retained, so far as they were allowed to do so, the social and political institutions of the Greek *polis*. Their loyalty to the Greek tradition and belief in their intellectual superiority ensured the survival of Hellenistic culture. Under the Roman administration they enjoyed a privileged position and it is to them that we owe the preservation of the many papyri of Greek literary works and artistic productions in the purely Hellenistic style.

The chief centre of the Hellenistic culture remained Alexandria. The city was deprived by the Romans of certain of the privileges which it had enjoyed under the Ptolemies, and throughout the first century its relations with the emperors were embittered. Disturbed though its civil life was, it continued to enjoy great prosperity from its port and to maintain its reputation as a centre of learning. It is unfortunate that relatively little of its ancient splendour has been recovered; the remains are for the most part below the present water-table and it is difficult to say to what extent the city retained its Hellenistic traditions in art and sculpture.

The point of greatest contact between the Hellenistic element of the Egyptian people and the old indigenous population was in the sphere of popular religion and funerary practices. The immigrants adopted Egyptian theophorous names and honoured, in particular, deities, like Harpocrates and Isis, who were considered as healers and saviours. In popular religion the Egyptian deities were assimilated to Hellenistic ones and representations occur in which Hellenistic dress is added to the traditional Egyptian iconography or Egyptian symbols to traditional Greek forms: Haroeris appears as a falcon-headed man dressed in the armour of a Roman legionary (fig. 91), sometimes seated on a horse spearing a crocodile; Hathor as a standing female figure with a cow's head wearing a long cloak; Anubis as a standing figure with a jackal-head and the accoutrements of Hermes; Isis in the guise of Demeter or Aphrodite. In Alexandria Egyptian deities were incorporated into Greek mystery religions and these had a wide vogue in Mediterranean countries. Particularly popular outside Egypt, but less so in the country itself, was Sarapis, whose cult was introduced by Ptolemy I Soter to form a common

Plate 18
Mummy case of
Artemidorus with
painted portrait
(*left*)

Plate 19
Painted portrait
of a woman
(*right*)

bond between his Greek and Egyptian subjects. Possibly the god was a hellenized form of Osorapis, the mummified bull whose cult at Memphis was well established before the Ptolemaic Period. Sarapis was given human form, his head similar to the Hellenistic concept of Zeus. By the Roman Period he was associated with Isis and Horus.

In funerary customs the Hellenistic element outside Alexandria adopted, as all foreign elements in Egypt hitherto had done, the

91 Figure of Haroeris in the dress of a Roman legionary

practice of mummification. Though the actual process of mummification was more often than not inadequately carried out, the decoration of mummies during the Roman Period was more elaborate than at any other time. The nature of the decoration shows that the dead man believed that as a result of the elaborate ritual which accompanied the actual embalming process he would experience the miraculous benefits which Osiris had enjoyed. Scenes from the myth of Osiris and from the various ceremonies conducted for him by Anubis are found painted on the linen shrouds enclosing the mummy or are depicted on the coffin itself (e.g. 21810, Plate 18).

It is clear from earlier practices, like the provision of linen cartonnage and gold masks (p. 165) and the emphasis of the funerary statues upon the features as compared with the treatment of the rest of the body that the survival of the individual personality was closely associated in ancient belief with the preservation of the individual features of the face. In the Dynastic Period neither the masks nor the statue-heads are true portraits of the individual but are idealized. With the Roman Period a new departure is seen in the provision of plaster-heads and painted portraits in a naturalistic style: in view of the date of their first appearance it is probable that the realistic element, which had always been a prominent feature of Roman sculpture, derives from Roman influence. The greater proportion of the painted portraits has been recovered from Hawara and Er-Rubbiyat in the Faiyum, and for that reason they are often referred to as 'Faiyumic portraits'. Examples have, however, been found in a number of sites from Saqqara in the north to Aswan. The earliest examples date from the first half of the first century AD, the majority fall within the second and third centuries, and perhaps about a quarter of the number belong to the fourth century, about which time the practice of mummification was gradually abandoned in favour of simple interment of the dead in their everyday costume.

The early portraits are painted on thin panels of cypress, usually about 43 cms high and 23 cms wide, and no more than 1·6 mm thick, roughly trimmed to a point or arch at the top; they were placed over the face of the mummy and secured in position by the bandages (29772, Plate 19). In later examples thicker panels are more usual, generally rectangular in shape and on average about 30 cms high and 20–23 cms wide. A smaller number of portraits painted on the linen shroud have survived, the majority representing young children (68509, Plate 20).

Some of the portraits, particularly during the fourth century, were executed in tempera. The pigments, most of which were well known in the Dynastic Period (see pp. 204 ff.), were mixed in water with the addition of an adhesive material, probably egg-white or gum, and applied with a brush, sometimes directly on the canvas, sometimes on a prepared ground of gypsum plaster or whiting (chalk).

Water-colours being easily damaged and the pigment affected by moisture or the action of the air, the medium chosen for the majority of the portraits was beeswax, to which the appropriate pigment was added in a coarsely ground state. It produced a more robust portrait with a luminosity and enrichment of colour reminiscent of modern oil-painting. The technique of painting in wax was already widely practised in the Hellenistic world, but it had not previously been employed in Egypt. The manner of painting is described by Pliny the Elder in his *Natural History*, xxxv. 31, 39, 41, where he uses the term 'encaustic'. So far as the mummy portraits are concerned, there seems to be no question of fusing cold wax on to the surface of the panel by the application of artificial heat; in the warm climate of Egypt it was possible to apply the wax in more or less liquid form by means of a brush, provided the work was quickly executed. The usual practice followed by the painter seems to have been first to out-line the head and the features in black or occasionally red wash upon a prepared white background or directly upon the wood. He then filled in the background in grey, running his brush freely round the outline sketch and covering the remainder of the background with long, full, horizontal or slanting strokes. The drapery and hair were painted in the same way. In some cases the flesh received similar treatment, but usually the wax was applied more thickly. There is still considerable doubt concerning the manner in which this effect was achieved. The coloured wax may have been poured and modelled on the panel from the bowl of a warmed ladle or worked in a creamy state with a hard blunt point, perhaps a brush stiffened by constant use. Another possibility is that the wax was simply applied with a brush repeatedly over the same area.

In the earlier examples, the impressionistic handling of the paint and the suggestion of movement in the pose derive from the tradition of classical portrait painting of which the mummy panels are almost our only surviving examples. The subjects are drawn usually with the face turned slightly to the left or right but sometimes frontally. They are never in profile. Head, shoulders, and the upper part of the breast are usually shown; examples executed directly on the canvas of the shroud might be full length. Gradations of the individual colour, the use of shading and of highlights, give the portraits a strikingly modern appear-ance; at close quarters the work looks casual; particularly noticeable are the heavy line of the eyebrows, the white streak down the nose, the thick red smear of the lips separated by a black line and the heavy shading under the chin. But from a distance of one or two metres these prominent features merge and blend with the background.

This tradition was still observed in the third century, but by the fourth there had emerged a different style in which there was a more formal geometrically balanced arrangement of the features and hair. The figures are almost invariably full-faced. The drawing is less assured, particularly around the mouth with its pursed underlip.

Both men and women are shown wearing the ordinary costume of daily life current throughout the Hellenistic world, consisting of a loose sack-like tunic, usually of linen but later also of wool, passing over both shoulders, with an opening for the neck and two projecting sleeves. The normal colour of the costume was white for men, and usually red, but also blue, green, and white, for women. It was decorated with two vertical bands (*clavi*) which in the eastern Mediterranean had no significance of rank. In the fourth century a coloured border appeared around the neckline of the tunic worn by women. One or two of these garments were worn. In portraits of the first and second centuries AD it was customary for men and women to be depicted with a loose garment of the same colour over the tunic, draped over either shoulder or wrapped around both. Women are almost always shown with necklaces and ear-rings derived from models current in the Hellenistic world. The arrangement of the hair and beards of the men and the coiffure of the women follow closely the fashions set by the imperial family at Rome, and provide one of the clearest indications of the date of individual portraits.

Portraits painted on the canvas shroud of a mummy can only have been painted after death, and probably the portraits on thick panels of the later series were for funerary use only. The degree of individual characterization of the best of the early first-century portraits suggests that they may have been studies from life, intended in the first instance to be hung in the lifetime of the owner in the living-room of his home. It is, however, noticeable that in nearly every case the subject is portrayed in the prime of youth and beauty, features at rest with a look of calm and serene repose. The probability is that at least from the second century most portraits were painted after death, the painter reducing the wide range of subjects to a small number of well-defined types.

The plaster portrait head-pieces are found from the beginning of the Roman Period until the middle of the third century. The majority come from Middle Egypt; they were used concurrently 92 Painted plaster mask with the painted panels. In the earliest type the head-piece was made hollow to fit over the skull which lay level with the body and it might be secured by cords passed through holes in the base. Gradually the head-piece was raised at an angle to the neck, to give the appearance of a man lying on a high pillow. The eyes were in the first place painted but from the second century translucent glass was commonly employed.

The emergence of the portrait masks is foreshadowed by the superimposing of naturalistic details on masks more or less in the Egyptian style, particularly in the treatment of the hair. The gold mask attached to the mummy of a young boy from Hawara (22108) is fashioned in the conventional way but an alien element is introduced in the realistic arrangement of the curly hair. In the fine mask of a woman, probably from Meir (26799), the hair falls in two ringlets on either side of the neck, possibly representing a more naturalistic treatment of the ancient wig associated with goddesses.

The representations of the head-pieces, like the panel portraits, follow the convention of the fashions set by the imperial family. Generally speaking, however, the modeller of the masks did not succeed in conveying the individual likeness of a person to the same degree as the portrait painter. A notable exception, which must be one of the earliest of the realistic masks, is the head-piece of a man found at Hu (Diospolis Parva) in Upper Egypt (30845; fig. 92).

The graves of the mummies fitted with plaster head-pieces or painted portraits were seldom marked with commemorative stelae recording the names of the deceased. Private funerary stelae, however, continued to be used in the Roman Period; some are carved in a purely Egyptian style with representations of gods, below which there is a short conventional text in the hieroglyphic or demotic script: others, like a stone stela with a Greek epitaph in elegiac verse mourning the untimely death of the child Politta at the age of five, set between two columns supporting a gabled pediment (1206), are in the subject matter of their texts and form of their decoration derived from Greek tradition. From the early Roman Period onwards, the two styles were intermingled; in the stela (59870; fig. 93), of a type found in great numbers at Kom Abu Billo (Terenuthis), the deceased is represented clothed in Greek style reclining on a cushioned couch with right arm outstretched, holding in the hand a libation cup. The attitude of the figure goes back in origin to the Athenian grave reliefs. The stela is given a mixed architectural setting with gabled pediment of the kind seen on Greek stelae set on two columns with lotus-form capitals peculiar to Egypt. 93 Funerary stela

In the background is the representation of the Anubis-animal. Similar stelae are found with the deceased standing, arms extended at right angles from the body and bent upwards at the elbow in the *orans* position.

In the fourth century AD, to judge from excavations at Akhmim and Antinoopolis, there was a radical change in the burial customs of the country. The dead person was buried in the worn-out garments of daily life consisting of one or two tunics and outer cloak of the type depicted in the mummy portraits and sometimes with cap, socks, leather belt, and sandals. Below the neck there might be a small crescent-shaped pillow of stuffed cut-leather (26565). Hangings were sometimes wrapped around the body as a grave cloth. The depth at which the bodies were buried varied, some being just below the surface, others over 3 metres. The body might rest on a wooden board or be placed in direct contact with the sand. Only occasionally was there any form of prepared substructure, or the marking of the grave by memorial stones. Though in some cases there was a perfunctory attempt to embalm by the use of bitumen, generally speaking the preservation of the body was due to natural desiccation owing to the circumstances of the burial.

With the final abandonment of the painted wooden coffins, of the painted burial cloths, of the plaster head-pieces, and the mummy portraits, the last lingering traces of the dynastic civilization disappear. It is difficult not to connect the change in the mode of burial with a fundamental change in belief. There is no indication in the burials of what may have taken the place of the ancient belief in the kingdom of Osiris and the efficacy of mummification. Perhaps the change was accelerated by the widespread adoption of Christianity throughout Egypt.

The history of the spread of Christianity in Egypt cannot be traced in detail in either the archaeological remains or the literary evidence. According to a tradition which goes back to the fourth century AD the church at Alexandria was founded by the evangelist Mark. No trace of this primitive church has survived; in all probability it was completely destroyed during the great pogroms against the Jews of Alexandria towards the end of the first century. Christians do not emerge as an effective, developed society, playing an important part in the intellectual life of the city, until the foundation in about AD 180 of the catechetical school by Pantaenus. The Alexandrine church was essentially Greek rather than Egyptian: its language was Greek, its leading figures were steeped in the tradition of Hellenistic thought and scholarship.

The diffusion of Christianity from Alexandria to the rest of Egypt seems to have been slow. Even among the many private letters in Greek found in Egypt there are only a few which can be assigned with certainty to a date before the end of the third century. Little progress was made, so far as we can judge, among the Egyptian-speaking element of the population. There are, for instance, few native Egyptians among the martyrs of the persecutions of the second century. The first patriarch at Alexandria who is said to have been concerned to convert the native Egyptians is Dionysius (247–264 AD).

In contrast with the apparent initial slow progress of conversion of the Egyptians, from the middle of the third century sudden and dramatic headway was made, which the persecution associated with the name of Diocletian failed to arrest. The persecution seems to have fallen particularly heavily in Egypt and it is from the date of Diocletian's accession in AD 284 that the Coptic church still reckons its years.

As a result of the need to provide the new converts with translations of the scriptures, the ancient native tongue of Egypt received fresh stimulus. Already by the end of the first century AD attempts had been made to write the Egyptian language in Greek letters supplemented by a fairly large number of demotic signs. The purpose seems to have been to render more accurately the correct pronunciation of spells and in particular the names of demons and magical words of power, since the texts are magical in content and largely unintelligible. The collection of spells written in a fine demotic hand probably of the third century AD, which goes by the name of the London and Leiden Magical Papyrus (British Museum 10070 and Leiden I. 383) contains about 640 words with transcriptions in Greek characters over the native script (fig. 94).

94 London magical papyrus

Though the original impetus to write Egyptian in Greek letters was not of Christian origin, the sudden emergence of Coptic (p. 88) and its standardization as a literary language, with a distinct grammer and regular orthography, was due to the need to supply translations of the scriptures in the vernacular. Its earliest use in this connexion is for glosses in Coptic of Greek words in a text of Isaiah and of a Greek–Coptic vocabulary of Hosea and Amos, both of the third century AD. The earliest surviving copies of books of the Old and New Testament date from the first half of the fourth century. Translations into Coptic from lost Greek originals of the Gnostics, found at Nag Hammadi (Chenoboskion), and of the Manichaeans in the Faiyum, both dating from the fourth century, show the establishment of heretical sects among the native-speaking Egyptians contemporaneously with the spread of orthodox Christianity.

The rapid adoption of Christianity by the Egyptian-speaking element of the population manifests itself in the remarkably quick hold which monasticism gained in Egypt. According to tradition the first hermit was Paul, who took to the desert at the time of the Decian persecution of AD 251. To escape the persecutions may have been the primary reason for the beginning of the monastic movement but undoubtedly a factor which must also be taken into account is the state of the Egyptian economy in the third century. In common with the rest of the Roman Empire, Egypt suffered from a general depression brought about by over-taxation and the consequent abandonment of the cultivation of marginal land. Conditions were aggravated in Egypt by the invasion of an army of seventy thousand sent by Zenobia, queen of Palmyra, in AD 268. At the same time the southern frontier, which had been undisturbed since the time of Augustus, was threatened by the Blemmyes, a tribe now in occupation of Lower Nubia. The word used of the solitary—anchorite—is also found in early pre-Christian papyri to describe one who withdrew his labour. A third factor which probably encouraged the movement to the desert was the climate and geography of Egypt: there was no lack of unoccupied desert to withdraw to and the warmth of the climate made it possible to live outside the villages without undue hardship.

The life of the solitary remained the ideal of Egyptian monasticism. The hermit was ideally pictured as one who went out to the desert to guard the valley settlement from the incursions of the demons who inhabited the wastes in a physical form. Food and drink were supplied to him miraculously by a palm which furnished twelve clusters of dates a year, one for each month, and by a spring yielding a cupful of water a day. His spiritual food was brought down by supernatural means from heaven itself and at the moment of his death he was visited by a fellow monk, who gave him spiritual comfort for his last and terrible journey and carried out the service of burying him.

Such was the ideal which is conveyed to us in simple narratives of the early hermits preserved in Coptic literature. In practice the rigorous life of the solitary was followed by few: a communal way of life with a set rule developed. The true founder of monasticism was Antony. According to the traditional life, Antony was born about AD 251. He came of a moderately wealthy Egyptian family and neither spoke nor read Greek. His retirement to the desert was said to be the result of hearing the passage in the gospel of Matthew read in church which relates how Jesus told the young man to sell all and follow him. The fame of his life attracted disciples and these he organized into a loose community in which each member had his own cell (*laura*), often some miles distant one from another; here each monk followed his own way of life, but the community met on Saturdays and Sundays for the celebration of the Eucharist. The lauriate system of Antony was that adopted in and around the Wadi Natrun on the western side of the Delta. Lying as it does close to the Mediterranean littoral, it was much frequented by those who came to Egypt to see the ascetics. An early collection of simple tales connected with the monks of these settlements known as the *Apophthegmata Patrum* was current in Greek, Syriac, and Coptic.

The model or pattern for western monasticism was, however, the more rigid rule of Pachomius, which according to tradition he received from the hands of an angel, a scene depicted in western medieval manuscripts. In the Pachomian system there was a relaxation of the rule of solitude and an insistence upon organized work. The monks were organized into houses according to trades, sleeping three to a cell and eating in a common refectory attached to each house.

During the fourth and fifth centuries numerous monasteries were established in the Nile Valley and in the Delta. Except for tax receipts, there is a marked decrease in the first century AD in the number of legal and business documents in the Egyptian language: it now reappears in the Coptic form, vast quantities of Coptic ostraca and papyri being recovered from monastic sites relating to the secular and religious activities of the monasteries and their relations with the surrounding laity. A selection of such ostraca is exhibited in the Fourth Egyptian Room (fig. 27).

The monks of Egypt were particularly loyal, at times fanatically so, to the patriarchs at Alexandria. The solid support which they gave to the patriarchs accounts to a large extent for the prestige and power of the Alexandrine Church at the oecumenical councils called to define dogma and suppress heresy. It also enabled the patriarchs to act contrary to the policies of emperors, by then ruling from Byzantium; in the course of the fourth century the church of Egypt developed strong nationalist feeling and this, as much as the doctrinal point at issue, led to the condemnation of the Egyptian Church at the fourth council of Chalcedon in AD 451 for its adherence to monophysite doctrine that in the person of Christ there was only one nature.

The bulk of the carved stonework from the monasteries dates from the fifth to the ninth centuries AD and consists of tombstones and decorated architectural fragments, few of which have been found still standing in position. Much of the material has no known provenance and there are many problems in connexion with its dating. The work is executed in limestone and sandstone, the tradition of work in hard stone having died during the third century. With the exception of a form of cross, derived from the *ankh*, the hieroglyphic sign for 'life' (fig. 95), there is almost no

95 Memorial stone for Pleinos

trace of the art of the Pharaonic Period. The style and subject matter of its decorative work can be traced back to the sculptured fragments found at Oxyrhynchus and Ahnas (Ehnasiya), which date from the beginning of the fourth century. The term Coptic is by general consent applied to this work, though for the most part it does not seem to have come from Christian buildings and may be considered as the last manifestation of Hellenistic work.

The carved relief of the architectural fragments of this early Coptic sculpture is drawn from familiar Hellenistic decoration, consisting for the most part of plant ornamentation and geometric designs seen at its best in friezes with acanthus and vine-leaf scrolls inhabited by birds and animals.

Particularly common at Ahnas are the friezes, niches, and other architectural elements with figure subjects in high relief, cut so deeply that at times they are almost detached from the plain background. In contrast with the general Hellenistic style,

96 Fragment of a niche with the head of a woman

the proportions of the figures show the clumsiness commonly associated with Coptic art, particularly in the small heads, conventional treatment of the hair, and the large eyes: the movements are angular and the forms sharply outlined. The subjects of the representations are drawn from the familiar repertoire of late pagan and classical mythology: Aphrodite, Herakles, Leda, Erotes, Nereids often riding on dolphins, Nymphs and other semi-divine powers, and personifications of the Earth, of the Nile, of Plenty (Euhemera), and of Good Fortune (Tyche). The style is illustrated by a female head of unknown provenance (36143; fig. 96) which formed the top of a niche.

When the Christian communities built monasteries and churches, they used the current decorative style incorporating the repertoire of motifs with which they were familiar. They were influenced in the course of time by the art of other Christian communities of the eastern Mediterranean. In general there was a tendency for the ornamentation to become more abstract, less naturalistic and less deeply cut. The decorative pattern of the friezes was simplified and monotonously repeated. The deep-cut relief characteristic of the Ahnas style disappeared, and figure subjects became uncommon except on tombstones. Free-standing sculpture is unknown.

Large numbers of Coptic tombstones, most of them dating from the seventh and eighth centuries, have been recovered. Neither in their inscription nor in their relief do they owe anything to the funerary stelae of dynastic Egypt, but clearly evolve from the style of the mixed Romano-Egyptian stelae of the third and fourth centuries (p. 246). The inscriptions carved upon them usually give the name and status of the deceased introduced by one of the common Christian funerary formulae, sometimes invoking the intercession of local saints (676). Only a few, and these of late date, contain more poetic compositions with reflections on death. If the date of the death is recorded, it is usually only by the year of an indiction, the cycle of fifteen years which was introduced at the time of Diocletian for administrative reasons (1328, 1801). Some stelae contain no more than the text; others are carved in flat relief, the common themes being the representation of the deceased standing with his hands raised in the *orans* position (1523), birds (618), foliate borders, crosses with and without an encircling wreath (1520), and the façade of a building rendered in an increasingly less naturalistic style (1328, 1801). In the late period the memorial stones are usually small with rounded tops or large slabs, rectangular in form or carved at the top with a gabled pediment. In the earlier period, up to the sixth century, there was more diversity of type: the upper part of a stela from El-Badari (1811), carved in the form of an *ankh*-cross, the loop filled with a chubby-faced mask and surrounded with a gaily painted decoration of vine stems and grapes, is of a type which seems to have been confined to Middle Egypt. The niche with a carved figure of a young boy (1795; fig. 97), which comes from a Christian necropolis at Oxyrhynchus, belongs to a type which, judging from the objects held in the hand of examples from Antinoopolis, was originally pagan, then adapted for Christian burials. Also from Oxyrhynchus comes a standing figure which presumably once stood in a similar niche (1841).

Some of the original impact of the Coptic sculpture is lost by the disappearance in most cases of all traces of its original colour which would have concealed the general lack of modelling and the absence of fine detail in the carving. The use of colour was an

97 Niche with figure of a young boy

essential part of the decorative nature of Coptic art in general and may best be judged from the textiles which have survived in quantity from the fourth century onwards, mainly in the cemeteries of Antinoopolis and Akhmim. The art of fine weaving goes back to Egypt to the Predynastic Period (see pp. 234 ff.), though relatively little has survived apart from plain linen weaves. The appearance of the textiles now in the fourth century AD is due to the change in burial customs described on p. 248.

Broadly speaking, the style of textiles follows the same lines as the stonework. The earliest of the larger tapestries show in their choice of subject, in their treatment of the figures, and in the naturalistic shades of colour, characteristics of late Hellenistic work. They are well illustrated in the two fragments of a large loop tapestry in wool on linen from Akhmim (20717; Plate 21) with a representation of two Erotes in a boat surrounded by a guilloche border at the corners of which are well-modelled masks within small roundels.

The evolution of the more specifically Coptic style is shown by the large tapestry in coloured wools and undyed thread on linen approximately 1·50 m. wide and 1·80 m. high with two lateral and one broad medial vertical bands, the intervening space being occupied by two large standing figures set against an open background studded with decorative rosettes (43049; fig. 98).

98 Tapestry with divine figures

The lateral bands show dancing male and female figures against a background of vine tendrils within a border of heart-shape pattern. The medial band has a formalized floral border and dancing figures with shields and flying cloaks enclosed within a scroll pattern. The large standing female figure, on the right of the tapestry, is wearing a long green skirt and blue-spotted red cloak. She draws a bow with her right hand and a quiver with three arrows is slung on her back. The male figure on the left wears a pointed cap of western Asiatic origin which is a mark of divine or heroic stature and is dressed in a short green kilt and red cloak fastened over his left shoulder. The female figure with bow and arrow is probably to be identified as Artemis, and the male figure with one of the heroes famed as hunters with whom she is associated in late classical myth, perhaps Actaeon, Orion, or Meleager. The treatment of the figures, with the stressed whites of the eye, heavy eyebrows, stylized treatment of the hair, and even rendering of the colour, marks the transition to the Coptic Period.

The bulk of the surviving textiles of the fourth to the sixth century consists of costume ornaments, with tapestry woven designs usually of dyed wools with linen threads for small details. Surviving examples show that there were different methods of arranging the ornamentation on the tunic, which in its essential form differed little from the costume depicted on the mummy portraits of the first four centuries AD. In its simplest form the tunic contained only two vertical bands running over the shoulders down to the hem and one or two bands ornamented in similar style around the cuffs (18198). A continuous broad horizontal band might run around the neck opening (21789). In more elaborate decorated costumes woven panels or roundels were added, usually on the shoulders or near the bottom corners at the front and back. In later tunics the bands are regularly shortened to about waist-level and terminated in a roundel or pendent ornament. Roundels are far more common than the square panels. The large oblong cloths (for example 21795) were probably used as an outer garment loosely draped over the shoulders like a cloak in the manner indicated in the mummy portraits. They were used also as covering at night and were faced with long loops for extra warmth.

The earliest of the costume ornaments are of intricate geometric patterns woven in purple wool and undyed linen thread (21516). They are characteristic of the fourth century. Purple was the standard colour used in the monochrome work. The designs for both monochrome and polychrome work were drawn from the repertoire of late Hellenistic art: fish, animals of the chase, particularly the desert hare and lions (21790),

Plate 20
Portrait painted on a linen shroud

baskets of petals and fruits (17172), trees, the most common of which was the vine-stem growing out of a vase or basket. Figure subjects are common, sometimes apparently drawn from popular stories of the classical heroes, identification of which is uncertain in the absence of detail; the figure of a nude man and woman set apparently in a meadow or garden (21791) may perhaps represent Herakles and one of the classical heroines with whom he was associated. The mythical creatures of classical invention also appear, like the half-human half-horse centaur or half-horse half-fish hippocampus. The scenes are often animated, leaping boy warriors with flying cloaks, dancing figures, with their heads tossed back, and mounted hunters (21802). Several elements, not necessarily harmonious, were combined in one piece, the central design enclosed by a surrounding border of intertwining stems, forming scrolls for further subjects (17172). Vertical bands were given a continuous decoration of figure or animal subjects within a border of interlaced pattern, particularly male or female dancers, shepherds holding a staff or a lion by the tail, and hunted animals (18198).

The earliest indication of polychrome tapestry for costume ornament is the addition of small detail usually in red (17171, 21791, 21795). The widespread use of polychrome weaving for this purpose probably dates from the sixth century. The range of subject and decoration remains similar to the monochrome patterns which are still found, but the treatment of the human figure shows a more specifically Coptic style. There is a tendency for schematic forms, large heads squashed down on the shoulders, the eyes large with prominent whites, the hair treated in stylized curls or stretched like a sponge across the top of the head. Hands and the lower part of the legs receive sketchy treatment. A characteristic example is the small square panel depicting a leaping warrior within a rectangular frame of coloured heart-shape petals (17176).

Christian subjects are rare before the seventh century and not common until the eighth. The figures are commonly woven on a red background, in a highly stylized but decorative form, which give the impression of having been built up from rectangular segments. The most common themes are haloed figures of saints, either standing or on horseback (18233). Scenes drawn from biblical stories, their subject not always readily apparent, also occur (18221).

The sequence of the textiles from the Egyptian burial grounds continues until the twelfth century, by which time the Christian church of Egypt had become a minority element in the population, not immune from persecution; the language itself was falling into obsolescence; by the eleventh century its literature lost

Plate 21
Fragments of
tapestry depicting
Erotes in a boat

its force and Arabic–Coptic grammars and vocabularies were first compiled. From the thirteenth century service books were regularly provided with Arabic translations, and by the sixteenth Coptic had probably ceased to be a spoken language even in the villages of Upper Egypt, its use being confined entirely to the recitation of the liturgy, for which purpose it is still read.

Similarly, after the ninth century, the art of the Copts is increasingly influenced by the Islamic world, until in much of its decoration only the presence of a cross or inscription in Coptic betrays its Christian purpose. Christian antiquities of this late period, which include remarkable examples of wood carving from the ancient churches of Cairo, are preserved in the collections of the Department of Medieval and Later Antiquities.

South of Egypt proper lay the independent kingdom of Meroe which had come into existence after the Twenty-fifth Dynasty in the seventh century BC. The kings of the Twenty-sixth Dynasty, the Persian emperors and the Ptolemies had not succeeded in bringing Nubia under their control; the Romans challenged the power of Meroe by a punitive expedition in 23 BC under Petronius, Governor of Egypt, who captured Qasr Ibrim and succeeded in sacking the capital, Napata, itself (p. 71). Though the treaty following this victory gave the Romans access to that stretch of Lower Nubia between Aswan and Hierosykaminos (the Dodekaschoinos), the power of Meroe over the rest of Lower Nubia was by no means broken. Roman influence remained only in the northern part, reflected in the completion or construction of a number of temples. The Meroites successfully petitioned for the return of Qasr Ibrim, a fortress valued not only for its strategic position but also, apparently, for religious reasons.

Knowledge of the expedition itself is derived from the detailed descriptions made by the classical historians Strabo, Pliny and Dio Cassius. At least one further expedition, recorded both by Pliny and by Seneca, took place between 61 and 67 AD. From this time onwards there was a gradual deterioration of Meroitic power in the south, evident in the less elaborate preparations for burial and in fewer imported goods. The chronology for this period is uncertain, the next firm date occurring only in a demotic graffito at Philae, which records that in AD 253 envoys were sent from Meroe with gifts for the temple, reflecting a special reverence for Isis among the Meroites. The decision made by the Emperor Diocletian in AD 296 to withdraw all his troops and to set the southern frontier of Egypt at Philae undoubtedly hastened the economic decline of Meroitic Nubia, and by the middle of the fourth century AD the Meroitic kingdom was at an end. An inscription of King Aezanes of Axum in

Ethiopia (AD 325–375) reveals that when he marched through the Butana, another nomadic group, the 'Noba', were already in possession of Meroe.

Such interventions in Meroitic history reflect the continuing influence of the Mediterranean powers. The forms and decoration of Meroitic pottery are particularly illuminating, for they illustrate vividly the combination of Mediterranean and African traditions. The British Museum possesses several fine specimens of Meroitic painted wares (e.g. 51615; fig. 99). The ancient religion and art forms of dynastic Egypt survived at Meroe until the fourth century AD and, although the Napatan royal cemeteries were abandoned in favour of burial at Meroe, the tradition of pyramid tombs continued (719; fig. 100). Fine metalwork was produced, examples of which may be seen among the bronze objects on exhibition (63585; fig. 101). The Meroitic kingdom evolved its own alphabetic script, which has been preserved for the most part in dedicatory inscriptions on stone libation bowls and similar objects. The inscription carved on a rectangular stela (1650) with the names of Queen Amanirenas and Akinidad and found at Meroe is one of the surviving texts of a more historical interest.

Following the disintegration of the Meroitic kingdom, Nubia was overrun by various nomadic tribes. By the fifth century AD

99 Meroitic pottery vessel

100 Carved relief from
a pyramid chapel
at Meroe

three distinct kingdoms, Nobatia, Makuria, and Alwa, had been
formed. Christianity penetrated slowly into Nubia from Egypt,
and finally in the middle of the sixth century AD the area was
formally converted by emissaries sent from Constantinople. In
spite of the Arab conquest of Egypt in 641, a Christian kingdom
continued to survive in Nubia until probably the early fifteenth
century but eventually succumbed to internal divisions,
renewed nomadic and Egyptian pressure, and declining trade.
Objects in the collection from Christian Nubia include a fine red
sandstone frieze (606) and a red sandstone capital (1636) from
the seventh-century cathedral at Faras, which was later to be
rebuilt and decorated with magnificent frescoes. Other artifacts
from the Christian period at Qasr Ibrim are part of the collections
in the Department of Medieval and Later Antiquities.

101 Bronze aegis

LIST OF THE PRINCIPAL KINGS OF EGYPT

(Overlapping dates usually indicate coregencies. All dates given are approximate.)

FIRST DYNASTY

c. 3100–2890 BC

Narmer (Menes)
Aha
Djer
Djet (Uadji)
Den (Udimu)
Anedjib
Semerkhet
Qaa

SECOND DYNASTY

c. 2890–2686 BC

Hotepsekhemwy
Raneb
Nynetjer
Peribsen
Khasekhem (Khasekhemwy)

THIRD DYNASTY

c. 2686–2613 BC

Sanakhte
Djoser
Sekhemkhet
Khaba
Huni

FOURTH DYNASTY

c. 2613–2494 BC

Sneferu
Cheops (Khufu)
Redjedef
Chephren (Khafre)
Mycerinus (Menkaure)
Shepseskaf

FIFTH DYNASTY

c. 2494–2345 BC

Userkaf
Sahure
Neferirkare Kakai
Shepseskare Isi
Neferefre
Nyuserre
Menkauhor Akauhor
Djedkare Isesi
Unas

SIXTH DYNASTY

c. 2345–2181 BC

Teti
Userkare
Meryre (Pepi I)
Merenre
Neferkare (Pepi II)

SEVENTH DYNASTY

c. 2181–2173 BC

EIGHTH DYNASTY

c. 2173–2160 BC

NINTH DYNASTY

c. 2160–2130 BC

Meryibre Achthoes I (Khety I)
Nebkaure Achthoes II

TENTH DYNASTY

c. 2130–2140 BC

Wahkare Achthoes III
Merykare

ELEVENTH DYNASTY

c. 2133–1991 BC

Tepya Mentuhotpe I
Sehertowy Inyotef I
Wahankh Inyotef II
Nakhtnebtepnefer Inyotef III
Nebhepetre Mentuhotpe II
Sankhkare Mentuhotpe III
Nebtowyre Mentuhotpe IV

TWELFTH DYNASTY

c. 1991–1786 BC

Sehetepibre Ammenemes I
1991–1962 BC
Kheperkare Sesostris I
1971–1928 BC
Nubkaure Ammenemes II
1929–1895 BC
Khakheperre Sesostris II
1897–1878 BC
Khakaure Sesostris III
1878–1843 BC

Nymare Ammenemes III
1842–1797 BC
Makherure Ammenemes IV
1798–1790 BC
Sobkkare Sobkneferu
1789–1786 BC

THIRTEENTH DYNASTY

c. 1786–c. 1633 BC

Sekhemre Sewadjtowy
  Sobkhotpe III
Khasekhemre Neferhotep
Meryankhre Mentuhotpe

FOURTEENTH DYNASTY

c. 1786–c. 1603 BC

FIFTEENTH DYNASTY
(Hyksos)

c. 1674–1567 BC

Mayebre Sheshi
Meruserre Yakubher
Seuserenre Khyan
Auserre Apophis I
Aqenenre Apophis II

SIXTEENTH DYNASTY

c. 1684–c. 1567 BC

SEVENTEENTH DYNASTY

c. 1650–1567 BC

Nubkheperre Inyotef VII
Senakhtenre Tao I, 'the
  Elder'
Seqenenre Tao II, 'the
  Brave'
Wadjkheperre Kamose

EIGHTEENTH DYNASTY

c. 1567–1320 BC

Nebpehtyre Amosis I
  (Ahmose)
1570–1546 BC
Djeserkare Amenophis I
  (Amenhotpe I)
1546–1526 BC
Akheperkare Tuthmosis I
1525–c. 1512 BC
Akheperenre Tuthmosis II
c. 1512–1504 BC
Makare Hatshepsut
1503–1482 BC

Menkheperre Tuthmosis III
1504–1450 BC
Akheprure Amenophis II
1450–1425 BC
Menkheprure Tuthmosis IV
1425–1417 BC
Nebmare Amenophis III
1417–1379 BC
Neferkheprure Amenophis IV
  (Akhenaten)
1379–1362 BC
Ankhkheprure Smenkhkare
1364–1361 BC
Nebkheprure Tutankhamun
1361–1352 BC
Kheperkheprure Ay
1352–1348 BC
Djeserkheprure Horemheb
1348–1320 BC

NINETEENTH DYNASTY

c. 1320–1200 BC

Menpehtyre Ramesses I
1320–1318 BC
Menmare Sethos I
1318–1304 BC
Usermare Ramesses II
1304–1237 BC
Baenre Merneptah
1236–1223 BC
Menmire Amenmesses
1222–1217 BC
Userkheprure Sethos II
1216–1210 BC

TWENTIETH DYNASTY

c. 1200–1085 BC

Userkhaure Sethnakhte
1200–1198 BC
Usermare-Meryamun,
  Ramesses III
1198–1166 BC
Hiqmare Ramesses IV
1166–1160 BC
Usermare Ramesses V
1160–1156 BC
Nebmare Ramesses VI
1156–1148 BC
Usermare Ramesses VII
1148–1141 BC
Usermare Ramesses VIII
1147–1140 BC
Neferkare Ramesses IX
1140–1123 BC

Khepermare Ramesses X
1123–1114 BC
Menmare Ramesses XI
1114–1085 BC

TWENTY-FIRST DYNASTY

c. 1085–945 BC

At Tanis
Hedjkheperre Nesbanebded
   (Smendes)
Akheperre Psusennes I
Amenemope
Siamun
Psusennes II

At Thebes (High Priests)
Herihor (temp. Ramesses XI)
Paiankh
Pinudjem I
Masaherta
Menkheperre
Pinudjem II

TWENTY-SECOND DYNASTY

(Libyan or Bubastite)

c. 945–715 BC

Hedjkheperre Sheshonq I
c. 945–924 BC
Osorkon I
c. 924–889 BC
Takelothis I
c. 889–874 BC
Usermare Osorkon II
c. 874–850 BC
Takelothis II
c. 850–825 BC
Sheshonq III
c. 825–773 BC
Pami
c. 773–767 BC
Sheshonq V
c. 767–730 BC
Osorkon IV
c. 730–715 BC

TWENTY-THIRD DYNASTY

c. 818–715 BC

Pedubastis I
c. 818–793 BC
Osorkon III
c. 777–749 BC

TWENTY-FOURTH DYNASTY

c. 727–715 BC

Tefnakhte
Bakenrenef (Bocchoris)

TWENTY-FIFTH DYNASTY

(Nubian or Kushite)

c. 747–656 BC

Piankhi (Piye)
c. 747–716 BC
Neferkare Shabaka
c. 716–702 BC
Djedkaure Shebitku
c. 702–690 BC
Khunefertemre Taharqa
690–664 BC
Bakare Tanutamun
664–656 BC

TWENTY-SIXTH DYNASTY

(Saite)

664–525 BC

Wahibre Psammetichus I
664–610 BC
Wehemibre Necho II
610–595 BC
Neferibre Psammetichus II
595–589 BC
Haibre Wahibre (Apries)
589–570 BC
Khnemibre Amosis II
   (Amasis)
570–526 BC
Ankhkaenre
   Psammetichus III
526–525 BC

TWENTY-SEVENTH DYNASTY

(Persian)

525–404 BC

Cambyses
525–522 BC
Darius I
522–486 BC
Xerxes
486–465 BC
Artaxerxes I
465–424 BC

Darius II
424–405 BC
Artaxerxes II
405–359 BC

TWENTY-EIGHTH DYNASTY
404–399 BC

Amyrtaeus
404–399 BC

TWENTY-NINTH DYNASTY
399–380 BC

Nepherites I
399–393 BC
Khnemmare Achoris (Hagor)
393–380 BC

THIRTIETH DYNASTY
380–343 BC

Kheperkare Nectanebo I
380–362 BC
Teos
362–360 BC
Snedjemibre Nectanebo II
360–343 BC

PERSIAN KINGS
343–332 BC

Artaxerxes III Ochus
343–338 BC
Arses
338–336 BC
Darius III
336–332 BC

MACEDONIAN KINGS
332–305 BC

Alexander the Great
332–323 BC
Philip Arrhidaeus
323–317 BC
Alexander IV
317–305 BC

THE PTOLEMIES
305–30 BC

Ptolemy I Soter I
305–282 BC
Ptolemy II Philadelphus
284–246 BC
Ptolemy III Euergetes I
246–222 BC
Ptolemy IV Philopator
222–205 BC
Ptolemy V Epiphanes
205–180 BC
Ptolemy VI Philometor
180–145 BC
Ptolemy VII Neos Philopator
145 BC
Ptolemy VIII Euergetes II
170–116 BC
Ptolemy IX Soter II
   (Lathyros)
116–107 BC
Ptolemy X Alexander I
107–88 BC
Ptolemy IX Soter II
   (restored)
88–80 BC
Ptolemy XI Alexander II
80 BC
Ptolemy XII Neos Dionysos
   (Auletes)
80–51 BC
Cleopatra VII Philopator
51–30 BC

NAMES OF THE PRINCIPAL KINGS OF EGYPT
(*including the Roman Emperors*)

During the Early Dynastic Period, the chief name (Horus-name) of the king was written in a rectangular frame called a *serekh*. The bottom part of the frame contained a design of panelling, and the whole was surmounted by a figure of a falcon–the god Horus. In the case of Peribsen of the Second Dynasty, the Seth-animal replaced the falcon, while the *serekh* of Khasekhemwy was surmounted by both falcon and Seth-animal. A second name sometimes accompanied the Horus-name, or was used independently; it was introduced by one or both of the two titles 'King of Upper and Lower Egypt' and 'The Two Ladies'.

FIRST DYNASTY

Narmer   Aha   Djer   Djet   Den

Anedjib   Semerkhet   Qaa

SECOND DYNASTY

Hotepsekhemwy   Nynetjer   Peribsen   Khasekhemwy

THIRD DYNASTY

Sanakhte   Djoser   Sekhemkhet   Khaba

From the Old Kingdom the Egyptian king normally possessed five names: the Horus-name, the 'Two Ladies'-name, the Golden Horus-name (of uncertain origin), the prenomen (preceded by the title , translated usually 'King of Upper and Lower Egypt') and the nomen (preceded by the title 'Son of Re'). The nomen was first used by kings of the Fifth Dynasty who were specially devoted to the worship of Re. Prenomens and nomens were regularly enclosed within ovals called cartouches, which depict loops of rope with tied ends. By having his name so enclosed, the king possibly wished to convey pictorially that he was ruler of all 'that which is encircled by the sun'. From the late Eighteenth Dynasty onwards additional epithets were regularly introduced into the cartouches. In times when the claim to the throne of all Egypt was disputed kings sometimes avoided the -title and used , 'the good god'. The names within cartouches are those by which a king is normally identified.

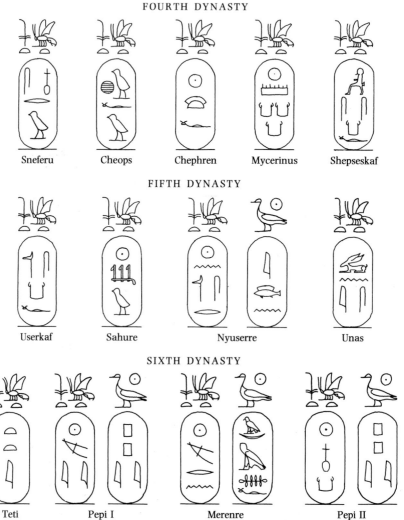

FOURTH DYNASTY

Sneferu   Cheops   Chephren   Mycerinus   Shepseskaf

FIFTH DYNASTY

Userkaf   Sahure   Nyuserre   Unas

SIXTH DYNASTY

Teti   Pepi I   Merenre   Pepi II

ELEVENTH DYNASTY

| Inyotef | Mentuhotpe II | Mentuhotpe III | Mentuhotpe IV |

TWELFTH DYNASTY

| Ammenemes I | Sesostris I | Ammenemes II |

| Sesostris II | Sesostris III | Ammenemes III | Ammenemes IV |

THIRTEENTH DYNASTY

FIFTEENTH DYNASTY
(Hyksos)

| Sobkhotpe III | Neferhotep I | Khyan | Apophis I |

SEVENTEENTH DYNASTY

Inyotef VII

Seqenenre II

Kamose

EIGHTEENTH DYNASTY

Amosis I

Amenophis I

Tuthmosis I

Tuthmosis II

Hatshepsut

Tuthmosis III

Amenophis II

Tuthmosis IV

Amenophis III

Akhenaten

Tutankhamun

Horemheb

NINETEENTH DYNASTY

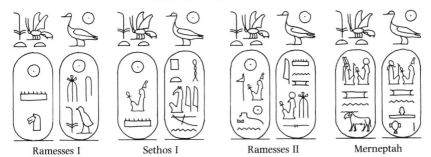

Ramesses I   Sethos I   Ramesses II   Merneptah

TWENTIETH DYNASTY

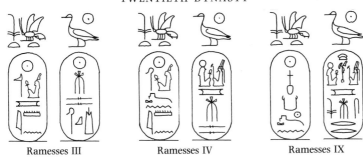

Ramesses III   Ramesses IV   Ramesses IX

TWENTY-FIRST DYNASTY   TWENTY-SECOND DYNASTY

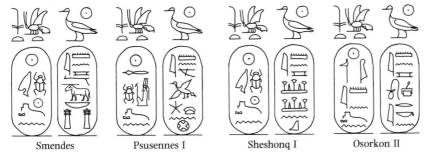

Smendes   Psusennes I   Sheshonq I   Osorkon II

TWENTY-FIFTH DYNASTY

Piankhi   Shabaka   Taharqa

TWENTY-SIXTH DYNASTY

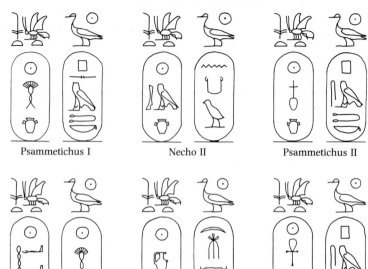

Psammetichus I   Necho II   Psammetichus II

Apries   Amosis II   Psammetichus III

TWENTY-SEVENTH DYNASTY

Cambyses   Darius   Xerxes   Artaxerxes

TWENTY-NINTH DYNASTY   THIRTIETH DYNASTY

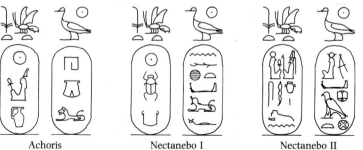

Achoris   Nectanebo I   Nectanebo II

MACEDONIAN KINGS

Alexander the Great   Philip Arrhidaeus

PTOLEMAIC DYNASTY

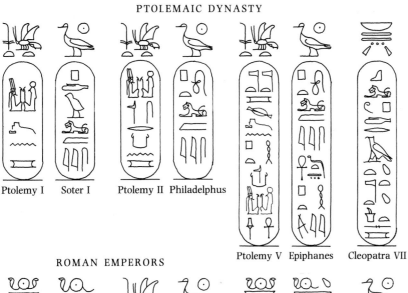

Ptolemy I   Soter I   Ptolemy II Philadelphus

Ptolemy V Epiphanes   Cleopatra VII

ROMAN EMPERORS

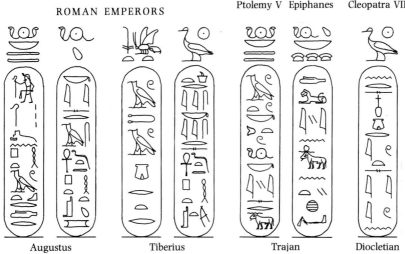

Augustus   Tiberius   Trajan   Diocletian

BIBLIOGRAPHY

CHAPTER TWO

E. Bevan. *A History of Egypt under the Ptolemaic Dynasty.* London, 1927.

The Cambridge Ancient History. Vols. I and II. 3rd ed. Cambridge, 1970–5.

Sir A. H. Gardiner. *Egypt of the Pharaohs.* Oxford, 1961.

CHAPTER FOUR

Erman (1927): A. Erman. *The Literature of the Ancient Egyptians.* London, 1927.

Gardiner (1909): A. H. Gardiner. *The Admonitions of an Egyptian Sage.* Leipzig, 1909.

Gardiner (1935): A. H. Gardiner. *Hieratic Papyri in the British Museum.* Third Series. London, 1935.

Glanville (1955): S. R. K. Glanville. *Catalogue of Demotic Papyri in the British Museum.* Vol. II. London, 1955.

Goedicke (1970): H. Goedicke. *The Report about the Dispute of a man with his Ba.* Baltimore, 1970.

Goedicke (1975): H. Goedicke. *The Report of Wenamun.* Baltimore, 1975.

Griffith (1900): F. Ll. Griffith. *Stories of the High Priests of Memphis.* Oxford, 1900.

Lichtheim (1973): M. Lichtheim. *Ancient Egyptian Literature.* Vol. I. Los Angeles, 1973.

Maspero (1915): G. Maspero. *Popular Stories of Ancient Egypt.* London, 1915.

Pritchard (1955): J. B. Pritchard. *Ancient Near Eastern Texts relating to the Old Testament.* Princeton, 1955.

Simpson (1972): W. K. Simpson (ed.). *The Literature of Ancient Egypt.* New Haven, 1972.

CHAPTER FIVE

J. Černý. *Ancient Egyptian Religion.* London, 1952.

S. Morenz. *Egyptian Religion.* Trans. A. Keep, London, 1973.

E. Otto. *Egyptian Art and the Cults of Osiris and Amon.* London, 1968.

S. Sauneron. *The Priests of Ancient Egypt.* London, 1960.

A. W. Shorter. *The Egyptian Gods.* London, 1937.

CHAPTER SIX

T. G. Allen. *The Egyptian Book of the Dead.* Chicago, 1960.

E. A. W. Budge. *The Book of the Dead.* London, 1909.

E. A. W. Budge. *The Mummy.* Cambridge, 1928.

G. Elliot Smith and W. R. Dawson. *Egyptian Mummies.* London, 1924.

W. B. Emery. *Archaic Egypt.* Harmondsworth, 1961.

I. E. S. Edwards. *The Pyramids of Egypt.* 2nd ed. London, 1961.

R. O. Faulkner. *The Ancient Egyptian Coffin Texts.* Warminster, 1973.

J. Garstang. *Burial Customs of Ancient Egypt.* London, 1907.

W. M. F. Petrie. *Shabtis.* London, 1935; reprinted Warminster, 1974.

CHAPTER SEVEN

A. Lucas. *Ancient Egyptian Materials and Industries.* 4th ed. London, 1962.

CHAPTER EIGHT

P. Du Bourguet. *Coptic Art.* London, 1971.

P. Shinnie. *Meroe.* London, 1971.

A. F. Shore. 'Coptic and Christian Egypt', in J. R. Harris, *The Legacy of Egypt.* 2nd ed. Oxford, 1971.

A. F. Shore. *Portrait Painting from Roman Egypt.* Rev. ed. London, 1972.

INDEX

INDEX TO THE COLLECTION NUMBERS OF OBJECTS MENTIONED IN THE GUIDE

Note: Numbers with asterisks refer to illustrations